PERFORMING THE WORD

Ronan Drury, Editor, *The Furrow*, 1977–

Performing the Word

FESTSCHRIFT FOR
RONAN DRURY

Edited by
Enda McDonagh

the columba press

First published in 2014 by
the columba press
55a Spruce Avenue,
Stillorgan Industrial Park,
Blackrock, County Dublin

ISBN 978 1 78218 197 2

Cover design by David Mc Namara CSsR
Cover image of St Kilian by Henry Flanagan OP, courtesy of
St Kilian's Heritage Centre, Mullagh, Co. Cavan.
Origination by The Columba Press
Printed by Scandbook, Sweden.

Contents

Preface

A Festschrift for Ronan Drury, Editor of *The Furrow* since 1977 and, prior to that, Review Editor from its founding in 1950, was long overdue, as I was informed by many in their letters accepting my invitation to contribute.

The invitations and acceptances were the easy part. The difficulties came with the editing and organisation of these essays for which I was fortunate to have the skilful assistance of my own secretary, Mary O'Malley, and that of the Secretary of the Classics Department at Maynooth University, Breege Lynch. Of course many others were directly or indirectly helpful, most notably Dr Kieran McGroarty of the Classics Department.

And there were the finances. Generous contributions from the four bishops approached for help, were a fine start. They were Fr Drury's own Bishop of Meath, the Bishop of Kildare and Leighlin, the Bishop of Killala and my own Archbishop of Tuam. A very substantial contribution came from the Maynooth Scholastic Trust. Various individuals and friends of Fr Drury and *THE FURROW* also contributed towards the project.

To all these, my sincere thanks. In all this, the President of Maynooth and various colleagues were encouraging and helpful. I must also thank the publisher, Columba Press, for their careful and timely production of the final volume.

Enda McDonagh
Maynooth,
October 2014

Introduction: Performing the Word

This volume is in itself an exercise in 'Performing the Word' as it seeks to express in human words its appreciation and understanding of the masterclass conducted by Ronan Drury as Editor for thirty-seven years of the public, published and indeed polished performance of the Word of God that we know as *The Furrow*. This tardy recognition is immediately occasioned by his reaching his ninetieth birthday this year. For sixty-four years he has been part of *The Furrow*, first as Managing and Review Editor and then, on the unexpected death of the Founder-Editor, J.G. McGarry, in 1977, as simply the Editor. The diverse contributors to this volume attest to something of the Christian vision of its two editors, their fidelity to the originating Word of God as manifest in Jesus Christ and their openness to the changing contexts in which that Word must be preached, heard and performed.

An editor of a journal such as *The Furrow* is to some extent like the conductor of a symphony orchestra. He must have a sense of the whole symphony, of the individual instruments and their playing and the capacity to integrate all this into a unified musical experience. One significant difference for editor of such journals is that their symphony is always unfinished and the editor is faced with the continuing task of combining integration with innovation. To complicate matters further the editor does not often know what the next month or certainly the next year will bring in fresh and positive contributors or in public or private criticism. And there is the difficulty for the editor that, unlike a Musical Director, he works in the immediate absence of his players/contributors, of his audience/readers. Such human, physical dimensions as presence and absence of people are very significant to the method and quality of all human communication, to the manner and effectiveness of Performing the Word.

I hope this volume, in the diversity of its valuable contributions, bears witness to the achievements of Ronan Drury in his demanding and lonely role as editor of *The Furrow* for thirty-seven years while never missing a single issue, come teaching, holidays, official reprimand, illness or bereavement. I should not overlook here his loyal and efficient secretary

Maria, who had some of her own serious illness problems and of course could not help with the difficult editorial decisions and other properly editorial work. However all of us contributors and readers owe her a deep gratitude for her own performing of the Word in her gracious fashion.

In this introduction I do not and could not seek to provide any kind of summation or synthesis of the richly diverse contributions offered here, still less of the overall work of *The Furrow*. Instead I try to reflect on some of the purely human as well as the theological dimensions of 'Performing the Word'.

As hinted here and elsewhere in the Festschrift, Performing the Word is a personal, indeed an interpersonal activity. And that involves personal presence, 'Real Presences', in the rich phrase of George Steiner. The 'Real' aspect is obvious or should be in face-to-face encounters. In some of these certainly the addressee may not be listening to the other, while it is not unknown for the addressing party to be no longer listening to himself. When 'Real Presence' on both sides has broken down, so has real communication, thus emptying the performing of the word however eloquent it might sound to a third party. Such failure exposes the complexity in all human communication or performance of the word which I am treating here as equivalents. This equivalence in turn demands a more searching examination of human presence, its expression and the recognition and reception of that presence.

The newborn baby is for most parents an unavoidable presence with its own powers of communication. The loving parents respond to that presence joyfully and lovingly in a variety of ways which include of course recognising and responding to its needs as it communicates them well before it has the words. But the coming of the words is an exciting and transforming event for parents and children and for their presence to one another. As the baby presence finds words, as the baby-flesh becomes word, whole new worlds are opened up. Important qualities of all speaking are also important for the learning baby speaker, love, discipline and style. These it learns from its parents, its other regular companions and its formal teachers of course. Love recognises and sustains presence. Discipline is essential to meaning in grammar, syntax and choice of word. Style is crucial to making presence acceptable and enriching. The gracious word and the creative image and metaphor make the message and the presence enriching for speaker and listener. The tone of voice conveys the love and is important in attracting and holding the attention of listener. All these move into another phase in verse, poetry and song. And so the gifted speaker approaches in many ways the singer or the musician and the gifted editor approaches the musical conductor.

The flesh made word in the learning baby is a long way from this pinnacle and most babies never reach or indeed come near that pinnacle as most singers or musical groups never approach the level of orchestral playing of the Berlin Philharmonic or other great orchestras. Ronan Drury had a double or treble role in the language area: speech-tutor particularly for those with speech defects, director and coach for would be preachers as priests; and editor of the monthly journal, *The Furrow*. In the last of these in particular the demands of style were significant and may have marked his editorial tenure out from that of his predecessor-founder who was far from indifferent to writing and speaking styles but would settle for substance even if he were still unhappy with the style. Ronan would always seek for improvement and had been known to return material for revision, because of its writing style inadequacies, to prominent and regular contributors, even bishops. His sense of style was far from a prettifying of language or any pretentious eloquence. It was language appropriate to the topic and in tone (its musical dimension) persuasive to discriminating reader and listener. No more.

The Miracle of Language and Miracles with Language
Without at this stage invoking the world of the supernatural and staying with the world of the human and the natural, the emergence of language in the evolution of humankind is so extraordinary and unique at least in its sophistication, that it might well be described as a miracle, at least a miracle of nature. This once for all event may have had its forerunners and parallels in other species but as of now we are not aware of any simple equivalent in the natural world. Similarly we might argue that it is a purely natural human achievement. Yet it appears primarily as gift which has of course to be developed on the basis of certain peculiarly human physio-logical and psychological gifts and in the presence of a human community of one or more, a further dimension of the gift.

Communication and presence may take many positive and enriching forms as well as many negative and impoverishing ones. Assuming conversation as a primary model it needs to be based on its linguistic relation conversion, its turn to the other. Otherness, involving mutual recognition and acceptance in word and engagement, is at the heart of true conversation, true presence to one another in human words. It is one of the miracles with words and comes in many forms, including that between writers and readers, and where appropriate includes editors. So it is proper to describe *The Furrow*'s editor, writers and readers as participating in an extended and unfinished conversation over some sixty plus years, at least as applying to one of the editors, Ronan. What this volume is attempting is another round of these conversations with a stand-in chairman.

Many other miracles with words might be listed. A favourite one of the editor honoured here would be the miracle of poetry. His love of poetry emerges perhaps only occasionally in his editorial work. It is well-known to friends and colleagues that he is very familiar with a wide world of poetry. In the right mood and in the right situation he can be persuaded to read or recite some of his favourite poems, adding a new dimension to presence and conversation. His sense of style in editing and preaching is undoubtedly influenced by his poetic sensibilities.

One last miracle with words is worth mentioning here. It is that of the healing and reconciling word. Ronan is a natural or should I say gifted peacemaker. His regular conversational gifts are witty and amusing beyond the average. Yet they feed into that important defusing of tension in certain fraught situations. For those individuals, hurt and suffering, he can be a healing presence by word and silence. Silence belongs with word as part of it in healing, support and companionship over time.

There are other aspects of word and presence which might be counted miracles in that sense of their unexpected and transformative appearance. Above all the 'love' dimension of all true presence and its words. Ultimately true words are words of love and require a loving style of expression which may well be anger in appropriate situations. 'Tough love' may be a cliché in speech but its equivalent may provide the first stage on the way to healing transformation and reconciliation for both parties. All this attention to the human word in its wonderful, miraculous life and its wonder-full usages is necessary preliminary for the theologian, academic and pastoral. Indeed in this context of *The Furrow* we are reminded that, at its best in word and concept, all theology is pastoral and all pastoral care including preaching and healing is, implicitly at least, theological. And so from baby talk and the flesh made word to theology or God talk and the Word made flesh.

The Word Made Flesh (Conversation and Community: Human and Divine)
Theology in its origins and tradition is wrestling with the ultimate. In the western tradition this ultimate is called God, to be affirmed and accepted or denied and rejected. In celebrating *The Furrow* and its editor we continue to affirm and accept that God, although conscious of the many difficulties associated with this position. In 'Furrow Time', as one contributor terms it, that affirmation and acceptance has been widely questioned and denied in Ireland as many contributors past and present have recognised. In the same 'Furrow Time', huge changes have occurred in the Irish and International Church, many of which *The Furrow* itself has been the herald and promoter. The most significant ones in the immediate context relate to return of the centrality of the Word of God in Scripture, in Liturgy and in Christian living. That return has been well covered in successive issues of *The Furrow* itself over its sixty years. These short reflections attend to inter connection between human aspects of the human word discussed earlier and some aspects of the Divine Word as truly present in the human community and in human words.

In the poetic Genesis account of Creation, Yahweh, by his presence, lovingly initiates the conversation with the human community by creating humanity in community and endowing it with the gift of communication in love 'talk', Bone of my bones and Flesh of my flesh as Adam addresses Eve as Yahweh lovingly creates and addresses both. All radically changes as the couple would be like Godself in eating of the forbidden fruit. Yet the conversation and its implicit conversion is to be maintained by the promise and power of Yahweh. The Hebrew Scriptures are an account of the fidelity of Yahweh to his promise, and the erratic response of Israel and humanity, leading to the child born of Mary, the Divine Word made Flesh, the Son of God become Man.

So we are reminded by the opening chapter of John's Gospel, in parallel to the opening of Genesis: 'In the beginning was the Word, And the Word was with God and the Word was God … And the Word was made Flesh and dwelt amongst us.' From Creation through the call of Israel to the Incarnation with God entering into directly human history and so into human conversation, Performance by and of the Word forms the upper level of that divine-human conversation. It is towards that level of conversation that *The Furrow* aspires. In Jesus' own words, 'Where two or three are gathered in my name there am I in the midst of them.' In its pastoral mission speaking and interpreting the Word of God so that it informs the life of its readers, *The Furrow* draws its readers into the presence of Jesus and the Father by the power of the Spirit. They are drawn into the heavenly conversation that constitutes our God, into the Trinitarian life of that God. So in all our serious attention to that evangelical mission in worship, prayer and sacrament, in speaking and writing, we do so in the presence and in the name of the Father, the Son and the Holy Spirit. Such is the grace that is ours in all our communication with others and not just in God-talk, although more evidently there. Such is the responsibility that is ours at whatever the stage of our development and whatever the topic of our conversation, spoken or written. So *The Furrow*, its editor, writers and readers, while their conversations in subject matter are more consciously concerned with God and other things in relation to God (Thomas Aquinas on theology), in form and style they must offer a model of conversation that expresses the Spirit and love of God. In a world where so much of the human verbal exchanges are exploitative or hate-filled, this is no mean responsibility. And it is one which *The Furrow* has tried valiantly to fulfil.

Performing the Word so graciously over the decades is a remarkable achievement for *The Furrow*, its editors and contributors. As this volume attempts inadequately to honour that achievement, it is fitting that it be dedicated to the current editor, Ronan Drury, on completing ninety years, over sixty of which have been immediately involved with the editing of *The Furrow*. Long may they both flourish.

Enda McDonagh

I. The Editor in Person

The Priest, the Editor and the Man of Many Talents

MICHAEL OLDEN

Rugby is very big in Ireland at this time. Most of us are happy to include it in our sports menu. When Ireland is playing a special match the nation almost comes to a halt. Outstanding players like Brian O'Driscoll are national heroes.

In his day, Ronan Drury played rugby. Occasionally I have heard him make mention of 'my rugby days'. The acute sporting exegete might, I fear, have serious difficulty in researching how long the rugby days lasted and if the farewell (or could it have been dismissal?) had any seismic significance such as was the case when Brian O'Driscoll departed the scene. But there are some similarities. Brian has his giant record of caps for international rugby. Ronan has ninety caps for living with so much vigour and zest stretching back to the days of his youth. And he has not finished yet! Ninety years of achievement in the stadium of life is a wonderful trophy to hold aloft. Most of Ronan's long life has been lived in the priesthood; most of his priesthood years have been spent in Maynooth College, seven years as a student and sixty years as a resident member of staff. He has been actively and directly involved with *The Furrow* throughout its entire life, first as Review and Managing Editor and then as Editor for thirty-seven years.

I had studied philosophy in University College Cork, so I was only a student in Maynooth for four years instead of the usual seven. One lacuna in my formation was that I never studied under Ronan Drury who, at that time, dealt mainly with the more junior students. This, for me, was a loss. My fellow classmates had the benefit of knowing far more about communication and voice production, very important in the work of a priest, than I knew. In fact, I had only one conversation with Ronan in all my student days. The senior theology students, as part of our homiletic training, had the unenviable task of having to compose a sermon and deliver it to more than two hundred fellow students and, most demanding of all, in the presence of one of the professors of homiletics, Gerry McGarry or Ronan Drury. It was usually quite an ordeal and I personally felt ill-equipped to be successful. However, when my first masterpiece had been delivered, Ronan took me aside and praised my sermon and its delivery with welcome words. He was critical here and there but hastened to declare that he was offering his criticism at a high level. To this day he cannot be aware of how much his gracious words and accompanying smile meant to me. With that conversation, the grimness of Maynooth began to give way to sunlight for me. I seriously needed to believe that happy humanity and priesthood could go together. That conversation, which Ronan probably never recalled, meant a great deal to a struggling student.

Fast forward to 1966. After studying in Rome for some years and after a period as curate in a parish in Waterford city, I found myself on the staff of St John's College, Waterford. One day the president informed us that Ronan Drury from Maynooth was coming to lunch. Mealtimes were always pleasant in our college dining room. It was a kind of clearing house for academic chat and all sorts of light and weighty gossip. The addition of a guest, especially with a personality such as Ronan's, induced an extra helping of banter and badinage. All too quickly he was gone. No-one quite knew why he had come. Years later he informed me that I was the reason for his visit. He had been dispatched south from Maynooth to discuss with the newly installed bishop of Waterford and Lismore, Michael Russell, who was a friend of his, the possibility of my being appointed to Maynooth as dean in the place of Fr Tommy Finnegan who was about to become president of Summerhill College, Sligo.

The outcome was that I found myself Junior Dean in Maynooth three months after Ronan's puzzling anabasis to Waterford. I have never forgotten the day of my arrival in Maynooth to take up my new post. As it happened, I was met on St Joseph's Square by two of the staff: Joe Hamell, vice-president, and Ronan Drury, who happened to be strolling together. They welcomed me warmly and, with characteristic Maynooth hospitality, they brought me into the professors' dining room for a cup of tea. However, before I could settle my nerves with the cup that cheers, they informed me that an election was soon taking place to appoint a member of staff to the Finance Council of the college. Now that I was a member of staff I should cast my vote. They steered me towards a ballot box and handed me pen and paper. Quite bewildered I asked their advice as to whom I should cast my vote for. They both agreed that I could vote for anyone I wished except X who, in Joe Hamell's words, would be a dreadful nuisance. It may be of interest that X later became a bishop! With that rather weird and abrupt lesson at the hands of Hamell and Drury, my career in Maynooth began.

From the day that I arrived, Ronan was a loyal and very good friend. He had fine instincts as to the appropriate formation which should be given to students for the priesthood. In those days Maynooth was not an easy place in which to work. This was especially true in the case of a young fellow who had only known the college for four years as a student. It was strict in discipline and the dean was expected to be the major agent of discipline. Ronan was a very enlightened help to me in my attempt to be priestly and human in my personal dealings with the students rather than relating to them by clutching the book of rules. Perhaps because of the great size of the college, relations between staff and students had been traditionally formal and fairly distant. However, by the time I arrived in 1966 healthy changes were beginning to take place. Several young men had recently been appointed to the staff and a fresh, more friendly atmosphere was developing. Men such as Denis O'Callaghan, Donal Flanagan, Gerry Meagher, Enda McDonagh, to mention but a few, were accessible to and personally involved with the students. And there were slightly more senior men such as Michael Harty, Ronan Drury and Tomás Ó Fiaich who helped in a strong way to create good fellowship within the staff itself and between staff members and students. People tell me that I was the first dean who did not call each individual student 'Mr' but used his Christian name. If so, I am pleased. And the idea was not mine but came from Ronan Drury. It was only one of many healthy ideas which came to me via Ronan. I really got to know him very well and I needed and valued his support and his enlightened comments. By no means was he an unserious man, but there was in him a pause for laughter, a superb wordsmith, unsurpassable in telling a story, humble and sharing in a very authentic way. He was a deeply humanising person as well as a hard worker. If I were asked who it was who created healthy change in the Maynooth College of that time I would place Ronan Drury at the top of the list.

Unlike most of us, who can be touchy or testy or tetchy when people make fun of us, Ronan always seemed to revel when he was the butt of jokes or got caught up in ludicrous or uncomfortable situations. He rarely, if ever, took offence or umbrage but entered into the fun with the crowd. It used be customary on Good Friday, the most solemn day of the liturgical year, when the powerfully moving liturgies of the day had drawn to a close, for the whole college community to assemble in the great College Chapel for the Stations of the Cross. The powerful life-sized Stations, done by Westlake, were very conducive and the choral contribution to the prayer service was always very moving. But, above all, it meant so much that each year Ronan conducted, always with excellent commentary, the journey of Christ with its fourteen stopping points of powerfully sad moment on the way to Calvary. Sometimes he scripted the commentary himself; sometimes he chose it from some well known author. One year I showed him a commentary written by the influential Swiss theologian, Hans Urs von Balthasar. He liked it and decided to use it as his text. Before the service began I thought it would be helpful if I informed the crowded chapel what text the main celebrant would use. So I went out and simply said to them that 'the Stations this year will be by Hans Urs von Balthasar'. There was a respectful silence. Then from the wings there appeared not Hans Urs himself as my silly introduction seemed to have indicated, but Ronan Drury clutching the booklet by the great man. The greeting by the students was highly jovial and scarcely suitable to the sombre occasion. Ronan joined in the laughter. I was the only fool in the chapel.

I met him one June afternoon as he returned from the ordination to priesthood of one of our students. It had taken place down the country. Ronan laughingly recalled to me that, at the beginning of the sacred ceremony, the bishop welcomed in a special way Fr DREARY from Maynooth. And, three times before the ceremony had concluded, the well-meaning but rather clueless prelate mentioned Fr DREARY again. One thing was and always will be for sure: Ronan was never ever 'dreary'. But he enjoyed the humour of it all.

Fr John McMackin was professor of English in Maynooth for most of his life. He was very correct and proper in behaviour and strongly stressed the need for correct social grammar. I think it was about the time of his seventieth birthday that I suggested to Ronan that he and I should take John out to dinner. I suggested the Red House between Newbridge and Kildare as a suitable venue for John's impeccable taste. Ronan agreed but wondered if the Red Cow might be more pleasant for John. At that time the Red Cow was little more than a small little pub with no pretensions and it certainly would not figure on John's list of acceptable eating places. Ronan had a wonderfully vivid imagination for the incongruous. Needless to say we went to the Red House.

Behind the fun and laughter Ronan has always been a seriously caring man to students, staff, the priests and people of his native Mullagh in Co.

Cavan (I doubt if he ever missed celebrating Christmas midnight Mass in Mullagh), to many friends all over Ireland. Of the many instances of his deep kindness one in particular stands out in my mind. His very special friend, Fr Tommy Waldron, parish priest of Claremorris in 1995 and a very gifted literary man, was visited by a painful and terminal illness. On several occasions Tommy was cared for in his declining months by Ronan himself in his rooms in Maynooth. After his death, Ronan engaged another special friend, Enda McDonagh, to write a beautiful article on Tommy in *The Furrow*, October 1995. I consider it one of the finest pieces which Enda has ever written 'Bruised Reeds and the Mystery of the Church. In Memory of Tommy Waldron'.

Since its inception in 1950, Ronan has been inseparable from *The Furrow*. The relationship began before he joined the Maynooth staff, while he was teaching in Knockbeg College, Carlow. The founder of *The Furrow*, Gerry McGarry, had, practically from the beginning, anointed Ronan as the special son with whom he could work and whom he could trust. It was an unerring choice. I am sure that Ronan himself, as he looks back over the years, cannot begin to quantify the amount of time which he has dedicated to his work for *The Furrow*. When Gerry McGarry decided to leave his chair of Homiletics in Maynooth and become parish priest of Ballyhaunis in 1969, he took the editorship of *The Furrow* with him and the workload on Ronan increased and became more complicated. There was endless telephoning and consultation between Maynooth and Ballyhaunis. The day-to-day office work and business of *The Furrow* fell completely on Ronan. But his loyalty to McGarry would not permit him to make heavy complaints. McGarry was very fond of Ronan and he could never have conducted *The Furrow* without him. They were indeed quite a duo. They were so different from each other in style but *ad unum* in their commitment to *The Furrow*, in planning every issue, in choosing the books to be reviewed, in attempting to cater for the large and varied readership which *The Furrow* had gathered over the years.

McGarry's death – killed in a car accident while on his First Friday Communion rounds on 4 August 1977 – was a great blow to Ronan.[1] Ronan was the closest of all to the founder of *The Furrow*. In a tribute to him in *The Furrow*, Ronan, though typically sparing in words and disciplined in treatment, cannot disguise his sincere admiration and deep sorrow. I feel it should be quoted in full:

'Canon McGarry, founder and editor of this review, died in a car accident in his parish of Ballyhaunis on the morning of the 4th of August.

In speaking here of the grievous loss *The Furrow* has suffered by his death I know that I am not speaking to strangers. If all life is an attempt to express oneself, every reader of *The Furrow* will have known this man who made its pages his unique personal expression. *The Furrow* was the patriarch's voice and all his writers were his prophets.

Readers will have known in the pages of his review the openness, the honesty, the courage, the integrity that made him so trustworthy an editor, the unambiguousness of his direction for a quarter of a century. If the Church in Ireland is today better informed and more articulate it is chiefly because he made it so. And in other countries too. The wide world was his parish.

In remembering, when each one goes beyond private memories of him, odd, affectionate, imitable, there remains the man of great spiritual strength, somebody supremely in touch with his own feelings, bearing the burden of being an editor – and the pain when there was pain – with the assistance of the ever-renewing Spirit. Urbane in opposition, arguing always with civility, forgiving. A man of standards. When he was right he did not see rightness in terms of victory or discomfiture; when he was wrong his perception of it was grateful and had no thought in it of defeat. His dedication was to the truth. He was a holy man.

Throughout his life Canon McGarry showed strong attachment to elemental Crafts, the holiness of making. Things to be sculpted and hammered, forged and fashioned. Even as editor this is how he saw himself, a maker. Indeed he had planned when he retired to make prayers, to give people the words in which they might talk to God. ('Yes' – and he would pause, staring, chin on chest – 'Homo Faber' he would say, relishing the sound and the idea.) In the tradition of the old Christian craftsman, he would have asked from us, at this time, of our charity, 'a Prayer for the Maker'.

Ronan Drury
Managing and Review Editor

It is a beautiful piece, saying as much about the writer as about the subject. I love the tentative build-up to the phrase: 'He was a holy man'. It can only be used of someone you love. The word 'imitable', I believe says a lot about the two editors and their deep relationship. Not long after McGarry's death Ronan was appointed editor of *The Furrow*. It was a choice which has never been regretted.

About the same time, October 1977, I was appointed President of Maynooth in succession to Tomás Ó Fiaich who had departed for Armagh. Thankfully, my friendship with Ronan remained strong, despite our changes of work and office. In fact we went on a very long trip together which literally took us around the world. The Columban Fathers, founded in 1917 as the Society of St Columban or as the Maynooth Mission to China, wished to underline their strong contact with Maynooth College. They invited me to visit many of their mission centres in the Far East. Kindly they went further and suggested that I bring a travelling companion. I asked Ronan to join me on the long journey. It had to be completed in two weeks as we both had commitments back in Ireland. We visited Hong Kong, Japan, the Philippine Islands. Ronan was the perfect companion and we had a lot of fun as well as performing serious visitations. We travelled out eastwards and returned from the west. When we arrived back in Ireland, Ronan suggested that we should do a similar journey the following year as we really only had time in one trip around the world to discuss half the eccentrics on the Maynooth staff.

Ronan has been editor of *The Furrow* for the past thirty-seven years. Over the years I have suggested to him that he should write more himself. But that was not his way as it had not been the way of his predecessor, McGarry. He has seen his role as that of the one who coaxes, encourages others to take up their pen. On very special occasions, and they had indeed to be special, when he felt that it was appropriate and responsible, has he expressed himself editorially. His pieces have always been masterly. I have mentioned and have felt the need to quote his telling piece on the death of Gerry McGarry. There were others such as the gently personal reflection on the sudden death of Cardinal Tomás Ó Fiaich in the June issue 1990, and the mustering of hope under pressure at the election of Pope Benedict XVI in the May issue 2005.

It is my hope and prayer that his steady and influential hands may continue to guide *The Furrow* as it ploughs its way with hope into sunlit and pleasant uplands in the years ahead. *Novate.*

In 'Furrow Time'
DES WILSON

For old men, the years between ordination and now – 'Furrow time' if you like – were often years of great hope. In the nineteen sixties more people were talking to each other in Northern Ireland than ever before. Conferences organised by Catholic groups were asking with more self-confidence for changes in church and state. Pragmatists as they were, their requests were well within existing church and state laws, customs and structures, asking for a more generous fulfilling of our laws, customs and rules rather than any radical change of them.

The Second Vatican Council filled some Catholics with foreboding as if it were opening the way to a more radical approach in church, perhaps admitting dangerous questions like whether the Church really could invalidate marriages, or whether transubstantiation instead of helping our understanding could now have come to mean the opposite of what it meant centuries ago, and perhaps suggesting dangerous answers. Whatever the intention of Pope John XXIII, the Council would not prove so daring, however strong the voice of the questioners might be. We talked about Dutch Catholics going into schism, not perhaps because they were asking such questions and suggesting answers but because they were doing it so publicly and with such urgency; transubstantiation was even being discussed in their weekly newspapers.

Continental Europeans, who had lived and suffered together in war and prison camps, were discussing what their differences, separate radio stations, separate schools, Protestant and Catholic clubs and publishing houses, had really done for them or for the Faith that had sustained or exasperated them during the war. An inquisitive visitor to Holland could find little to be frightened about. More frightening was the tendency among Christians elsewhere fearfully to disregard the injunction of Jesus Christ not to be afraid, so many of them seemed afraid even to reveal what they were thinking.

We envied French Catholics their well produced magazines and other publications and reflected forlornly on our *Irish Ecclesiastical Record* in which 'Parochus' and 'Sacerdos' had been so regularly rewarded for their full page of questioning with a curt Latin reply from Rome, 'Negative', 'Positive'. We looked with respect also at the Continental Christians' books with their pages uncut, knowing it was worth more than the bother of page cutting to read what was in them, especially as the Church in France became our model of what Catholics can confidently do for the best and yet fail without seeming to notice it. Jacques Duquesne firing a broadside, then receding into the background, to return again quickly to the fray, became a popular instructor and a warning light. Dariel, Rouet, Pierrard, Vilain, rendered the same service by recognising the real world, always demanding but often spiritually and materially impoverishing, in which their priests lived. We were shocked to find that, for all its expertise and history of faithfulness, the church in France was in a crisis which had passed unnoticed until the nineteen forties and even later. Could we then ever find ourselves asking a question similar to that of Godin and Daniel: Is France Mission country? We were not impatient for change in those days; we remained patient even without it.

Our patience was loyal but unfortunate and had to wait long for its reward. When the new Irish Catechism for Adults arrived in 2014 we saw that our church authorities were stirring in the direction we hoped they would go in those patient hopeful years. The eternal pains of hell had gradually faded from our preaching until, apparently to only a few people's surprise, a Catholic archbishop conceded that 'hell is possible'. In the New Catechism Limbo had disappeared into, well, into limbo, hell written about in terms of eternal death rather than eternal punishment, thus leaving the way open to believing in a God who mercifully ceases to sustain human life rather than a God who punishes His own beautiful creation eternally. Those who with sorrow had failed to find a formula to suggest how our God of infinite love could serenely contemplate the eternal suffering of His children could breathe more easily, hoping we had found not a solution to our problem but a cautious step towards one. Perhaps there might be an existence in which such divine opposites could exist together but in our world where our logic ruled, we could hardly find it in our hearts to insist on it.

Although we did not like to admit it, it was the people, the faithful, the multitudes, who seemed to be exploring what our faith means, testing its vitality in the harsh conditions of our everyday life, adjusting their understandings, perhaps hardly knowing they were doing it, perhaps moving as the Spirit willed. Cardinal Newman would probably have sympathised with them. After all, when Jesus came preaching it was to the multitudes, the masses, the people of God he preached most of the time. So to discover His message it is reasonable for all of us to go there too.

We came to realise more clearly that while we knew, or thought we knew, what our church teaches, we were not so sure about what we believed. Those who thought the Second Vatican Council might help us in this were disappointed; but we, the faithful, have our own way of moving towards new interpretations, even new laws in our church. We understand now that less understanding need not mean less believing.

For us in the northeast of Ireland, the nineteen fifties and sixties were a time of optimism, the thawing of relationships, the emergence of more reasoned discussion about religion, our thirst for certainty giving way to a glad taste for the reality and dignity and beauty of difference. Religiously we were moving from a desire to convert to a desire to understand and appreciate and perhaps to share. And for our encouragement Cardinal Bea said we should talk about all that without asking leave to do so.

There was a backlash of course. Reconciliation became a word which might not be used in mixed company for fear of a backlash against even talking about it. 'Fundamentalists' in Northern Ireland and the United States of America joined forces, learning from each other how to identify and fight common enemies whom they really could not know because they would not talk to them. Compromise and reconciliation, words of peacemaking, became weapons to beat the heads of enemies. The Bible, someone said in a broadcast, had become a quarry of stony sentences to hurl at each other. Distressing as that might be, some who had come into the Roman Catholic Church because of its certainties were even more distressed to find their fellow Catholics sitting with them around conference tables not rejoicing in their certainties but sharing each other's doubts.

Eventually though, whether people would remain confident that the Church had anything of value to offer or would walk away in sorrow or in anger often had to be decided in the whirlpool of our local war; so the experiences of Christians in Latin America, or in Camden New Jersey, or wherever else people did not just be miserable but were made miserable, would become painfully intrusive here in Ireland. A cold war took place between Christians who wanted the full force of the indignant Nazarene Preacher to be brought to bear on our life and governance and those who accused them of preaching a 'socialised gospel'. We lost some of our most intellectually gifted priests in that cold war. Saying we lost them though is hardly accurate. Through broadcasts, writing and conversation we tried to frighten fellow Christians, especially our leaders, into recognising the magnitude and meaning of the flow of people away from all the churches. We thought this would jolt us all together into action to reduce the flow. It came as a surprise then to hear a greatly respected churchman say, 'The people who are leaving, we are better without them; when they go we shall have a foundation of solidly believing Catholics with whom we can start re-evangelising.' In time we realised that this was the idea not of one church leader but of church leadership; it took much longer to see that we were sometimes assisting the departure from our church, by tightening the rules instead of loosening them, to encourage people to stay with us. Telling everyone the good news, sympathising with their understanding of it, nourishing and fostering our growing understanding lovingly, carefully and forgivingly might not, it seemed, be a method of the new evangelising.

If so, we might forget that, especially after the horrors of the Second World War, we had accepted more and more that others, including the pagans, had virtues too. Sending missionaries abroad should not, but might one day become uncomfortable, if we felt the need of missionaries for ourselves. Cardinal Tomás Ó Fiaich accepted that possibility and was unperturbed by it; some ecumenical clergy though, when our streets became battlegrounds, were aghast that, as they put it, 'Black soldiers have to man our streets to keep us in order.' Later, Blessed Mother Teresa's Sisters would learn how real that shame at needing missionaries was. What was happening in our war-wounded streets and the hesitant response to it in our Christian churches, told us how sorely we, at the very least, needed fresh inspiration in our life. Our great question then was not what the Church could do to help other people but whether we Christians had anything useful to offer a suffering world whose suffering we now realised included our own.

So we posed the refreshing and healthy question: 'We know what our Church teaches, but do we know what we really believe?' There was often a difference between the two and we needed to know how wide and deep the difference was, otherwise we might try to live by formula rather than by the Spirit. Whether we accepted or neglected the words of the Second Vatican Council we needed to feel sympathy with the impulse that created it.

We had become used to ironies in our public life – Trinity College refusing to accept Catholics and then, when accepted, Catholics refusing to come in; or a tentative notional movement away from centralisation and towards diffused authority in the church while at the same time there was, and is, a political movement towards centralising political and financial power in Europe, in the Dáil, in the Westminster Parliament, in the world, often the same people approving diffusion of authority in the church and centralisation in politics. There were disappointments too, and these were more difficult to bear because they represented so much hopeful work which had proved emptier than we thought; and disappointment may come in old age when we're not as strong as we used to be.

The struggle against torture was one of them. Would Vatican II condemn torture outright and end for all time the equivocal attitude of church people towards it? The Council did and we were grateful. The United Nations did. But, although the Catholic attitude was clear and the consent of Nations was clear, it was still possible to torture. So when our neighbours were tortured, what we had theorised about in the sixties, we had to be active about in the seventies. But worse was to follow. By the year 2014, governments were unashamed once again, announcing that torture was admissible because it produced information necessary for national security. Public opinion had been with Vatican II against torture but now there appeared little opposition, even from the People of God, to powerful governments who used it as if it were normal. It gave a foretaste not just of immoral things to come but of an indifference to them we had thought would never paralyse God's people again. Our morality was being given a new basis, not by closeted theologians or by the insights of God's people but by governments and corporations.

However, as the world becomes darker, with almost continuous wars, based on the idea that death is the best solution to problems and life is not for everyone, the Catholic church is entering into a new age in which its message can become as fresh as it was in the beginning, a message of hope to a jaded world that has tried everything and resolved nothing. The Church was often said to be before its time, behind the times or not in tune with the times. But its founder was like that too; is our church then what the Lord intended it to be and if not can it become so? To the delight and relief of many, it has become possible to talk and write publicly about such things, resolutely defying the silencers when necessary. But it should not have taken so long to happen.

One of the attributes *The Furrow* inherited from the wisdom of its founder, J.G. McGarry, has been its serenity. No show, no glitter, gracefully presenting itself with neither old greyness nor new self-assurance; with no promises of solutions to come but a quiet invitation to think now. J.G., facing the future with courtesy and foresight, had a vision of a whole church. Our devotional life was provided for lavishly if not always temperately; our emotional life was too. With many stimulants borrowed from abroad, our liturgical life was frequently at yet one more experimental stage, but our intellectual life would not be given similar luxuries. It was still possible in the nineteen seventies and even much later for preachers to stir a congregation with the words, '… and some of these so-called intellectuals …' The Curé of Ars was proposed to diocesan priests as a role model, particularly because he found holiness without much formal learning. So our Furrow time has often been a lean time for thinkers and writers, who recognise how many roads both rich and impoverished lead to sanctity; and who insist there is room for intellectual willingness to explore and describe the divine value in all of them. That Christians could and should be among the intellectual leaders in the world, illuminating the divine quality of everything in it; this we probably recognised, but that all of us should rejoice in it, we were reticent about that. Humility seemed to allow emotion and devotion but the preacher's words about 'these so-called intellectuals' has sent a chill of apprehensiveness into many an anxious heart and many a gifted mind. Most often we had less reason for regret over bad things done than for so many good things neglected, including our natural exploratory vision enhanced by the Holy Spirit.

Fr Alex Reid in his quest for peace would not say simply, Where a few are gathered together … he would say, 'Where we, politicians, paramilitaries, saints, doubters, neighbours are gathered together, there is the Holy Spirit hovering in the midst of us …' It will be a sad day when we aim for renewal by getting rid of the unsatisfactory sisters and brothers rather than challenging the Holy Spirit to be as good as His word and keeping them with us, safe in the family. After all, we were never promised we would always be good, we were promised that when we were bad, we would have the inspired knowledge of what to do about it.

For us old folk who have watched the new furrow being ploughed, one reason to wish to live on in this earth, perhaps the only compelling one, is our desire to see the beautiful inspirations lying dormant in our churches come alive.

'Now Lord you can send your servant away in peace. I have seen ...'

Letters to Ronan

A N N E T H U R S T O N

1 Kensington Villas
Easter-tide 2014

Dear Ronan,

When I heard about the idea for a Festschrift I was delighted for you and honoured to be invited to contribute. I hope you will forgive a somewhat personal response.

When the request arrived I had been musing on a possible piece to send to you. I owe much to *The Furrow*. In many ways I cut my theological teeth, so to speak, by writing for *The Furrow* and thus, I wanted you to know that I would be conferred with my PhD from Trinity in the summer of 2014. That journey started many years ago when I encountered Seán Freyne (of blessed memory to Furrow readers, among countless others) in the parish of Rathmines. Seán encouraged both the study of theology and writing for *The Furrow*. At that stage we both had young families and were involved in the liturgy in the parish and my first article for you was based on that experience. As I completed the BD amidst the chaos of family life I wrote pieces which often attempted to integrate the experience of the academic study of theology with the lived experiences of faith. One of those pieces 'There was a birth ...' eventually became part of my first book. All of this I note now to demonstrate the significance of your encouragement and your readiness to accept pieces which at times went beyond the boundaries of conventional and 'clerical' expectation of what was acceptable for Furrow readers.

While completing the doctoral dissertation, our two daughters were married, and now I am a grandmother and that experience, of a totally new and surprising grace, will, I expect, seep into the writings that follow from this stage. What I want to do in the following two letters is to revisit a couple of those early pieces published over twenty-five years ago and consider how things have changed in the theological and personal landscape.

But this first letter is principally one of gratitude for your discerning wisdom and encouragement. When I submitted pieces of writing I used to look forward to a phone call and that unmistakeable voice and I knew if I heard the words 'I like it' or 'I think it's good' my heart would lift. Then some gentle suggestions from the editor would follow about various possible modifications. If all goes according to plan, this book and these letters will come to surprise you and demonstrate in some small ways the debt your Furrow writers as well as readers owe to you.

Anne Thurston

1 Kensington Villas
Ascension-tide 2014

Dear Ronan,

In this letter I have decided to revisit my first offering for *The Furrow* on 'Family Mass' published in 1987. It is a strange experience to read something written twenty-seven years ago and realise also that our youngest child, then three, has just celebrated his thirtieth birthday. It would be easy to be nostalgic about what I see now as almost a kind of 'innocence' in that piece. This was the eighties; we were idealistic young families with a strong sense that we had a role and mission in the Church. It was also the year of the first major gathering of Pobal Dé, driven by the energy of the indefatigable Seán Mac Réamoinn and the report is published in the same issue. This was all before … This was before the nineties and the beginnings of the exposure of the abuse of children and young people by priests, and the cover-up by bishops and those in authority. *The Furrow,* no less than any other religious journal, moved to record the dark days of what Enda McDonagh called the 'wintertime' of the Church. The shock was seismic. And, as most Irish families are linked though blood or friendship with priests, it was impossible to escape connections with abused or abusers. Among the many woefully inadequate early responses from the authorities was the idea that these abusing priests were just a 'few rotten apples' and once the Church was rid of them everything would be well. What was not recognised was the level of dysfunction in this 'family'. Even now, with all the safeguards in place, I still miss this dimension: families are not 'pure' and cannot be purified by ridding themselves of those who have brought shame and disgrace. There are two moves necessary, each equally difficult: the first most importantly is the recognition and identification with the suffering of the abused; the second is to find ways of including the abusers in the family of the Church lest they, in their isolation, resort to the same practices in other places. One never 'trusts' an abuser again but the call to 'love' them, in however tough a manner, remains as a scandal, and I use the word advisedly.

I don't wish to make this topic central to my revisit for a number of reasons: others may deal with it more adequately but also because now, in 2014, it appears that springtime has returned to the church, with the 'oversight' of the bridge-builder Francis, and his declaration that 'I prefer a Church which is bruised, hurting and dirty because it has been out on the streets, rather than a Church which is unhealthy from being confined and from clinging to its own security' (Pope Francis, *Evangelii Gaudium*, #49). This way of describing Church allows for its flaws and failings to be part of its self-description rather than a notion of a 'pure and spotless bride'.

What I wish to do for the remainder of this letter is to reflect on what family means (with the help of that description) and how that might be related to how we celebrate the Eucharist. I find the concept of a children's liturgy, which I fear is what most attempts at 'Family Mass' now mean, inadequate. It already suggests something to be outgrown and the inevitable question is what will replace this when one has outgrown childish things? To give our early venture its due, we were conscious of this fact, and, our preparation for liturgy always had elements of adult catechesis about it.

But first to family: two things prompted my reflection on this topic. The first was the experience of becoming grandparents. This happened two years ago and again a few weeks ago and with another expected shortly and it has reshaped our lives. I look at a photo taken early in May of my husband greeting the newest arrival, Imogen Katherine (eight days old) while the first, Evie (two years old), sat on his knee. I realised that his hand was on the child's head in a gesture of blessing. The prayer of Simeon resonated. In a very real sense, one is both in awe of this new life and aware that as this child grows we diminish. Their birthdays lay down a marker for our death-days. This is not intended to be morbid but in fact there was an odd yet fitting coincidence in the fact that, on the birth of our first grandchild, we also paid a fee for our burial plot.

There is also an entirely new experience of love which seems to me to have a closer analogy (than sometimes possessive parental love) to what we might want to say about Divine love. Firstly, there is the sheer grace and gift of the love and trust from the child, unbidden, undeserved, simply given. The way it catches one unawares is in turn beautifully caught in Heaney's poem 'Album'. He describes three attempts to embrace his father and then admits 'it took a grandson to do it properly / to rush him in the armchair / with a snatch raid on his neck, / proving him thus vulnerable to delight.' That wonderful phrase 'vulnerable to delight' captures the experience so perfectly: joy, love, render us vulnerable. I recall my own father, an undemonstrative parent, reserved in his manner, rendered equally vulnerable by one of my daughters who, quite simply, 'disarmed' him. The breaking down of his defences was achieved through similar 'snatch-raids' without purpose or guile. The affection returned is, in a similar way, without 'intent'. The grandparent is free to love without wishing the child to be anything other than she is; she is loved for herself, and it is this 'freedom to be' which renders the analogy to ways in which we try to speak of God's love.

However, I digress; how does this experience help to reshape an understanding of family? Surely it simply reinforces the notion of close family bonds and thus leaves one within the usual contours of the domestic. Not quite; one of the things that struck us when our first grandchild arrived was the fact that she shared genetic codes, not just with us, but with her other grandparents who had, as it were, an equal part, biologically and affectionately with this child. Yet these others were in a real sense 'strangers' to us. We meet these in-laws of our daughters at weddings and christenings but they are not part of our lives. I am making much of an obvious and simple fact: the creation of families requires in the first instance an embrace of a stranger. This 'other' becomes son-in-law, daughter-in-law and, if one is lucky, these 'legal' bonds become a 'human chain' of affection, and this extends outwards to include others. Somehow it was most marked for us when we recognised that, unlike becoming parents when this is 'our' child, becoming grandparents required a stretching of that 'our' – this was 'their' grandchild. So my intention in beginning with this thought is that 'family', even in its simplest definition, is a continual demand to embrace 'otherness' and include the 'stranger'. Pious descriptions of the 'holy family', or references to the model of the family at Nazareth that ignore the turbulent embrace of the 'stranger' at its heart, give a false impression of a unit that is modelled on internal cohesion, rather than on openness to the rupture of grace. The other difficulty in terms of the 'nuclear family' is the impression that this small unit is self-contained and self-sufficient. This is far from the truth and, in fact, I believe that it is an unnatural state; and, having recently observed the struggles of first-time mothers with their infants, I think there is much to be said for an extended tribe of willing (great) aunts and (great) uncles, cousins and friends, as supporters and nurturers of these new parents and their offspring. Family works not by closing in but by opening out.

For some time I have imagined a scenario which I now learn has become a reality in Europe: namely that the very old and the very young are intentionally brought together in community. One of the most profound losses of old age is the loss of intimacy, the loss of touch. A depressing prospect for many elderly people is being confined to homes where their only company is that of others in the same state. I had imagined a set-up where homes for the elderly would be built next to nurseries so that those arriving and those departing could exchange blessings. This is apparently already happening in Germany where 'multi-generational' houses are being built: 'the elderly get a social hub and the children get a story read to them' according to a report in *The Times* (3 May 2014). According to the report, small children don't have the fear of dementia that adults have and are unself-conscious in the presence of others of limited capacity.

So my first idea, in terms of reframing family, is to step back so that the foremothers and forefathers are included; so that the wise elders are embraced and not treated as a separate category. It is not without significance that the gospel of Matthew opens with a genealogy, which includes significant disruptions, and the gospel of Luke opens with the experience of the older cousin Elizabeth, which provides a framing for the Annunciation to Mary, a detail which is often missed in the separatist accounts of Mary's holiness.

Let me now push out the boundaries of what constitutes 'holy families' a bit further. This time I do it with reference to some recent reflections by Werner Jeanrond – also well known to Furrow readers, and now master of St Benet's in Oxford. Werner was reported in the British press as offering a new and radical concept of the Christian family and challenging traditional teaching. In subsequent correspondence, he referred me to an article in the *Oxford Mail* in which he suggests that the concept of the nuclear family is a fairly recent one and yet often understood as the primary form of family and 'misunderstood as a sacred institution'. Happy families of father, mother, son and daughter are played out commercially in advertisements for houses or holidays, but also set up as 'idols' by churches too. The reality of how families are actually constituted and now function in Western cultures is very different. So the question is: what model should guide our moral compass when we talk about family?

Jeanrond returns to biblical concepts of family and suggests that these are not governed primarily by biological considerations but transcend such and refer to larger households consisting of 'relatives of different degree and generation, visitors and workers, helpers and slaves.' He argues that 'here table-fellowship makes the family'. He might also have cited Luke 8.21, 'my mother and brothers are those who hear the word of God and do it', in response to the comment, 'your mother and brothers are standing outside, wanting to see you'. The apparent downgrading of the biological tie also suggests an alternative rendering of how family is constituted.

Jeanrond asks about how we include the increasing numbers who live alone, and who is in and who is out of our categories? What about 'patchwork families', he asks? Where do single mothers fit in? Where do same-sex couples find their place? Where do the divorced and re-married or those separated belong? In one example, of what Jeanrond might describe as a 'patchwork family', a single mother is bringing up her two children with the help of her half-sister, and two 'grandmothers': one biological and the other her former step-mother who has retained bonds of care and friendship with her former step-daughter. What might seem on the surface as a set of rather complex relationships in an apparently dysfunctional family, is in practice a network of nurturing care for these children. These kinds of complex unconventional patterns exist and so a set of different questions arise about how one enables the flourishing of children and of adults in such circumstances and, it seems, that giving, what Jeanrond describes as, 'critical attention and loving support' is a good way to begin.

From a theological perspective what is important is the recognition, again citing Jeanrond, 'that Christian witness is not bound to particular culture-specific models of family life'. So rather than seeing these ideas as the Church succumbing to the prevailing culture, one might see the Church as providing alternative models for growth and grace, without undue concentration on the 'nuclear model' of the 'Christian Family' as the only form to be upheld as promoting holiness. Gospel teaching is an invitation to break out of the confines of the self and through the breaking of the bread, to break open to others.

The revelation of how table-fellowship reconstitutes the meaning of family was brought home to me by a three-year-old Indian boy some years ago. It was Christmas day and we had invited a young Indian family, whom we had met that morning, to join us. It was one of those 'risks' that we almost didn't take and, which once taken, became a gift for us. The family had turned up at the church unexpectedly just to see how 'Christians celebrate Christmas' and we got into conversation outside afterwards. This was their first Christmas in Ireland and they thought they would go into town and find somewhere to eat. Picturing the bleakness of the city on Christmas Day, we asked if they would like to come to us instead. Our son had spent time in India and promised he would try and make something spicy to eat, if they would help him. Their small boy, Subodh, very easily and happily settled in the house, while the parents joined our son in preparing the vegetables and adding spices, which of course bore no resemblance to what they would make, but was a gesture. In the preparation of the food, the guests relaxed and that nuanced balance between the vulnerability of guest and host shifted from one side to the other. Some hours later, we sat at the table, extended now, to include the 'strangers' who had become our table-companions. We exchanged words of welcome and greeting and the small child whispered something to his mother who very shyly told us what he had said. He had pointed to my husband and said to his mother, 'grandfather'? The different colour of the skin was not noticed by the child, the strangeness of food, of language, of custom was not noticed by the child, but what he observed or felt was 'family' and the fact that he noted this at the table, was for us the grace of the moment. This honorary conferring of 'grandparenthood' before the biological event was a gift. Such moments of illumination are rare and, as I said, we almost missed it; the words of invitation almost didn't reach my lips and I could have been left with 'if only' regrets for the rest of the day. 'I wonder what they did?' 'I wonder if we should have …' Yet that day, with a Hindu family, we were graced with the opportunity of learning the meaning of Christmas and the meaning of table-fellowship. Every gathering around a table to break bread and share food – particularly when it includes others, those strangers who become guests – has the potential to shape the meaning of the Eucharist so that it becomes not just something we proclaim but something we practise and something which in turn shapes us. This connection needs more explicit articulation and celebration in the Sunday gathering.

I have been circling round the ideas of 'family' and liturgy and I want to conclude this letter by asking how we might reshape our notion of family so that we don't become imprisoned by an icon which has become an idol and which, instead of enabling the breaking open of ourselves as gift and grace to one another, contributes instead to a closing off and a demarcating of the pure and impure. This, I suggest, is a false reading of the Eucharist community which is made up of the flawed and failing, the imperfect, the patched up and patched together families who seek the nurturing and sustaining grace of communion. Every Eucharist is a 'Family Mass' in this wider sense of inclusiveness.

So Ronan, it is hardly surprising that I would have different reflections on that topic at this point. There is much more I could say in terms of participation in liturgy and I still believe that that early experience was significant primarily in terms of a catechesis for the participating adults – it led me to the study of theology!

Warm wishes,
Anne

1 Kensington Villas
Pentecost 2014

Dear Ronan,
For my third and final letter in this response to your *Furrow* Festschrift, I am going to steal a title from Seamus Heaney and talk about 'the age of births'. This also returns me to the essay you published in January 1998 'There was a birth ...' Heaney's phrase comes from his poem 'Route 110' in *Human Chain* and is dedicated to a grandchild, Anna Rose. The concluding section XII begins 'And now the age of births' and finishes with the beautiful lines 'As her earthlight breaks and we gather round / talking baby talk.'[1]

In 1998 I could write with memories of my own experience of having given birth and I attempted to draw some of that very bodily experience of blood, sweat and tears into what I considered to be the sanitised descriptions of the birth of Jesus. Now looking back I find my essay once again too innocent of some of the very painful realities of the birthing experience. In the month of April, a second granddaughter arrived and two grandnieces were born and in July of this year, a third grandchild is expected, so to say that I am once again in the age of births is no exaggeration. Now, at this remove, I realise again the precariousness and fragility of human life and how each birth is and was a difficult transition for both mother and child, and how the prayers of gratitude that go up after safe arrivals are deeply felt. Walter Brueggemann talks about Israel's familiarity with babies and births, our foremothers and fathers watched the moment in which 'the newborn inhales breath … begins to live and cry … They knew that the baby did not invent that breath. The baby received it and took it in … such breath is a gift.'[2] It was through the response of the two-year-old elder sister to her two-day-old sibling which suggested a slight revision to the lines of Psalm 139 'I praise you for I am fearfully and wonderfully made.' Evie gazed with wonder at her new sister and took up one tiny hand and examined it and then reached over and took up the other hand and checked it too, and then did the same with her feet, and announced that the baby was out now and in her gaze I imagined these words: 'For it was you who formed her inward parts;/you knit her together in my mother's womb./I praise you for she is fearfully and wonderfully made.'

From the perspective of grandparenthood, watching these births and babies is a restoration of that impulse to praise. I note how both Seamus Heaney and Michael Longley have written poems dedicated to, or about, their grandchildren. The last poem in *Human Chain* is called 'A Kite for Aibhín'. And in the case of Longley these poems have an explicit tenderness to them: in fact the collection *A Hundred Doors* has a poem dedicated to each of his six grandchildren. 'The Leveret' dedicated to Benjamin begins and ends 'This is your first night in Carrigskeewaun' and tells of how he, the poet-grandfather, will 'introduce you to the sea'. When he comes to grandson number four he wonders 'How can there be enough love to go round'; but there is; he rejoices greatly when the first granddaughter Catherine arrives, followed by the 'sixth swan', Maisie. Longley, talking to Kate Kellaway of *The Guardian* says, 'what suffuses these poems is love. But I had to be careful of becoming soft-centred. There is a hardcore in the grandchildren poems. The darkness, which inevitably awaits us all, is there in each one of them.'[3] And, as I suggested in my first letter, part of the intense joy and tenderness we feel at this second time of births is that these birth-days also lay down markers for our death days – the small wrinkled feet suggest long journeys of arrival and departure.

I think it is this awareness of the darkness (not just of the inevitability of death but of the sorrows as well as the joys which shape all lives) that changes how one writes about these things at this stage of life and this also is where conversation about faith begins. Even as I write about the joyful aspects of this 'age of births', I carry the thoughts of a young woman, the same age as my daughters, who was widowed some few months ago and who has just given birth to a child who will never know her father.

So I want to bring these things – poetry, grandchildren, faith in darkness and light, together in my final letter of this series. In that final beautiful poem 'A Kite for Aibhín', Heaney describes the kite carrying farther and higher until 'string breaks and – separate, elate –/ The kite takes off, itself alone, a windfall.' Longley, in one of the tributes to Heaney, described 'windfall' as one of the beautiful words in the English language. In this context it loses all commercial connotations and becomes pure gift, blown by the wind. The other aspect that strikes the reader is how the kite-flier stands 'longing in the breast and planted feet', that combination of being both grounded and yet with a pull towards something else. Then 'the string breaks' and there is rupture and rapture when 'separate, elate –/ the kite takes off, itself alone, a windfall.' The breaking of the string suggests the cutting of the cord at birth, and that letting go which is a continuous part of the parenting process. In the case of grand-parenting, we gaze with wonder at these new lives and there is a particular intensity to our awareness and joy, and part of that may be the knowledge that we will not see how these lives unfold to their fullness but we see their promise. In Longley's poem 'The Leveret' he names the things he wants to show his new grandson so there is this urge to pass on what is good, what matters. Longley imagines the child having heard the wind while in the womb and asks if he hears it now, 'Do you hear the wind tonight, and the rain/ And a shore bird calling from the mussel reefs?' He offers words of reassurance 'we may meet the stoat … But don't be afraid.' In 'Route 110' Heaney comes with a bunch of stalks as 'a thank-offering' like 'tapers that won't dim as her earth-light breaks'; Longley picks wildflowers and places them in water 'That will bend and magnify the daylight.' The urge to give praise and thanks is paramount.

Longley introduces his grandchildren to the wonders of Carrigskeewaun in the expectation and hope, I suspect, that closeness to a landscape such as this, will give them roots which will nourish and sustain them. Here in the city I read stories to my grandchildren and show my small grand-daughter the garden; she watches the clouds move across the sky and distinguishes between the Luas bell and church bells. We sit at the table together and I tell her 'I was writing about table-fellowship earlier'; she gives me a serious look, 'yes' she says, and asks to taste my bread; 'of course', I say, and break a piece off for her.

What shape will their faith take? We have no idea. What I do note though is a desire on our part to pass on the traditions which have given shape and form to our lives. I also know that this passing on, like that of Longley, will be in the form of invitation, of showing, 'Tomorrow I'll introduce you to the sea' or 'The leveret breakfasts under the fuchsia / Every morning, and we shall be watching.' We human creatures construct or create the meaning of our lives, but we also believe that we participate in traditions of meaning and thus each new human creature does not have to begin again but is inserted into sets of symbolic meaning which they in their turn will absorb, critique, modify. Hand-me-downs were very much a part of my childhood. They are less common in a disposable age, but with a greater ecological awareness they may return; but part of grand-parenting is to hand-down what is treasured in possession, in matter and in spirit.

In her novel *Gilead*, Marilynne Robinson's character, the pastor John Ames, speaks about the faces of the infants he baptises, and how he feels that each one is a blessing: 'There is nothing more astonishing than a human face … it has something to do with incarnation. You feel your obligation to a child when you have seen it and held it. Any human face is a claim on you, because you can't help but understand the singularity of it, the courage and loneliness of it. But this is truest of the face of an infant.' The baptism of our first grandchild was a chaotic affair and the 'sacred' memory I carry, is the way the child lay in her father's arms and did not take her eyes from his face. I thought as I watched them: she is certainly making her claim on him. Now at two years I see how she continues to read faces, alert to every change of expression and what it might mean.

The philosopher Levinas speaks about the call of the human face as an ethical call and Robinson gives this notion flesh: to hold an infant child and look at its face is to know such a call. As these small creatures reintroduce us both to the fragility and the wonder of human life, in turn we want to draw them in to the practices and rituals which have sustained and nourished our lives, made sense of its pains and its joys. And if the parents choose a sacramental life for their children you want them to do this because, citing Ames again, 'There is a reality in blessing ... it doesn't enhance sacredness but it acknowledges it.' The urge to give thanks and praise after the birth of a child calls for a 'Thanks be to God' in some shape. Our own words always seem inadequate to these occasions and the rhythms of something like Psalm 136, with its litany of 'for his steadfast love endures forever', places our thanksgiving into a cosmic context.

The three new human persons who arrived at Eastertide into our wider family are all girls. They come into a world now far more hospitable and welcoming to female children than the time of birth of their grandmothers. I do not know if any of these three will be shaped in Catholic communities and I wonder whether in their lifetime that Church will be reformed in such a way as it may also become fully hospitable to their gifts. I know that this grandmother will find it difficult, if not impossible, to justify exclusion from ministry and leadership in the Church to the small bright girl child who already at two years seems determined to 'lead'. I know too that when she comes to ask me 'why', and the 'whys' are beginning, I chose to study theology, my answer will have notes of loss and regret as well as pride and delight. In particular I regret the very limited, very occasional opportunities, to preach the word despite years of nurturing it through the study of theology, imbued with female experience.

Furrow readers may have noticed a shift in my lines of interest over these twenty-five years. I have not re-visited 'What do women want?' (1992) and recent pieces are more likely to speak of poetry than protest. Is this an escape, an avoidance? After a time it became wearying to speak about 'women and the church', it sapped energy. I turned to work on things that would reenergise, that would enable conversations about faith and practice at a fundamental human level. I continued to explore and draw on the social and cultural experience of being female, but I sought writers and poets who were readers of the human condition and who would draw me towards its mysteries and depths with full awareness of its ambiguities. In October 2012, you published a piece called 'Divining the Gaps', which contrasted poems by Seamus Heaney and Dennis O'Driscoll. At that year's end Dennis was dead, and the following August Seamus Heaney's heart burst open and he too died. What another has called O'Driscoll's psalms of lament in his last collection are now a haunting memorial, and Heaney's *Human Chain* collection is scoured for the last words of wisdom. O'Driscoll, in the final poem of *Dear Life*, 'Nocturne Op 2' takes us to the very edge of darkness, 'which seems the very point', but Heaney leaves us with both uplift and 'fall' in that last word of 'Kite for Aibhín', 'a windfall'.

Like Longley, I too want to introduce my grandchildren to the sea, but I hope too that they will be readers of parables and of poetry, hearers of stories and singers of songs, and this, alongside the swiping of screens, at which from a very early age, they are adept. For now we sit at the table talking and sharing food, passing on habits of grace and gratitude, as we wipe up spills, clean snotty noses, and wonder and rejoice at how blessed we are:

> So now, as a thank-offering for one
> Whose long wait on the shaded bank has ended
> I arrive with my bunch of stalks and silvered heads
>
> Like tapers that won't dim
> As her earthlight breaks and we gather round
> Talking baby talk.

And now finally I would like to bring such a 'bunch of stalks and silvered heads' to celebrate your ninety years Ronan, your 'silvered head', and your ploughing of this Furrow which has enabled many to gather round talking not so much 'baby talk' but spirited conversation about the many and varied things of matter to the pilgrim people of this Furrow parish.

Warm wishes and profound thanks,

Anne

Hope for Religious Education:
Was Danger Mulally on to Something?
THOMAS GROOME

It is a privilege to contribute an essay to a Festschrift in honour of Fr Ronan Drury. As for many others who contribute to this volume, I'm sure, this also lends me an opportunity to repay a long-standing debt that I have to Fr Ronan, if only by way of an explicit and public 'thank you.' My debt of gratitude goes back nigh fifty years to when I was a seminarian in St Patrick's, Carlow (1962–8).

At that time, Fr Ned Dowling, Senior Dean in Carlow and a great friend of Ronan's, was in charge of the twice yearly drama production. Not being much of a thespian himself, Ned would bring Ronan down from Maynooth to tutor the cast before the performance of each play. He had amazing creativity and expertise in this regard; if Ronan hadn't taken the path he did, he might well have been a successful Hollywood director. Being a performer in many of the plays during my time in Carlow, I benefited greatly from his tutoring. Indeed, whatever aplomb I may have had in the public arena across the years, is due in no small part to his tutoring. So thank you, Fr Drury.

From the dramas of my youth as well, I have a particular memory that will lead me into the theme of my essay in his honour. My favourite role to play by far was that of Danger Mulally in John B. Keane's play, *Many Young Men of Twenty*; I believe we performed it in the Spring of 1967. Fast forward some thirty years to 1998; when I submitted my first essay to *The Furrow*, Ronan responded with, 'Dear Danger'. I was flattered that he still remembered me in that role.

Like himself, however, I chose a different stage for my vocation, that of an educator-in-faith. Now, as honouring him prompts me to revisit memories of my drama days, a few lines from a song that Danger sings in the play come back to me and, upon reflection, I recognise them as naming well the signs of hope that I wish to suggest in this essay. Much as Ronan has lent hope through *The Furrow* across these many years, I have worked to keep hope alive for the Church's ministry of catechesis.

Hope for religious education has grown all the more challenging in our time. As Charles Taylor well describes, 'the conditions of belief' have changed radically from old Christian cultures that encouraged faith, to contexts within the time of a 'secular age' in which the culturally favoured position is for an 'exclusive humanism'. Taylor calls it *exclusive* in that it excludes any reference to the Transcendent, nor does it nurture the human aptitude for transcendence.[1] Yet, in spite of the greater challenge, I recognise at least two significant signs of hope for catechesis that seem a little more evident in our time. The first is a new found emphasis among Catholics on *the historical Jesus* (in many ways, the defining theme of Pope Francis) and the second is the emergence of a pedagogy that seems more likely to promote the integration of *life and faith* into *lived faith*.

Remembering that I should, 'give reason for the hope that is in (me)' (1 Pet 3:15), I will lay out these hopes briefly here and my rationale for them. But first, as the pleasant task of honouring Fr Drury caused me to revisit the memory of Danger Mulally, I recalled a song that Danger sings in *Many Young Men of Twenty*. It summarises well I think, my two signs of hope, namely a personal relationship with the historical Jesus that encourages an everyday faith. The song comes at a dramatic moment, when Danger, finding himself on the ropes of life, kneels before a crucifix, and sings to the Crucified:

> They crowned Your head with thorns, they brought You misery;
> You died upon a Cross, high up in Calvary;
> There is no other love for me;
> You will be mine for all eternity.
>
> Round here they laugh an' call me 'Drunken Danger!'
> But I have you in spite of Keelty town;
> The greatest pal that ever walked a roadway;
> The only Man who never let me down.

In many ways, Danger had it right; Christian faith calls first and foremost to friendship with Jesus, and then to the deep conviction that the relationship with him must be lived out daily. I find warrant for my two hopes in the Church's more recent catechetical documents; they state them more elegantly, of course, but no more persuasively than Danger did.

A Turn to The Historical Jesus
Traditionally and comparatively speaking, Catholic Christians have been far more focused on the Christ of faith than on the Jesus of history. There

are a number of reasons for our neglect of the historical Jesus. Let me cite just a catechetical one. *The Catechism of the Council of Trent* (1566, also known as *The Roman Catechism*) was framed around the Apostles' Creed, the Sacraments, and the Commandments – in that order. So, for the beliefs of Catholic faith, the *Catechism* simply took each article of the Creed and explained it. Subsequently, the great national catechisms (Maynooth, Baltimore, etc.) followed the same pattern of 'creed, code, cult.'

The Creed's article 'born of the virgin Mary' is followed immediately by 'suffered under Pontius Pilate.' In other words, it skips entirely the public life of Jesus. As a result, you'll find nary a word in any of the traditional catechisms about Jesus' feeding the hungry, healing the sick or any of his other works of mercy and love. The historical Jesus is simply absent. Likewise the traditional decades of the Rosary, long the operative Christology for Catholics, move from the fifth *Joyful* mystery 'The Finding in the Temple' (when Jesus was twelve) to the first *Sorrowful*, 'The Agony in the Garden' – again, skipping the praxis of the historical Jesus. (This was before Pope John Paul II wisely added the *Luminous Mysteries*, lending at least some focus on the public life of Jesus.)

The Church's recent catechetical documents have consistently recentred Christology and lend fresh highlight to the historical Jesus,[2] though without diminishing the Christ of faith. Patently, the two are the same person, and our faith needs emphasis on both. A now classic summary is offered by the *Catechism of the Catholic Church* (echoing Pope John Paul II's *Catechesi Tradendae* of 1979). The *Catechism* makes clear that the centre of our faith is not the Bible, the sacraments, the commandments, the church and so on, constitutive as are all these aspects. Instead, 'At the heart of catechesis we find a Person, the Person of Jesus of Nazareth, the only Son from the Father' (*CCC* #426). Note well the equal emphasis on both.

So, as Pope Francis is heralding so well, Christian faith must first centre on and imitate the praxis of the historical Jesus. Essentially, our faith calls to discipleship to that carpenter from Nazareth who walked the roads of Galilee, preaching radical love – even of enemies – feeding the hungry, caring for the poor of all sorts, healing the sick, expelling evil from people's lives, welcoming all to the table, claiming to be 'the way, truth and life' (Jn 14:6), all to announce the in-breaking of God's reign. Like the people in his home town synagogue of Nazareth on a Sabbath, we must 'fix our eyes on Jesus' as 'this very day' he claims to fulfill the radical messianic prophecy of Isaiah 61:1–2. He was the anointed one who brought 'good news to the poor … release to the captives … sight to the blind … freedom to the oppressed' and proclaimed 'the year of the Lord's favour' (Luke 4:16–21).

As the *General Directory for Catechesis* summarises, all evangelising and catechising has the defining purpose 'to put people in communion and intimacy with Jesus Christ' (*GDC* #80). This, however, does not mean a solipsistic 'me and Jesus' solo faith but an 'apprenticing' (a favoured term in the *GDC*) of people in discipleship to Jesus within his community of disciples, the Church, so that they come to a 'full and sincere adherence to his person and the decision to walk in his footsteps' (see *GDC* #53 and *passim*). Nor should we fall into a Christomonism as if Jesus is the beginning and end of Christian faith. Instead, he is the key to how we come to know and share in the Trinitarian life of God. As always 'the Word of God, incarnate in Jesus of Nazareth, is the Word of the Father who speaks to the world through his Spirit' (*GDC* #99).

The ultimate essence of Christian faith, then, is to live like Jesus, within a community of his disciples, with all the compassion for human suffering, mercy for sinners, and care for the poor that advances the realising of God's reign 'on earth as in heaven.' As Pope Francis summarises so well, 'The Son of God, by becoming flesh, summoned us to the revolution of tenderness' (*Evangelii Gaudium* #88).

Of course, our catechesis must also reflect the centrality of the *Christ of faith*. This very same Jesus was also the divine presence among us as one of ourselves, the Son of God, the Second Person of the Blessed Trinity, our Savior and Liberator. By his paschal mystery, Christ conquered sin, personal and social, and even death. Now, and by the power of the Holy Spirit, God's saving work of humankind continues through him. So, not only does he model how disciples are to live, but 'God's abundant grace in Christ Jesus' (1 Tim 1:14) now makes it possible for us to at least approximate so living.

However, why does this rebalancing of the Jesus of history with the Christ of faith offer new hope for evangelisation and catechesis. I believe the person of the historical Jesus is the most appealing feature of Christian faith in our 'secular age'. To propose *the way* modelled and made possible by Jesus can still appeal powerfully to people's deepest desires to live well.

As such, focusing on Jesus, the Christ, can lend a persuasive apologetic that appeals to personal conviction much more than a coercive one that relies simply on authority (e.g. of the Church), or is based on a system of reward and punishment – our standard apologetic for so long. Again, Francis is leading the way. He says that we need 'a creative apologetic which encourages greater openness to the Gospel' (*EG* 132), one that 'appeals to freedom' (*EG* 165) by offering God's 'healing and liberation' in Jesus Christ (*EG* 89). As if echoing the song of Danger Mulally, Francis writes that our primary proclamation to people must be that 'Jesus Christ loves you; he gave his life to save you; and now he is living at your side every day to enlighten, strengthen and free you' (*EG* 164).

Bringing Life to Faith to Life

The second sign of hope I see for educating-in-faith is the increasing popularity and growing employ of a pedagogy designed to encourage people to bring their lives to their faith and their faith to their lives. Some such approach is now implemented in a number of major catechetical curricula throughout the world and, as I suggest below, seems to be favoured by the Church's own *General Directory for Catechesis*.

The Second Vatican Council declared that the 'split' which Christians maintain 'between the faith which many profess and their daily lives deserves to be counted among the more serious errors of our age'.[3] This statement highlights the need to teach Christian faith in a way that encourages people not simply to know about it but to consistently integrate 'the faith' into their daily lives. Though it favours the language of 'experience', the *GDC* states repeatedly that catechesis must teach the faith handed down in ways that relevantly engage people's lives and that encourage their integrating life and faith into lived faith.

The *Directory* states: 'every dimension of the faith, like the faith itself as a whole, must be rooted in human experience' (*GDC* #87). For 'experience promotes the intelligibility of the Christian message'; in fact, 'experience is a necessary medium for exploring and assimilating the truths which constitute the objective content of Revelation' (*GDC* #152). In consequence, catechetical education is most effective when it integrates with human experience. Its starting point, 'faith formation must be closely related to praxis; one must start with praxis to be able to arrive at praxis' (*GDC* #245).

For almost forty years now, I have been attempting to develop, articulate, and practice *a life to Faith to life* approach to Christian religious education and catechesis. I have written about it more formally as a 'shared

Christian praxis approach.'[4] I now often refer to it with the more user friendly *bringing life to Faith and Faith to life*.[5] But let me point to the praxis of the historical Jesus and precisely to his pedagogy.

I believe that Jesus' favoured pedagogy was to lead people *from life to Faith to life-in-faith*. He did so by:

- Beginning with people's own lived reality
- Encouraging their reflection and often a new perspective on their lives
- Teaching them his Gospel with authority
- Inviting people to see for themselves, to make his teaching their own
- Encouraging their decisions for lived faith as disciples

Beginning with People's Lived Reality: Jesus almost invariably began a teaching event by inviting people to look at their present lives in the world. He turned his listeners to their own experiences, to their feelings, thoughts, and values, to creation around them, to the beliefs, practices, attitudes and mores of their religious tradition and culture, to their work and social arrangements, to their joys and sorrows, fears and hopes, sins and goodness – to life. His favourite teaching method, of course, was his use of parables in Matthew, Mark, and Luke, and through allegories (e.g. the Good Shepherd) or 'signs' (e.g. wedding at Cana) in John's Gospel. All of these begin with symbols of everyday life that would actively engage people as they recognised their own lives and stories.

Encouraging People's own Reflections: Second, Jesus invited people to think about their lives and often in a whole new way. He wanted his listeners to recognise that great things like the reign of God and their own eternal destiny were being negotiated in the ordinary and everyday of life. He wanted them to reflect critically on the falsehood of hypocrisy, the emptiness of ritual detached from doing God's will, the lack of faith in hating any group or class, the unconditional love of God, regardless of one's worthiness.

In prompting people to reflect on their lives, Jesus often invited them to turn their perspectives upside down. None of Jesus' first hearers would have expected the Samaritan to be neighbour, nor the father to welcome home the prodigal, nor Lazarus to go to the bosom of Abraham and the rich man to hell, nor the prostitutes and tax collectors to enter the reign of God before the religious leaders. Such reversals were Jesus' way of getting people to reflect critically, perhaps to change their minds and hearts, to see their lives and possibilities with fresh hope and in a whole new way.

Teaching his Gospel with Authority: Third, from the very beginning of Jesus' public ministry, people recognised that he 'taught them as one with authority' (Mk 1:22). Clearly, Jesus took strong positions in teaching his Gospel. He deeply appreciated his Jewish tradition, never intending to abolish the Law and the Prophets but 'to make their teaching come true' (Mt 5:17). Yet, he also claimed the authority to propose a new vision for living as a people of God. 'You have heard it said ... but I say ...' (Mt 5:21–22).

Inviting People to See for Themselves: Fourth, Jesus taught in ways that invited people to recognise for themselves the Good News he was proposing, to take to heart and personally embrace the truth he was teaching. Jesus often blessed those 'with the eyes to see and the ears to hear.' Referring surely to more than physical seeing and hearing, he wanted people to open themselves up and make their own the spiritual wisdom he was teaching. He waited for the Samaritan woman to come to see for herself, and see for herself she did: 'Could this be the Messiah?' (Jn 4:29). The same became true for her friends as they came to recognise him themselves. 'We have heard for ourselves and we know that this is truly the Savior of the world' (Jn 4:42).

Encouraging their Decisions for Lived Faith: Fifth, Jesus' invitation to discipleship – to lived faith – was ever on offer. The intended outcome of his whole public ministry was that people might decide to live for the reign of God by following his way as disciples. Jesus was adamant that to belong to God's reign, people cannot simply confess faith with their lips, saying 'Lord, Lord,' but must 'do the will of my Father in heaven' (Mt 7:21). That surely requires decision. Jesus even went so far as to say, 'Whoever does the will of God is my brother and sister and mother' (Mk 3:35). From his opening statement inviting people to 'repent and believe in the Gospel' (Mk 1:15) to his farewell discourse, 'live on in my love ... keep my commandments' (Jn 15:9–10), Jesus invited people to decision for lived faith.

Though Jesus' pedagogy of *life to Faith to life* is evident throughout his public ministry, nowhere is it more patent than with that stranger on the road to Emmaus (Lk 24:13–35). Note how he engages their lives and draws out their reflections on their traumatic story and shattered vision. Only then does he share the Story and Vision of the faith community – 'beginning with Moses and all the prophets' (v. 27). Yet, he never tells them what to see but waits for them to come to see for themselves, whereupon they freely decide to return to Jerusalem and re-engage their lives in faith. The more we can approximate such pedagogy – *life to Faith to life-in-faith* – the more effective our religious education will be.

At least, this is another of my hopes. Through the thousands of pages of *The Furrow* that he has published, Ronan Drury has also kept such hope alive. *Ad multos annos*!

Communication and the Church:
A Memory and a Meditation
JOHN HORGAN

If you walk down the Via della Conciliazione from St Peter's, and wander into the warren of little streets on the left-hand side of that grandiose thoroughfare, you might come across a small nondescript building that is, nonetheless, unmistakeably a church.

Nothing strange about that, you might think: Rome has plenty of them. But this is a church with a difference. It is the Roman footprint of the Moravian Church, cheekily adjacent to the Vatican, and boasting – even more cheekily – on an inside wall, facing the congregation, the inscription: *Lux lucebit in tenebris*.

It was there, at some stage during the first Synod of Bishops in 1967, that I attended a public meeting addressed by the diminutive, feisty French Dominican theologian, Fr Marie-Dominique Chenu. Fr Chenu was already famous as a key member of the progressive Le Saulchoir monastic community in Paris, and the author of a book on that monastery and its theology which had been condemned by the Holy Office more than a quarter of a century earlier. Now, he practically levitated as he denounced the Vatican's attempt to roll back the advances which had been made in the relationship between the Church and the media during the Second Vatican Council, which had ended two years earlier.

'*Tout blocage de communication*', he declared in ringing tones, '*est un péché contre le Saint-Esprit!*'

The circumstances in which he uttered this call to arms could hardly have been more apposite. Vatican II, two years earlier, had been marked by an extraordinary relaxation of the relationship between bishops, priests and media generally. In 1967, as the first Synod opened, it was immediately apparent that the Canute-like propensities of the Vatican bureaucracy had again reasserted themselves. Information about the Synod dribbled out in costive, uninteresting summaries prepared by the Vatican Press Office. There were no press conferences – Pope Paul VI himself had even given one during the final session of the Council – and scraps of unofficial information were being devoured by the hungry, multitudinous press corps.

The relationship between Church and media generally has always been on a bit of a see-saw. In Ireland, specifically, it was slow in developing.

Before the council, the mainstream media reported bishops' pastoral letters, and that was about it: Fr Michael O'Neill, writing in *The Furrow* in 1958, noted that 'even the clergy find much of it dull and repetitious.'[1] The advent of John XXIII created a stir: some of his encyclicals – notably *Pacem in terris* – were reprinted by some national media in their entirety. But no media organisation, with the exception of RTÉ, sent journalists to the first three sessions of Vatican II: Kevin O'Kelly did news and, at intervals, the irrepressible Sean Mac Réamoinn contributed more detailed reports and interviews, but that was all.

The national newspapers did not send reporters to Rome until 1965, when the Council was ending. Almost without exception, however, Irish journalists in Rome in 1965 (and here I must count myself among the guilty parties) had little or nothing to do with the Irish hierarchy or their *periti*, closeted as they were in the Irish College. Other bishops (not least Irish missionary bishops like Donal Lamont from Antrim and Umtali, and James Corboy SJ from what was still 'Southern Rhodesia') were so much more available and – we assumed, perhaps wrongly – more interesting or at least more approachable and laid-back. The Council as a whole was, when contrasted with the over-formal and largely unexplored relationships between Irish media and Irish bishops, the embodiment of the scriptural narrative: 'The wind bloweth where it listeth, and thou hears the sound thereof but canst not tell whence it cometh, and whither it goeth: so is everyone that is born of the Spirit.'[2]

Communicating the Council later became, in a sense, a post-conciliar apostolate in which clergy and laity could all, at least theoretically, participate to some degree, even though it quickly became evident that the religious orders were, in this respect, much more adventurous than their colleagues in the diocesan ministries. The work of people like Br Paul SVD of Donamon with The Word comes to mind, together with that of the Columbans. And of course there was *The Furrow*, whose *lares et penates*, JG McGarry and Ronan Drury, probably did more to re-invigorate Irish public discourse about the challenges facing the Church in the world than many of those who had a more formal responsibility in that area.

It was hardly an accident that both men were professionally involved in homiletics, and the index of the magazine demonstrates, beyond argument, the positive interest of its editors not only in the communications media as such, but in the creative and communicative arts of television, theatre, cinema and radio. In this sense, the post-Conciliar initiatives taken by *The Furrow* and its editors in breaking down the barriers of clericalism, verbal obscurantism and one-way communication were building on already well established and tested foundations. This showed, too, that in communications, actions can speak as loud as words – in this case, the actions of McGarry and Drury in identifying, and giving the immeasurable hospitality of their pages to lay and clerical communicators who were notable for the efficacy of their communicative skills. If these skills did not always evoke assent, they demanded engagement; and the *populus dei* was the beneficiary. Both men, in the words of a friendly chronicler, saw openness of communication and the renewal of the Irish Church as 'inextricably interlinked'.[3]

After the Council, the kind of courage and creativity exemplified by *The Furrow*, its editors and contributors, began to spread like a benign bacillus. The Redemptorists started their magazine *Reality*, edited with the help of a lay advisory board. The unforgettable Mission Study Week in Navan in 1968, fuelled by the latter order's legendary hospitality, was a reminder, if reminder was needed, of how much of the creative, communicative and theological energy of the Church in Ireland had flourished in foreign fields, compared to the sometimes stony ground of home, and of the greater freedom enjoyed by religious compared with secular clergy. More than that, it sowed the seed of the critically important idea that dissent was not disloyalty – that the emergence of what might be called, in parliamentary parlance, a loyal opposition, was a growth to be cherished rather than stamped on.

In time, too, the lay element of that loyal opposition began to find its voice, and the communicative dialogue increasingly involved the laity. There was, for instance, a largely lay discussion group in Dublin, known colloquially as 'Flannery's Harriers' in jocose homage to the energy and personality of its guiding Dominican spirit, Austin Flannery OP. This began to meet, much as Christians used to do in the catacombs, first in James White's apartment above the Municipal Gallery of Modern Art in Parnell Square and later in the more plebeian surroundings of the upstairs lounge in the Clarence Hotel. Visiting speakers, both clerical and lay, came to engage with disputatious Harriers like Jack Dowling of RTÉ and Desmond Fennell.

Outside Dublin, growth may have been slower but was no less significant. People like Jack Peters in Galway generated lively discussion groups to spread the awareness of Conciliar matters. After one of these, at which the then Bishop of Galway, Michael Browne, had met a torrent of criticism from lay people about the Church's teaching on contraception, he invited Jack to the episcopal residence, sat him down with a glass of whiskey, and inquired: 'Jack – what makes these people tick?'

Archbishop McQuaid not only appointed a press officer – a gentle, ex-Irish Independent journalist named Osmond Dowling – as the first ever diocesan press officer, but invited scores of journalists, including some the clerical Church might have regarded as deeply suspect, to a special Mass in Clonliffe to celebrate Communications Day. At this Mass Sean Mac Réamoinn and myself served as altar boys under McQuaid's watchful gaze, and it was followed by a huge reception at which strong drink was served to those who wished to partake, along with the tea and sandwiches.[4]

There were, it seems to me on reflection, three different things happening during this period. One was adaptation, on the part of the Church, to the demands of the late twentieth century media. This was, to put it mildly, uneven, but in all the major newspapers, and in RTÉ, there was an openness to the new ideas, to new theology, and – probably more significantly in the long run – to the idea that the range of topics now open for discussion had been extended exponentially, and that status did not automatically confer authority.

Some of the steps were painfully slow: I have a vivid recollection of the first RTÉ religious discussion programme to feature an atheist, a man who was, for this purpose, surrounded and generally patronised by a bevy of well-intentioned Christians, some of whom plainly had difficulty in taking him seriously. At the other end of the spectrum were the television appearances by people like Austin Flannery and Feargal O'Connor, who offered vivid insights into the options for the Church in the world, and in the media, that left little room for doubt about the critical arguments that would take place in the future.

The second thing that was happening was the development of an unspoken but real rivalry between the pulpit and the camera and microphone. The pulpit, effectively, was no longer the only show in town. The flashy, glitzy world of the broadcasters – particularly in television – demanded (and got) public attention even as the pulling power of the pulpit began to wane. It was hardly accidental that the responses to a survey of its members carried out by a recently founded association of Irish priests[5] provided strong evidence that the majority of respondents, had they not opted for the priesthood, would have liked to take up a career in media. At this level, and for some of those involved at any rate, the issue was less one of the Church learning how to work with the media, and more one of the Church marshalling its forces to establish a bridgehead in the terrain of public discourse on which the voices of its clerical office-holders had previously been unchallenged but were now questioned at every turn. The danger of this model, of course, was – and is – that the attempt at colonisation of hostile intellectual territory by the Church would, in the long run, be no more successful than other, physical colonisations carried out for simpler political or economic motives.

The third thing that was happening was more inchoate and is still an area in which developments are continuously taking place and in which the future is still to a degree unclear. This is the extent to which the Church is facing the challenge involved in seeing itself less as an institution that communicates (or fails to communicate) in purely technical or strategic terms, and is prepared to re-imagine itself more as an instrument of communication in its own right, as a living, breathing organism whose very essence is communication. If it is true, as has been said, that we must love one another or die, is it not equally true that we cannot love each other without communicating with each other?

If we begin to look at the church more in this light, the relevance of Père Chenu's warning becomes ever more apparent, and some of our more contemporary issues may appear in a different light. The Church's problems of discipline, of organisation, of ministry, of status and of power, if viewed in a new context in which the demands of communication and a refreshed concept of service provide a new litmus test, may appear quite differently to us, and their solutions more achievable.

Of course, it forces us, in turn, to confront new or at least renewed definitional challenges: what exactly is it that we think we ought to be communicating and why? Starting with the Beatitudes would not be a bad idea. But even attempting to answer those questions will, with luck, drive us back to our roots and should also, in the process, help us to redefine our modes of communication, our structures, our relationships with ourselves and others, and even many of our supposed values, in ways that may make some of our old internecine squabbles, both intra and inter-ecclesial, seem at best superfluous and at worst ridiculous. For the future, let communication and the *sensus fidelium* proceed, if not always hand-in-hand, at least side-by-side.

Encountering The Furrow

EÓIN DE BHÁLDRAITHE

When I studied theology in the monastery (1958–63), *The Furrow* was a great assistance in what now, looking back, seems like an intellectual awakening. There were several articles advising that we abandon long-held Catholic positions and practices and adopt a more contemporary view. I remember, in particular, going back a few times to read a piece by Enda McDonagh on Jesus as our Shepherd. My first foray into controversy was in *The Furrow*, 'Joint Pastoral Care of Interchurch Marriages'. Some background information, like a flashback in a film, will be necessary to explain the significance of this.

I was lucky enough to be sent to Rome just after ordination, rare in our Order, and so was able to continue study without a major break. I attended the University run by the Benedictines, mainly attracted by the reputation of Cipriano Vaggagini. He withdrew from teaching, however, just as I arrived. He had written the first draft of the Liturgy Constitution and was deeply involved in re-drafting it as the debates proceeded. He was replaced by Magnus Löhrer of the monastery of Einsiedlen. This new man had decided that ecumenism was the up-and-coming thing and was deeply influenced by his fellow countryman, Hans Küng. His Benedictine confreres were perhaps a little worried by his approach and commented that we were all absorbing his doctrine, 'like little Abelards'. I remember deciding at the time that there would be plenty of scope for ecumenical rapprochement when I came back home.

The burning issue at the time was our mixed marriage laws. Both parties had to sign a promise that all the children would be reared as Catholics. Since this became law in 1908, there was a great diminishment in numbers for the Protestants. As a precaution they had to try to keep their young people from mixing with Catholics. A new document was issued by the Holy Office in 1966 which caused great resentment outside our church.[1] So I settled down to write my own theology of mixed marriages. Pope Paul VI took up the matter personally and issued a new document in 1970, *Matrimonia mixta*.[2] Now there was no promise expected from the non-Catholic and the Catholic promised to do 'all in his power' to have the children Catholic. I remember Archbishop Simms welcoming the fact that one of his flock would not now have to promise anything but it took a long time for this to sink into the RC mind. The Archbishop of

Canterbury said that the new legislation would be helpful, 'so long as it is acted upon to the full'. I wrote that, considering the rights of the Protestant party it was not in the power of the Catholic to ignore those and so, sometimes, a decision to have all the children Protestant was permissible and legitimate. David Woodworth, Church of Ireland minister, wrote commending my views as it would now be more possible to allow the young people of both sides to mix.[3]

I submitted my essay to the *Irish Theological Quarterly*. I also submitted a follow-up article to *The Furrow* on the clergy of both sides working together to help mixed marriage couples. Meanwhile ITQ would not publish the matrix essay and asked for certain revisions. I was naive enough to believe them. After long labour in revising the text they still refused. This meant that *The Furrow* piece remained without a desirable context.

At the time the monastery was newly founded in Dublin archdiocese, so it was important for the new superior to cultivate good relations with Archbishop McQuaid. Just before this (early 1968) he had forbidden Michael Hurley to give a public lecture in Milltown Park, so the superior asked me not to mention Hurley. But it was still a quandary for him as to whether he should allow publication. I wrote to the editor, Canon McGarry, explaining the situation. He wrote back to me a letter intended mainly for the superior's eyes. The essay, he said, was a fair effort to implement the Pope's document and the reaction of the Irish bishops to the same was inadequate. So he recommended publication.

The article got little enough attention. Fr P. J. Brophy (Carlow) had written shortly before that to say that in the ecumenical age, a church should be prepared to die and so the Church of Ireland should accommodate itself to our laws even if it meant the end for them. I countered that to assent to one's own demise would indeed be like the martyrdom of Jesus but to desire the end of another church was more akin to murder. Brophy took it rather well and on one occasion while visiting in Carlow College, he offered me a lift back to the monastery. His bishop Patrick Lennon was driving, so the opportunity was not to be missed. 'Why couldn't the bishops be more lenient on mixed marriages?' 'I have really nothing to do with it,' he said, 'Cardinal Conway decides on that issue and he says that if things were to be more lenient, they would run the risk of losing control of the Catholics.'[4]

Canon McGarry had much good advice to offer to a young writer. Finish your essay in every way and make sure that it is right politically. Then leave it for a time and you will come back to it with a fresh mind. Later I began to write on other topics. McGarry advised me to restrict myself or people would say, 'This fellow is on to everything'. I didn't take his advice with the result that I have spread myself too widely and so much of my work is shallow and ephemeral.

Likewise Cardinal Heenan in England had been strongly defensive of the Catholic legislation. So when he died in 1975, the English bishops allowed a more generous arrangement. I heard one bishop claim that they did not realise that the 1970 document meant a change in the law. But the fact is that the change in the law was not so easy to discern: it would allow the continental bishops to make the change they wanted without disturbing the Irish or British bishops. The other regulation of the time (1972) on sharing the Eucharist was similar: it should not be given to anyone who had easy access to a minister of their own church. This clever law had little to do with the theology of the Eucharist but it allowed Church of England people to receive communion while on the Continent and forbade them to get it at home. This proviso was dropped by Pope John Paul in 1995.

Cardinal Conway died in 1970 and his successor was anxious to see an improvement. The Irish bishops eventually published a new directory in 1983. Reputedly, Cardinal Ó Fiaich had to use a lot of persuasion to get it past his fellow bishops. The main statement was; 'The obligations of the Catholic do not, and cannot, cancel out, or in any way call into question, the conscientious duties of the other party.' That left an opening for a decision to have some or all of the children reared in the church of the other partner. But of course the ideal was that they be reared with 'double belonging'.

Canon McGarry died in a car accident in 1977. The people of Ballyhaunis were surprised to see twelve bishops at his funeral. 'We had a saint living among us, and we did not know it', one woman said to me. At the Mass, the Archbishop of Tuam said that he was happy to tell everyone that one of the last letters written by McGarry was an effort at conciliation with somebody who was offended by something in *The Furrow*. It was widely believed that this referred to a letter to Bishop Eamon Casey of Galway. Joe Dunn, a priest of Dublin diocese, was famous at the time for the programmes on current church affairs, shown on Irish TV and known by their Gaelic name, *Radharc*. He had written an article, probably at McGarry's request, saying what kind of person was needed for the diocese of Armagh, then vacant. Did we want a great theologian? No! Did we want a competent administrator? No! Did we want someone who could sing a song and say damn and bloody on television? No! Bishop Casey thought that this referred to himself, as it probably did, so he phoned McGarry's bishop, Joseph Cunnane of Tuam to complain. Cunnane discussed the matter with McGarry who agreed to write a letter of conciliation to the offended bishop.

This is a good illustration of McGarry's character.

Ronan Drury was soon appointed as the new editor of *The Furrow*. There was a certain rejoicing that the editorship had returned to Maynooth. By now Austin Flannery was editor of *Doctrine and Life* and it was to him one should send controversial material for publication. My most important essay ever was, I think, on Pope John Paul's teaching on violence during his visit here (*Doctrine and Life*, 30 [1979], 634–55). I sent it to Bishop Cahal Daly who kindly read it and was duly influenced by my arguments; at least I never again felt uncomfortable with his approach.

In 1983, the new canon law was promulgated. The few loopholes in the old law were firmly closed. There was, however, a special canon which allowed a bishop to dispense from any ecclesiastical law. So I wrote a note of four pages explaining that, for *Doctrine and Life*. However it was not to be published.

We were now an abbey and the new abbot was a scripture scholar and was friendly with Archbishop Ryan. The abbot told the bishop that he was worried about my writings. So the latter said that he could always ask Bishop Donal Murray to censor my writings. The first application was to this short note for *Doctrine and Life*. It could not be published, they said, as it would raise expectations among the Protestants that could not be fulfilled. I asked where I could publish, so they suggested a lecture to the canon law society of Great Britain and Ireland. Professor Urrutia from the Gregorian was present and he endorsed my view of the new power of the bishop. Later Bishop Murray came to see the abbot and said that my essay could be published as long as it was outside Ireland. To this four-page note I added the substance of the article originally intended for *ITQ*. So the four pages expanded to a thirty-two-page article in *The Jurist* and is now regarded as required reading on the matter. This was now my position. I could publish anything outside Ireland but at home strict censorship was required.

At this time I was privileged to do a lecture tour of eight of our monasteries in the United States. On return I wrote on 'Church and Monastery in USA' and offered the essay to Austin Flannery OP. Without asking me, he divided the article in two and published the bit on church politics as the leading article in *Doctrine and Life*. I had described the Eucharist I experienced at the conference of *Societas Liturgica* in Philadelphia. A Lutheran minister celebrated the Eucharist while all the leading Catholic liturgists took Holy Communion. I said that the practice was common in the USA but, this was a mistake, and I realise now that it was only done in meetings of *Societas*.

The morning it appeared, the new Archbishop of Dublin, Kevin McNamara, phoned the abbot complaining about shared communion. He countered that Bishop Murray had censored it. McNamara said that censorship would have to be more rigid in future. He was soon succeeded by Archbishop Connell. When he saw the system of censorship to which I was subjected he thought it was a great idea and soon imposed censors on other people. The best known case is Brian D'Arcy: according to Brendan Hoban, it is 'indescribably sad' that 'his writings now have to go through an official church censor before they can be published.' A few other priests are in the same position.

Then unexpectedly I was chosen as abbot of Bolton for a six-year-period. That entailed a great change. It would not look well to be banning an abbot, so gradually all restrictions both inside and outside the Order were removed.

II. The Pilgrim Church

The Tacit Reform of Vatican II

GABRIEL DALY OSA

At the Second Vatican Council a change took place that was in some ways the most momentous achievement of the council; but its texts make no explicit mention of it. In practice the council abandoned the *mandatory* Thomism imposed on the church by Pope Leo XIII in 1879, thus freeing a distinguished theological school of thought to exist in its own right (as its originator would have wished), commending rather than commanding its adoption. It also freed proponents of other philosophies to pursue their studies without official harassment.

Just as, eight years earlier, some members of the Church of Ireland claimed on the morrow of its disestablishment that 'Today the Church goes free', authentic Thomists might have felt similarly when the majority of the fathers at Vatican II showed that they no longer felt obliged to use neo-scholastic language in their deliberations and documents. Pope John, in his opening words to the council, had told them that they should not be concerned with anathemas and other condemnatory acts. 'Nowadays however, the Spouse of Christ prefers to make use of the medicine of mercy rather than that of severity. She considers that she meets the needs of the present day by demonstrating the validity of her teaching rather than by condemnations.' The council complied in a manner that amounted to a silent revolution, and it had momentous consequences, not merely for theologians but also collaterally for the entire church.

Ronan Drury succeeded J. G. McGarry as editor of *The Furrow* during the period when Vatican II was having its effect on the church at large. *The Furrow* played a significant part in communicating the conciliar vision to Irish Catholics. The reception of a council can be a complex matter, and we easily underestimate the problems it may have to solve. It was not an easy time to be editor of a Catholic journal, knowing that gimlet eyes were watching what you allowed to appear in your pages. With the passage of half a century, we are freer to assess the situation today than sponsors of change were in an age that was still grappling with the challenge held out by an innovating council.

Led by its bishops, Catholic Ireland was not a place where new theological ideas had circulated with much excitement or at any depth before the council. The Irish bishops had made little contribution to conciliar debates; and on the whole they were not at ease with the new theology. An article that Vincent Twomey SVD contributed to *The Irish Catholic* mentions the case of an Irish bishop who, when asked how he got on at the Second Vatican Council, is reported to have replied: 'Well, it was really all a bit of a waste of time. They talked about nothing but theology.' To what extent this comment reflected the general attitude of Irish bishops who attended the Council is uncertain; but theology had not played a notable part in the life of most Irish clerics.

This may seem too sweeping a judgement; for there were some voices to be heard and authors to be read who were open to the excitement of what was happening on the continent of Europe; but they were not representative of feeling in the church at large. To be more precise, it was not that the Irish bishops lacked an interest in theology; it was that they expected theology to be the faithful repetition of unchangeable truth. They were theologically educated in the period when neo-scholasticism was in the ascendant. They were used to the support given by that system to a notably authoritarian attitude to church governance. They were accustomed to being heard, deferred to, and to being obeyed.

Vatican II came as an unexpected upheaval for which Catholics were unprepared. Archbishop John Charles McQuaid will always be remembered for his attempt to reassure his flock at the end of the Council that 'No change will worry the tranquility of your Christian lives.' This assurance suggests that the wish was father to the thought. Other bishops may have hoped for something similar.

Their flocks were accustomed to being told what they should believe and how they should behave. Their beliefs were officially enshrined in language that came from a long-forgotten age. They had worshipped liturgically through the medium of a dead language. Their church played a pervasive and unquestioned part in their lives; but serious theological questions rarely occurred: there were too many confident answers available.

Since Ireland's bishops were largely unaware of the questions that other European theologians were raising at the council, they were to some extent out of their depth and failed to see the point of such questions. Consequently they did little to educate their flocks in what the church was trying to do at Vatican II, and they resented what a well-informed corps of journalists was writing and speaking about the council. They were ill-at-ease in the sort of church that was emerging at and after Vatican II. The essentialism of the theology they had been taught favoured managerial control and obscured the pastoral relevance of the new theology. As a result, the changes brought about by the council operated at a very superficial level in the popular mind. No wonder the bishops were disturbed by what was happening. To them it must have looked like the disintegration of the system in which they had been educated.

Archbishop John Charles McQuaid's assurance that the council had done nothing to disturb the tranquillity of his listeners' minds gives a clue to how he would react to the excellent journalists who wrote, spoke about and explained the work of the church in council. He wrote to Roland Burke Savage SJ, editor of *Studies*: 'I am dismayed by the facile ignorance of the journalists who are writing about the documents that have cost us years of work, and by the more facile dictation in regard to what we bishops must now do.' The archbishop clearly regarded the work of these journalists as a kind of *lèse-majesté*, performing a task that should be exclusively episcopal. They were in fact the first indication of a lay Catholic input into the life of the modern church, and they were putting it up to theologians to respond to the situation that they were revealing. Many theologians responded by lecturing at seminars, writing in journals like *The Furrow* and *Doctrine and Life*, and in general studying the new theological ideas generated by the council. We are fortunate today to have an increasing number of lay theologians, many of whom speak with greater freedom than their clerical colleagues are often able to do.

The moral standards of Irish Catholics had been formed, less by conscience, than by obedience to authority. If that authority were to be in any way compromised it would damage the moral and religious consciousness of the faithful. That is what seems to have happened, mainly due to failure to react adequately to clerical child abuse. Moral consciousness needs to arise out of inner conviction rather than as a response to external authority which has been shaped by a theological system that promoted 'extrinsicism'. The scholastic character of the Catholic understanding of orthodoxy in the late nineteenth century church began with Leo XIII in his encyclical *Aeterni patris* (1879):

> Let carefully selected teachers endeavour to implant the doctrine of Thomas Aquinas in the minds of students, and set forth clearly his solidity and excellence over others.[1]

Pope Leo was determined to tidy up the philosophical eclecticism prevailing at that time in the Catholic Church, so that it might present a more convincing face to a hostile world. He chose the thought of St Thomas Aquinas as the instrument that would lead away from the philosophical free-for-all which was at that time, in his view, weakening the stance of the church towards the world; and it would give it a firm, unified and coherent foundation for action. His appeal to medieval thought was timely and in convenient harmony with nineteenth-century Gothic romanticism.

Not unexpectedly, there was reaction to the Leonine programme. It came from the Modernists at the end of the nineteenth century and the beginning of the twentieth. One of the most prominent Modernists, George Tyrrell, an Anglo-Irish Jesuit, in an act of ecclesiastical suicide, wrote an article in the London *Times* shortly after the publication of Pius X's encyclical, *Pascendi dominici gregis* on 8 September 1907: 'Whereas, *Pascendi* tries to show the Modernist that he is no Catholic, it mostly succeeds only in showing him that he is no scholastic.'[2] In this article, Tyrrell put his finger on the main point at issue in the Modernist controversy, though not many anti-Modernists would have recognised it. The Modernists wanted to show that one could be a good Catholic without being a Thomist. It was a very reasonable argument; but it expressed a view that was not shared by Pope Pius X:

> We therefore desired that all teachers of philosophy and sacred theology should be warned that if they deviated so much as a step, in metaphysics especially, from Aquinas, they exposed themselves to grave risk.[3]

Interestingly, Pius extended the same principle of reform to music in the liturgy, giving the instruction that plainsong and classical polyphony should replace the theatrical music that was redolent of the 'profane' world and ill-fitted the sacred words of the liturgy. His native Italy, the home of opera, was notorious for the operatic treatment of sacred texts sung in the liturgy. Pius's Instruction on Sacred Music, *Tra le sollecitudini*, of 1903, (the first year of his pontificate) made plainsong the model for all liturgical music. Musical eclecticism was in his eyes similar to philosophical eclecticism and needed to be reformed. The reform was motivated by a desire to segregate the church from the world by withdrawing into a secluded island of holiness. In Christianity, there is a balance to be kept between withdrawal and engagement, and Pius clearly believed that the time had come for withdrawal from a degenerate world.

After World War II, the theologians advising Pius XII were disturbed by the philosophical problems thrown up by Existentialism, which appealed to some Catholic theologians as a corrective to scholastic essentialism. Furthermore, some French theologians, mainly Dominicans, were approaching the question of Tradition from a historical perspective. Rome did not like what was happening. In 1950 Pius XII issued an encyclical, *Humani generis*, possibly drafted by Sebastian Tromp SJ of the Gregorian University in Rome,[4] reaffirming the Leonine position with disturbing clarity:

> All these [modern] opinions and affirmations are openly contrary to the documents of Our Predecessors Leo XIII and Pius X, and cannot be reconciled with the decrees of the [First] Vatican Council.[5]

Papal teaching from Leo XIII's *Aeterni patris* down to Vatican II made it very clear that the Catholic Church was not merely recommending, but requiring fidelity to, neo-scholasticism, and especially to the philosophy of Thomas Aquinas, as *obligatory* Catholic orthodoxy. So effective was the tacit reform brought about by Vatican II, that Pope John Paul II was able to write in 1998:

> The Church has no philosophy of her own nor does she canonise any one particular philosophy in preference to others.[6]

This can be fairly described as a sensational development! John Paul was in no sense a liberal pope, but he accepted that Vatican II had made a crucial difference to the church's outlook on the relationship between faith and philosophy. This acceptance revealed that the council had dispensed with neo-scholasticism as a *necessary* philosophical foundation for Catholic theology. Vatican II did not abandon the teaching of Thomas Aquinas, as has sometimes been incorrectly claimed; it abandoned the imposition of his thought as indispensable for Catholic orthodoxy. The distinction is important; but no less important is the fact that a momentous change, not explicitly mentioned in its documents, did occur at the council. The nature of the change marks an historically significant moment in the life of the church and its theology. Vatican II was an experience before it was a set of documents; and it is the experience that animates many of us today who are fortunate enough to have lived through a momentous four years in the life of the church.

No great fuss was made over this radical change brought about by the council; yet it was a major achievement made tacitly rather than expressly in response to Pope John XXIII's vision of *aggiornamento*. Catholic authority is averse to admitting discontinuity in its teaching. John had made it plain that he wanted a change in language and style from that of previous councils. It was a momentous change, because Vatican II showed that style and language were not a merely collateral effect of substantial change; they were a vital element in it.

John O'Malley, the American Jesuit historian, in his fine book, *What Happened at Vatican II*, makes this point with clarity and vigour, when he points out that the council, by not employing scholastic language, moved from abstract metaphysics and grand conceptual schemes to the humble acceptance of mystery. 'In so doing it largely abandoned the Scholastic framework that had dominated Catholic theology since the thirteenth century.'[7] In a word, Vatican II was a reaction not merely to neo-scholasticism; it made a break with the entire scholastic movement set in train by the discovery of Aristotle's philosophy and its employment in the framing of Christian doctrine.

The Modernists had offered the first significant challenge to neo-scholastic orthodoxy and Rome adopted a fiercely adversarial attitude to them. Between the condemnation of Modernism and the meeting of Vatican II, people who knew little about what the Modernists had said routinely labelled any theological position in the Catholic Church that differed from scholastic orthodoxy as unacceptably 'Modernist' – an automatic vilification. For over half-a-century the official church was deprived of attitudes and convictions that are unexceptionable today.

Apart from the Modernist critique of neo-scholastic hegemony, perhaps the most notable contribution to Christian theology made by theologians like Lucien Laberthonnière and philosophers like Maurice Blondel was 'the method of immanence', an awareness of the need for an inner dimension in apologetics (or fundamental theology, as it would be called today) where the neo-scholastic method had focused on evidence, miracles, fulfilled prophecies and other extrinsic phenomena.

Laberthonnière, a dedicated proponent of the method of immanence and a sworn enemy of scholastic 'extrinsicism', wrote a sentence in 1904 that he later described as the core of his philosophical and religious position that one of his biographers has described as 'critical mysticism':

We do not set out from knowledge so that faith may follow. We believe as we know and we know as we believe. The outcome is a complete transformation of the soul.[8]

It has been pointed out that the French authors of *Gaudium et spes*, Vatican II's Constitution on the Church in the Modern World, were strongly influenced by Pascal's preoccupation with the *'faite intérieure'*, the interior, subjective aspect of faith which relies less on evidence and more on the logic of a yearning heart. Pascal wrote in his *Pensées*: 'That is what faith is: God perceived by the heart, not by the reason.'[9] We can see what Laberthonnière meant when, in a daring phrase, he described Pascal as a 'positivist of interior reality'. This profession of voluntarism was a return to St Augustine's restless heart in search of eternity. For Augustine, human beings are defined by their capacity for desire, which precedes all purely rational thought. Neo-scholastics ridiculed what they saw as irrational sentimentality. It is no accident that many scholastics entertained a deep suspicion of Augustinianism, which they correctly saw as impugning their 'extrinsicism'. The defeat of mandatory scholasticism opened up the possibility of a return to an interiority that had been ruled out at the highest level in the church by the anti-Modernist campaign.

Lucien Laberthonnière, a Modernist reformer, censored by the Holy Office, makes an ironic companion of an authoritarian pope! Nonetheless, he and Pope John Paul II share an intriguingly similar view of the relationship between faith and reason. Laberthonnière, who hated the effect that Aristotle had had on Catholic theology, was treated with heartless disregard for justice and forbidden to publish; John Paul was a pope of undoubted authority and orthodoxy. Neither of them takes any notice of the general thrust of Pius X's encyclical *Pascendi*; and in John Paul's case, it signals an end to the anti-Modernist crusade.

When, in *Fides et ratio*, Pope John Paul II wrote that the church [no longer] canonises any one philosophy to the exclusion of all others, he was implicitly declaring that the church has no competence to prescribe a philosophy in the manner of his predecessors. Much that the Modernists had striven for is delivered here.

The Second Vatican Council was clear that matters of strict Christian faith may be said to be permanent; however, the theologies and politics that are associated with them are always changeable, and in point of fact have manifestly changed. In this world we are pilgrims who are living in changing times and different cultures. We are not settlers with a fixed abode; and we can agree with Newman that to be perfect is to have changed often.

Priesthood, Authority and Leadership
MICHAEL A. CONWAY

Introduction

After a number of decades during which any idea of authority was identified with limitation, the misappropriation of power, and the suppression of creativity, there is in contemporary Europe evidence of a new awakening to the essential positive role that authority might play in family, community, workplace, social, and, indeed, ecclesial life.[1] This transition to a more positive understanding of authority is indicative of a change in our culture that has important consequences for an ecclesial ministry that would seek to nurture the Gospel in the European context, a context that has a specificity that is not evident elsewhere. The change has to do with authority, with power, with leadership, and with trust. This short essay is an initial attempt to understand the changing dynamics in our culture, and to suggest how leaders in ministry, particularly priests, might begin to reimagine leadership in this emerging context.

I. A Fixed World Order

If we look to the recent past, what we see is a certain common understanding of how authority, leadership, and power worked together. Various sectors of society were apportioned different competencies and these in turn handed over to a spectrum of persons who were then deemed responsible. Thus, for example, in matters of health the doctor, the midwife, and the nurse had the appropriate authority and the concomitant power to act on the other's behalf in matters medical. In issues of the law, the Garda, the solicitor, and the judge were in the positions of responsibility. In matters of faith and morals the responsible person was most often understood unilaterally to be the local priest. He was charged on behalf of the community with maintaining the religious life of the parish and, indeed, at least striving to maintain a certain level of moral decorum in the parish. For most people, this structuring of communal life was virtually an absolute and any idea of questioning this was, practically, unthinkable.

This basic way of understanding social structures and communal order was a well-established one that had its proximate roots in the medieval world order, where each person in society had his or her place with a well-defined role that was designated for life. Society, reflecting this order, was highly structured. This, in turn, reflected a neo-platonic understanding of the cosmos, where everything had its fixed place in a divine order that was structured according to a hierarchical principle.[2] And, of course, this could not be altered. This was its primitive attraction: the divine order being realised here on earth. Thus, for Leo XIII, for example, the medieval world order was what he termed the 'Golden Age' and when he thought about 'Church' this was his ideal. It was a top-down model, where everyone had a place, knew where it was, and, crucially, knew also everyone else's place! Any attempt to change things disturbed the entire structure of the world order, and this, in turn, threatened everyone. Communal stability depended on everyone knowing and acting according to their position. It could not be otherwise. Around you, others depended on you being where you ought to be; you could not act in isolation, and if you did, you would have to be dealt with severely or removed from the community.

In this model, more than anyone else, it was the priest who was at the centre of the local parish life. He was the leader and authority figure at the centre of communal action and with enormous power. Further, for this model, moral direction and religious education were in the form of *instructed conscience*. This was mandated by the bishop (himself a link in an over-powering hierarchy) in his diocese and carried out by the priests and to a lesser extent the teachers in the parish. People were taught what was to be believed, how they ought to act, what was right, what was wrong, and this was deemed to maintain the correct ordering in, for example, a parish community.

Of course, even with a little theology, it was always recognised that there was an element of voluntary cooperation in all of this. There was an awareness that the act of faith, for example, was worthless if it were not a *free* act. But this very freedom, the 'voluntary element,' so to speak, had such little wriggle room, that it was practically non-existent. Freedom in any real sense around religious or moral ideas was an ideal rather than a reality. There was an enormous over-simplification of moral prescriptions and an extreme lack of trust in lay-people in terms of dealing with the complexities involved in decision making.

The model, at least to the degree that it was, and still is, operative, reflects, on the one hand, an authoritarianism and, on the other hand, an *infantilisation* of others.[3] One group in society, those in positions of authority and leadership, assumes 'power over' others, and another group behaves, or is forced (sometimes subtly) to behave in a fashion that is a good deal less than reflecting mature, competent, responsible adults. To be a 'leader' in such a world is to be entangled in a web of often dubious expectations, of paternalism and of vicarious responsibilities. It is profoundly unhealthy on many levels. It places those in leadership in positions that go well beyond appropriate boundaries and legitimate competencies.

II. Personal Freedom and Diversity
In general European culture, this authoritarian model has, for the most part, completely collapsed. The collapse was precipitated to some degree by another powerful dynamic in Western culture, namely, the emergence of 'personal freedom', a discovery, so to speak, of the 'voluntary element' that I mentioned above. This has now come to the fore as a central value in how we understand ourselves and the structure our lives. It is a definitive achievement: one that has been hard won over an extended period of time, beginning with the so called nominalist controversy of the late Middle Ages, given an enormous impulse through the Reformation, and hammered out between the Enlightenment and the Romantic movements of the eighteenth and nineteenth centuries. It is important to recognise that this is not something that has suddenly arrived from nowhere and is now knocking on our doors. It has been emerging over a very long period in the European Christian tradition and, curiously, nowhere else. The surprising thing is how quickly, in the last few decades, it has spread in the general culture. It now means that personal freedom, the subjective, the singularity that is each person, and the narrative history of the individual, can no longer be treated as accidental or ancillary and subsumed under any so called 'objective' system, be it economic, political, moral, or religious.

When tensions now arise between an external authority, such as Church teaching, and personal conscience, the trend is clearly against an exclusive exterior voice and in favour of an interior trusting of one's own conscience. There is nothing strange about this in contemporary culture; it simply expresses the idea of 'moral autonomy', which is a core value in a liberal democratic culture. In our European (and, indeed, North American) culture, this is neither a localised phenomenon nor a passing phase. In matters of faith, of religion, of spirituality and of morals, people decide increasingly for themselves in the final instance. This is understood as a matter of integrity and authenticity. In our personal lives, subjectivity now counts, singularity matters and no decision has value unless the crucial voluntary component is explicitly given a real place. This has not always been the case; it is this that is new. The more traditional discourse on religion and morality focused on the objectivity of doctrines and teachings and on passing these on to others, usually in a downward direction.

Now, a by-product, if you like, of this fact is an *enormous diversity* of expression vis-à-vis religion. Some are heavily engaged in the local parish and are fully at home there; attend Mass regularly and so on. Some have a more marginal relationship to the stable, visible Christian community. Some will be leaving shortly, only to return to regular community involvement in a few years. Some will reconnect when they have children, when they get ill, or when death knocks at their door. Some will never come near the Church again. Some will find another Christian group where they will feel more at home (and their numbers are increasing). 'Belonging' is now no longer a simple either/or, an 'in' or an 'out'. There is a spectrum of positions: always, never, sometimes, occasionally, sort of, when needed, never but glad it's there, and so on. It is the diversity that is now striking, and it is a significant factor in contemporary living.

III. Freedom and Dignity

This has enormous implications in terms of effective leadership at parish level, where there is increasingly very different expectations when it comes to being a leader in a community. In line with the above, people now increasingly engage with parish, with Church, and with religion, and with the 'practice' of religion very much from their own subjective centres. They decide for themselves what that engagement will be, and in this, they have achieved significant freedom. They cannot any longer be frightened or shamed into religious conformity. Those of us who are leaders in ministry are well aware of this: people can leave if they wish; and return if they wish; they can move around between parishes; and, increasingly, they simply put together a religious or spiritual profile for themselves that best suits their own needs. Spiritual or religious leaders are no longer in a position of 'command and control.' We now have to recognise, respect, and engage with this new found freedom. We cannot make demands and have expectations that bypass the voluntary element. It is a limit point for us, and we need to learn to recognise it and mark it. And people need to know (and it needs to be clear in our discourse) that we are, at least, conscious of this *or they will never trust us*. This is what makes our leadership so utterly different from that in, say, a workforce or a company or a business where there are legitimate expectations built into the contract itself of the work environment, and these necessarily suspend or modulate the 'voluntary element'.

The dynamics of a work environment cannot and do not transfer into life in general for a parish situation. The days of telling people 'what to do' and 'how to live' are over. Now the interesting thing is that they are over not because of some political expedient (whereby the Church must adapt in order to survive). They are over because they no longer correspond to how we understand the dignity of the individual human person, whose life and action is always singular, personal, and only ever said once. We cannot and should not ever speak for another, who is capable of doing so for themselves. At Vatican II, this became more and more apparent as the Council progressed: Thus, in *Gaudium et spes* we read: 'There is a growing awareness of the sublime dignity of human persons, who stand above all things and whose rights and duties are universal and inviolable.' And among those rights the document named: 'the right to act according to the dictates of conscience and to safeguard their privacy, the right to just freedom, including the freedom of religion' (26). This 'growing awareness' was also affirmed in the very first sentence of the council's last document, *Dignitatis humanae*: 'People nowadays are becoming increasingly conscious of the dignity of the human person' (1). This idea that there has been a *development in* our recognition of the dignity of the human person is expressed in the statement: 'the leaven of the Gospel has long been at work in people's minds and has contributed greatly to a wider recognition by them in the course of time of their dignity as persons' (12). We have hardly even begun to draw out the implications of this new awareness.

IV. Authority in Community
Regarding 'authority', it is evident that we have a deep need for authority. It is an immensely creative power for the individual and in a community, and we seek it out and we search for it at all levels in life and in many different places. We require authorities to structure and to shape our world.

People who stand out for us, who affirm us, and whom we aspire to emulate are vital if we are to realise our full potential.

In terms of religion, faith, and parish life, where the acknowledgement of personal freedom is increasingly recognised to be an inviolable norm, *authority* is very definitely a two-sided reality: on the one side, it is claimed, among others, by priests (and bishops) as leaders, but, on the other, it is recognised, welcomed, and accepted by those whom it might serve. If it is not accepted then it no longer exists. Or better it merely exists in the minds of those of us who might claim it. It becomes, however, unreal, imaginary, and lifeless. It is not real in that full, authentic, life giving sense of the word. Whereas you can give someone power, you cannot give authority. It is a characteristic of an authentic leader-in-community; and it requires essentially that communal recognition. An authority that is not recognised and accepted by others or that alienates others is a pseudo-authority. To be a healthy, life creating leader in ministry is to be someone with authority in that real living sense, and it is this that we urgently need to understand if we are to be effective leaders at parish level (or in our various ministries). Leadership is a vital service in a community. We are moving from positions of 'command and control' to positions of participation, of affirmation, of enabling, and of encouraging. Necessarily, this requires a fully developed ability to listen with integrity and to learn from others in the common project that is community.

V. Authority in Transition

Leadership and authority are in transition. It is no longer possible to treat others as objects that might be manipulated or moved around in the name of some larger reality, however one might define or justify it, against their expressed or even tacit wishes, and without real exchange and engagement. This means that those in positions of authority and leadership need to recognise the importance of listening, of hearing, of accompanying, and of responding. Not to do so is to violate something fundamental that we are discovering about ourselves. This is an enormous change for the family, social, cultural, and Church fabric of our society.

And this is a dilemma that we find ourselves in at the moment. On the one hand, we need authority (and derivatively leadership), and, yet, on the other hand, the way that authority works for us is changing and must change. And we know that we cannot repeat the patterns that we have inherited. The fixed authoritarian and non-consultative forms of the past are no longer viable in a contemporary European context. They do not draw that agreement that they would need to embody the hopes that communities have and the affirmation that they require as they journey toward the future. And this is vital: authority is intimately connected to the future and, indeed, to hope: personal future, communal future, Church future, society future. As opposed to authoritarianism that attempts to coerce, disenfranchise, and manipulate others, real, living authority is open, transparent, and just in meeting others. We are beginning to recognise that we need healthy, strong, affirming, just, wise and enriching authority. And, in particular, in our parishes, we need priests who embody this powerful presence for everyone. This is a service in the very best sense of this word (see Mt 20:25–8). My concern is not so much that priests as leaders are going to fall back into the oppressive dynamics of tribal authoritarianism (and, for some, this is a possibility), rather my concern is that we may be fearful about taking up our distinct and important place as affirmers of the future. There is no doubt that most of us do not wish to repeat the dynamics of the past, but there is a danger that we would avoid altogether anything to do with authority beyond the very minimum that is required of us.

We are gradually moving from structures that were based culturally and socially on power over others to *a new form of authority and leadership* that is based on the structures of gathering and empowering others. The only form of authority that has a future in our culture, and for which, in terms of the Christian community, priests have a special role to play (and it's not exclusive of the leadership of lay men and women) has to do with *solidarity*. It is a matter of bringing and holding people together, while respecting difference and personal freedom. It is not directed towards a union that requires *uniformity* or that aspires to uniformity but, rather, is directed towards a solidarity that appreciates the individual person as a singularity with a unique identity. The credibility of authority and leadership in contemporary European culture rests on the ability to maintain solidarity in freedom; be that in a family, in a community, or in an ecclesial setting. Ultimately, this is to realise that the world belongs to God, and it is to trust in each person's, in each family's, and in each community's journey into God.

A Gallican Strain?

BRENDAN HOBAN

Bishop Michael Harty of Killaloe once remarked, after a bishops' meeting in Maynooth in the 1960s, that Irish bishops had forgotten how to say 'No' to Rome. More than a century after Cardinal Paul Cullen's 'Romanisation' of the Irish Catholic Church, it was a prescient insight. A century earlier, in 1867, Archbishop John McEvilly of Tuam, one of Cullen's cheerleaders, had remarked to a friend, 'I always regarded as certain, as anything in this world can be, that Rome is always right.'

The gap between the two views is instructive. The first comment emanated out of a strain of Gallicanism that had virtually disappeared in the Irish Church; the second gloried in the success of Cullen's ultramontane revolution.

Gallicanism, in simple terms, emphasised the autonomy of local churches at the expense of the papacy. Because it has its roots in early French nationalism, and characterised the life of the Catholic Church in France at certain periods, with a complex of doctrines and practices advocating the restriction of papal power, it was called 'Gallicanism'. In Ireland it was first formally propagated in the writings of Frenchman, Louis-Gilles Delahogue in Maynooth College, though a strain of what, in hindsight might be contrived as 'Gallican', stretched back into earlier centuries.

Ultramontanism, in simple terms, an attachment to and conformity to Rome, was the polar opposite of Gallicanism. For the ultramontane, the centrality of Rome and papal authority was everything, becoming the only acceptable mark of real Catholicism. The Church was a monolithic beacon in a dark world, an institution that insisted its adherents would march in step with the drumbeats of the Vatican.

The incompatibility of the two contrasting visions of Catholicism came into open conflict at the first Vatican Council in 1870. The Ultramontane Party triumphed when the dogma of papal infallibility was defined, what historian Eamon Duffy described as 'a defiant symbol of the spiritual claims of the pope in the face of a hostile world'.

John MacHale, Archbishop of Tuam, a Gallican, was one of the few bishops at the Council who voted against the Decree on Papal Infallibility. Though he was careful to accept it afterwards – and was already, as he remarked at the time, all too familiar with the notion of the infallibility of parish priests – the concept of papal infallibility and the prospect of external 'interference' it brought with it didn't sit comfortably with MacHale's independent and forthright approach. MacHale, for many different reasons, wasn't comfortable either with the influence of Cardinal Paul Cullen of Dublin, or what has been called the 'Cullenisation of the Irish Church', which involved not just the celebrated 'devotional revolution' but the gradual 'Romanisation' of the Irish bishops, Ultramontanism in full flight. Cullen, like one of his predecessors Archbishop John Patrick Troy half a century earlier, would became the great 'king-maker', presiding over what John H. Whyte called 'a definite, centrally-directed policy on the selection of bishops'.

While Cullen was in thrall to Rome, anxious to extend its culture, worship and centralising policies to the Irish Church, MacHale, the first Irish bishop to be educated in Ireland for centuries, was cut from a very different cloth. Awkward, stubborn, recalcitrant, MacHale was, in comparison with Cullen, something akin to a Gaelic chieftain, presiding over an ancient tribe. While MacHale was careful – as bishops needed to be – not to be found wanting in appearing loyal to Rome, and could manipulate Rome as effectively as other similarly ambitious clerics, he instinctively distrusted Cullen's Romanisation policy and seemed more at ease with a Gaelic, pre-Tridentine, folk religion. MacHale understood, in a way Cullen did not, the depth and resilience of a form of popular or folk religion which had thrived over the centuries – and, to some degree, continues to survive, despite the best clerical efforts to institutionalise it – a religion of the people rather than of the institution.

So despite the significance of the Council of Trent, Irish Catholicism, particularly in the west, remained 'Irish' as distinct from 'Roman' because the implementation of Trent was effectively scuppered by the Penal Laws. The effect of this – a blessing in disguise – was that Catholicism survived as a popular religion rather than as a way of life identified with the ruling class.

It was only towards the end of the eighteenth century – two centuries on from Trent – that a Tridentine reform of Catholicism became possible. While historian Patrick Corish suggests that the Tridentine fabric was fairly well in place in Ferns diocese by 1775, in other dioceses, like Killala in the far west, that consummation would be delayed for most of a century. With few churches, few priests and what was later described by historians as 'a culture of indiscipline' in the far west, an independent spirit at odds with the Tridentine ethos of control and regimentation survived and sometimes prospered among people and priests.

Rome seemed much further away from Belmullet than from Bunclody. For example, when MacHale's successor as bishop of Killala, Francis Joseph O'Finan, a Dominican, arrived from Rome in 1835, and at his first meeting with the Killala priests, he described them as 'a conventicle of Jansenists' and instructed them to discontinue their political machinations, MacHale sensed that the confrontation between Roman rectitude and Killala resistance would end in tears – as it did when O'Finan, the worst for wear, was recalled to Rome two years later.

While it might be argued that MacHale was, less a convinced Gallican than an awkward Lahardane man, who was always right and who manipulated all around him to get his own way, he opposed Cullen's devotional and Roman revolution, though he was soon isolated by the appointment of ultramontane suffragan bishops like Laurence Gilooly of Elphin and Hugh Conway of Killala, and the undermining by Cullen of his influence in Rome. Yet the influence of the Gallican strain continued. If MacHale had lived, given the nationalist fervour that characterised his life, it might be surmised that he would have supported the Plan of Campaign (1886) and Cullen, if he had lived, would have opposed it.

The Plan of Campaign was a strategy, devised to force Irish landlords to reduce their rents, as two successive poor harvests and a decline in agricultural prices had brought many tenants to the point of ruin. The Plan, as historian Emmet Larkin pointed out, paid scant respect to 'the sanctity of contracts and the rights of property' and was denounced as immoral and subversive. The Conservative government in England pressured Pope Leo XIII to officially condemn the land agitation and the boycotting that attended the Plan and to forbid the Irish bishops and their clergy from supporting it. Eventually in May 1888, the Pope did condemn the Plan but the Irish bishops, in an unusual display of independence, refused to enforce the Roman condemnation and, in Larkin's words, 'cooly opted instead for the maintenance of the clericalist-nationalist alliance' that had produced the Plan.

Roma locuta est (Rome had spoken) – but Rome was ignored. The Irish bishops had rightly judged that they could not oppose the will of the people. The Plan of Campaign effectively sounded the death-knell of landlordism in Ireland and demonstrated that the MacHale factor – that indefinable independent spirit that smacked of Gallicanism – trumped the Cullen line of loyalty to Rome at all costs. Few would doubt but that episcopal support for the landlords at that key juncture would have, into the future, significantly damaged 'the good of religion' as well as relationships between bishops and people, bishops and priests, priests and people.

Ultimately, of course, Cullen's ultramontanism would triumph, as a respect for and devotion to Rome – its ways, its policy and its leader – became a defining and central characteristic of the Irish Church. Even the Second Vatican Council, which should have been a triumph for Gallicanism, and which attempted to redefine the papacy's relationship with the local Church, was regarded as little more than a blip as soon, through the influence of Pope John Paul II and later Benedict XVI, ultramontanism was on the march again, sweeping all before it.

Even the unexpected arrival of a Gallican pope, Francis I, has not moderated the force of ultramontanism, as reactionary forces within the Vatican, now that they've recovered from the shock of Francis' appointment, are marshalling their forces to neutralise and defeat the Gallican threat once again. Closer to home, there's no hard evidence to support the accusation that any Irish bishop will adopt the 'Gallican' vision of Pope Francis I, apart from the standard, predictable, knee-jerk, formulaic, ultramontane response to whatever the pope says.

The foregoing is an effort to create a context for understanding the long decline of the Gallican strain and consequently of the independence of the Irish Church. Since the Plan of Campaign, a historian would be hard-pressed to find one example of an Irish bishop making a stand on an issue of importance and declaring, even sotto voce, that they knew better than Rome what was for the good of religion and Catholicism in Ireland. Yet despite the overwhelming triumph of the ultramontane spirit in the Irish Church, throughout the centuries, slivers of resistance to Roman hegemony echoed the independent Gallican spirit of the Irish Church, as far back as the Middle Ages.

The Calendar of Papal Records, mined by church historians like Edward MacHale in Killala and Liam Swords in Achonry, attest to an ongoing, lively, independent spirit in the Irish Church. It is clear from the records that Rome struggled to exercise control over the Irish Church as claim and counter-claim by clergy – often a toxic mixture of fact and fiction – in search of more lucrative benefices made their way to Rome. It is clear too that Rome adopted a relaxed approach to the traditions and practices of the Irish Church, encouraging investigations and issuing dispensations without any real hope of influencing the practices of the medieval Irish Church. The authority of Rome was casually swept aside when it suited. For instance, when Innocent IV sent John de Frosinone to collect a tax on the incomes of the Irish clergy, for the relief of the Holy Land, ordered by the Council of Lyons in 1245, he didn't expect that the Cistercian bishop of Achonry and his colleague in Killala would end up excommunicating the papal envoy.

The Irish reactions to the reforms of the twelfth century, when officially, celibacy became mandatory, attest both to the geographical distance from Rome and the penchant of the Irish Church in the Middle Ages for devising 'Irish solutions to Irish problems'. Stable sexual relationships, as historians now attest, between clerics and women persisted long after the twelfth century reforms. Priests and monks continued to have sexual relationships with life partners, described as 'concubines' rather than spouses and clerical concubinage, a half-way house between marriage and fornication, was such a long-standing practice that it was regarded as the norm.

Despite the efforts of the First Lateran Council in 1123, celibacy among the clergy, as Liam Swords has written, was 'to remain little more than an aspiration for some centuries to come'. At least two bishops of Achonry were fathers of families as were some abbots of Boyle and some of their children in turn became bishops, monks and priests. At least ten clerics in Achonry in the fifteen-century were recorded as sons of priests. And it wasn't just Achonry. It took the Irish Church an unconscionably long time to come to terms with celibacy.

Rome did not seem to be unduly perturbed by sexually active priests and issued the appropriate dispensations liberally as the need arose. While it was accepted that clerical concubinage was to be discouraged, and Rome tolerated what it called 'fornication' (concubinage), it tended to draw the line at what it called 'notorious fornication' (sexual activity outside of concubinage), and it continued after a fashion to put pressure on bishops to remain celibate. In Roman terms, technically though unofficially, 'fornicators' were tolerated but 'notorious fornicators' were discouraged.

An example of Roman efforts to reform the Irish Church and to exert discipline on bishops and priests, not least in the matter of celibacy, was the appointment in the sixteenth century of Irishman, David Wolfe SJ, as papal commissary. He arrived in Ireland in January, 1561 and his initial report was optimistic, noting that he had dealt with over a thousand lay dispensations in six months. However, he found the clergy less responsive, with a number of the bishops countering his order to abandon their concubines by challenging his authority as papal commissary and refusing him the right of visitation to their churches.

Despite the extraordinary turnaround with the unexpected presence of a 'Gallican' bishop in Rome, the ultramontane doctrine has so embedded itself in the Irish Church that now it can be argued we lack the resources and personnel to respond to the huge expectations that attend the present pontificate. After centuries of seeking to obliterate the stain of Gallicanism, the irony is that in the present dispensation, whatever slivers of Gallicanism remain need to be unambiguously cherished.

There is, of course, little evidence of this in the Irish Church. A few years ago an Apostolic Visitation decided that the presence of 'dissident' priests was part of the problem of the Irish Church, and predictably and shamefully, a number of priests were named and disciplined. A Gallican strain, even a measure of self-respect in the Irish Church, would have forced our bishops to stand up to the counter-productive, even bullying tactics of Congregation of the Doctrine of the Faith (CDF). Yet, there wasn't even a teaspoonful of protest from the leaders of the Irish Church, with one Irish bishop saying that the CDF was 'in dialogue' with the priests concerned.

Picking off independent-minded priests and bizarrely threatening them with excommunication provoked an abject silence from Irish bishops when we expected, as we should, that the bishops would protest at the blanket condemnation of decent men, who had conspicuously made a huge contribution to the Irish Church over several decades. As if, after all that had happened in the last few decades, and not least the very reason the visitation took place, that part of the solution to the problem of the Irish Church was to silence voices that held things up to the light.

The introduction of the new missal, a liturgical delinquency inflicted on the English-speaking Catholic world by the conservative forces in the Vatican, was scandalously nodded through by weak-willed bishops, Irish and others, who lacked the courage or the nous to realise, despite the voices that were raised to the contrary, that the new translation would effectively damage the scaffolding of worship in the Irish Church, even if it indulged the esoteric interests of a tiny minority of ultra-conservative Catholics, lay and clerical.

During the long winter time of the pontificates of John Paul II and Benedict XVI, there was little sympathy with or respect for a Gallican voice in the Irish Church. Our tradition of undue deference to Rome wasn't questioned; finding our own voice as a church, or articulating our particular needs was regarded with deep suspicion; dissent was a synonym for disloyalty.

Whatever independent spirit was left in the Irish Catholic Church had few opportunities to keep the Gallican flag flying and few platforms from which to raise it. It is a tribute to *The Furrow* that for over six decades it has facilitated alternative voices, despite no doubt causing many an episcopal eyebrow to be raised and generating much episcopal unease. Its semi-official position in Gallican Maynooth has not just retained a prophetic presence at the heart of the Irish Church but provided a light in dark and dismal times. Louis-Gilles Delahogue would be well pleased.

The Reform of the Church in
Her Missionary Outreach

GERRY O'HANLON

Why does mission demand reform?

Our title is taken from the first topic that Pope Francis discusses in his Apostolic Exhortation *Evangelii gaudium* (*EG* 17, November 2013). Francis knows that nowadays 'documents do not arouse the same interest as in the past', but stresses that what he is trying to express here 'has a programmatic significance and important consequences' (*EG* 25).

Mission involves being sent, it is outward looking. However, does not church reform suggest something introverted, even self-referential and narcissistic? This is the kind of niggling question which many may ask – think of the faithful in the pews, looking to the Church for comfort and even inspiration; think of bishops (including here in Ireland) and busy priests, struggling to maintain the *status quo*. But Francis is convinced that mission and reform are inextricably linked: why?

One can express this 'why' in two main kinds of ways. First, there is the commonsense (and biblically rooted) insight that one must try to practise what one preaches. And so, for example, if the Church wants to preach with authenticity about global financial reform, it must attempt to put its own financial house in order; if it is serious about the dignity of every human being, it must be seen to deal justly with clerical sexual abuse; if it considers dialogue essential (with states, with society, with other believers, with all men and women – *EG* 238 ff), then it must encourage dialogue within its own ranks.

A second way to understand the link is to draw on the principle of sacramentality.[1] The church understands itself as a kind of sacrament (*EG* 1), a visible sign of the invisible presence of Jesus Christ and of the invisible presence of the triune God. In its proclamation of God's kingdom to the world, it must try to embody kingdom values in its own inner life – values like justice, the equal dignity of all the baptised, the principle of subsidiarity (developed in Catholic Social Teaching and related to the Conciliar notion of collegiality), the preferential option for the poor.

Of course Francis understands that we are always a church of saints and sinners. However, while we should use this eschatological horizon (the tension between the 'already and not yet') as grounds for a more inclusive church (of, among others, so-called progressives and conservatives), we should never use it as a pretext for failing to tackle known defects, defects which can too easily fail to 'attract' (*EG* 14) people to Jesus Christ and, instead, serve as a deterrent, an anti-sign.

At the heart of his approach is a simple but profound grasp of the essentials of Christian faith, of the Good News – that Jesus Christ shows us that God is a God of love and mercy who saves us, sinners and needy as we are; that Jesus is particularly close to the poor and suffering, who are first in his kingdom; and that all this is a matter not just for relief, or strategic and organisational planning, but for sheer joy. In this context he observes that what the Church needs most today is 'the ability to heal wounds and to warm the heart of the faithful' (Jesuit Interview, September 2013, p.8).

Francis draws on Paul VI and on the Second Vatican Council (*EG* 26) to promote his 'dream' (like Martini, whom he admires so greatly) that the missionary impulse would be 'capable of transforming everything, so that the church's customs, ways of doing things, times and schedules, language and structures can be suitably channelled for the evangelisation of today's world rather than for her self-preservation' (*EG* 27). This renewal of structures, he goes on to say, is 'demanded' by pastoral conversion (*EG* 27).

What sort of reform?
The kind of required reform is clear enough and has been amply indicated by Francis himself. Principally – and key to all else – we need to move in the direction of a more decentralised and collegial church at all levels (*EG* 16; 32; 19–33). This will mean granting effective and not just affective authority to Episcopal Conferences, as well as a more autonomous role to the Synods of Bishops. We can learn about this practice of synodality from other Christians, including the Orthodox (*EG* 246; SJ interview, p.11). It will also mean real, and not just token, consultation with laity, who should also be part of decision-making (*EG* 102). This includes women, who should have a more incisive and visible presence in the Church (*EG* 103). All this transcends what Gerard Mannion has called the strategy of 'negative subsidiarity', operative until recently in the church, by which responsibility for defects has been offloaded at local level in order to deflect attention from the failings of central authorities.[2] Francis himself has begun

this process of a more collegial church by convening the Council of eight Cardinals and by promoting the church-wide consultation in preparation for the next Synod of Bishops.

Closely connected to this principal reform is the inclusion of the 'sense of the faithful' as *a locus theologicus*, a source of truth in the formation and reception of church teaching. This is true of popular piety (*EG* 126), of the experience of the poor (*EG* 198), but applies also to all the faithful, who are holy thanks to the anointing of the Spirit, which makes them infallible *in credendo* (*EG* 119), in believing. This insight, giving rise to a more participative notion of 'thinking with the Church', has potentially radical consequences. One thinks, for example, of the widespread dissatisfaction of the faithful with aspects of ecclesial teaching on some issues of sexuality and gender. This leads to the kind of situation where between bishops and others a spirit of reciprocal pretence seems to prevail: 'you pretend to teach me, and I'll pretend to learn'.[3] May this now be assessed in a more critical theological light rather than being dismissed on purely sociological grounds? Ladislas Orsy notes how a seemingly secular movement – the demand for human rights – became a source for the Conciliar Fathers in the composition of the Declaration on Religious Freedom of Vatican II, so that 'they acknowledge the common sense of humanity as a *locus theologicus*, a legitimate source for theological information'.[4] The upcoming Synod on the Family will be a test of how seriously the Church is prepared to take the commonsense of its own baptised faithful.

These two major strategic reforms, concerning governance and teaching, will require appropriate structural expression at all levels. They can lead to the kind of more open and inclusive church which Francis wants (*EG* 27), in which dialogue is valued (*EG* 238 ff – our culture 'privileges dialogue as a form of encounter' – 239) and a reformed Roman Curia operates in service of the pope and all the bishops, of particular churches and of bishops' conferences, and not as 'institutions of censorship' (SJ interview, p.11). Meanwhile there will always be particular issues that have to be dealt with – one thinks, for example, of the already mentioned reform of the Vatican's own financial operations and of the crucial issue of sexual abuse. Above all, there is the option for the poor, 'primarily a theological category rather than a cultural, sociological, political or philosophical one ... this is why I want a Church which is poor and for the poor' (*EG* 198).

How to go about reform?

I take it as given that reform involves strategic and tactical planning, personnel management, the creation of new procedures and structures and so on. We have already seen some of this – for example the Council of Cardinals, the consultation prior to the upcoming Synod, new personnel, reforms in areas like finance and sexual abuse. All this, and more, will need to continue, but I want here to address further the underlying dynamic, the spirit of the reform. I will do so in four points.

First, Francis, true to his intuition that mission and reform belong together, insists that we are engaged here in God's work, in the realm of grace (*EG* 12; 22–24; 112; SJ interview p.4). The primacy and initiative are always that of the God who is *semper maior*, always greater, whose ways are wonderfully mysterious and surprising, who lets the tares grow together with the wheat, who cannot be coerced by our more straight-line, results-oriented thinking. We need, then, to proceed in a way that blends humility (and indeed humour) with zeal and planning, to imitate the paschal way of proceeding of Jesus Christ who 'emptied himself' so that all might be brought along, be saved.[5] We do this all the more easily when we ask to live in the graced state of being aware that we too are sinners ('I am a sinner whom the Lord has looked upon' – SJ interview, pp.1–2), that it is all too human to resist change, that conflict is endemic to human affairs. This graced perspective introduces a certain tenderness to what might otherwise appear only as a field of battle, it allows us to speak of the need not to avoid but to 'caress conflicts'.[6]

Above all it insists that all our planning and action towards reform be subject to a profound process of personal and communal discernment (*EG* 43; SJ interview, pp.3–7). This discernment will involve, in a spirit of prayer, consideration of the issue at hand, the scriptural foundation, the resources of the tradition, and also the 'signs of the times', the voice of the poor and those of all the faithful, a privileging of the view from the periphery over that of the centre.[7] Prayer in this context includes a weighing up of thoughts and feelings, of what St Ignatius calls 'consolation' and 'desolation', as we try to put on ever more the 'mind of Christ', drawn by the Holy Spirit. Church renewal and reform are likely to remain a somewhat 'zero sum', fruitless game between progressives and conservatives unless this faith perspective takes root and is not merely a pious veneer without real substance.

Secondly, Francis likes to insist that change is less likely to take place in haste and with grand gestures, but more with patience, time and the introduction of processes which lay the foundations for real, effective change, which bear fruit in significant historical events (*EG* 222–5; SJ interview, pp.3–7). As with the temptations of Jesus and his kenotic response, Francis is cautioning against recourse to the default position of power and self-assertion: instead 'you can have large projects and implement them by means of the smallest things. Or you can use weak means that are more effective than strong ones, as Paul also said in his First Letter to the Corinthians' (SJ interview, p.3). His own policy of de-centralising power, of trusting in collegial governance, is very much of a piece with this purposeful but less forcibly controlled approach. The Lord, as Elijah discovered, is found not so much in the mighty wind, the earthquake or the fire, but rather in 'the sound of a gentle breeze' (1 Kings, 19:9, 11–13).

Thirdly, there is a need for both attitudinal and structural trans-formation. Francis will be aware of the judgement of the 34th General Congregation of the Jesuits in 1995: 'Our experience in recent decades has demonstrated that social change does not consist only in the transformation of economic and political structures, for these structures are themselves rooted in socio-cultural values and attitudes'.[8] He himself notes that 'changing structures without generating new convictions and attitudes will only ensure that those same structures will become, sooner or later, corrupt, oppressive and ineffectual' (*EG* 189). And so 'the first reform must be the attitude' (SJ interview, p.9), our approach must not be that of business managers wishing to wield power (*EG* 95–96), and yet 'convictions and habits of solidarity … open the way to other structural transformations and make them possible' (*EG* 189). And so, as noted, we require more collegial structures for governance and teaching in our church, but we require also to move towards these in a prayerful and patient way, not substituting grand gestures for more lasting reform. Francis himself is proving a good model in terms of initiating both attitudinal and structural change.

Fourthly – and crucially for us in Ireland – there is the call to missionary conversion of each particular church, to undertake a 'resolute process of discernment, purification and reform' (*EG* 30). This will mean that bishops encourage means of participation and dialogue, 'out of a desire to listen to everyone and not simply to those who would tell him what he would like to hear', sometimes walking behind his flock, allowing them 'to strike out on new paths' (*EG* 31; SJ interview, pp.8–9). The papacy itself and Episcopal conferences need this same conversion and reformation (*EG* 32). We need to be 'bold and creative in this task of rethinking the goals, structures, styles and methods of evangelisation' in our respective communities, we need under the leadership of the bishops to engage in 'a wise and realistic pastoral discernment' (*EG* 33). We must not succumb to the temptation of 'an ostentatious preoccupation for liturgy, for doctrine and the Church's prestige but without any concern that the Gospel have a real impact on God's faithful people and the concrete needs of the present time' (*EG* 95). We must not, in short, be content 'to have a modicum of power' and 'rather be the general of a defeated army than a mere private in a unit that continues to fight' (*EG* 96). When one observes the platitudinous response of most Irish bishops, and of the Episcopal Conference as a whole, to requests for a more dialogical church, to attempts from organisations like the ACP and ACI to engage with real issues, one cannot but be struck by their serious lack of cooperation with the renewal and reform agenda of Francis. Yet, conscious of the difficulty we all have with change, perhaps it is wise also to temper the necessary language of critique and condemnation with Francis' own preferred language of encouragement and invitation. The pope has been crystal clear in his desire for ecclesial reform. Leadership at local, national and regional level is crucial to this call: it is not too late to respond, so please, bishops of Ireland, let's get started!

Conclusion
The motif on the cover of *The Furrow* (the journal Ronan Drury has served with such distinction for so long) since 1961 is:

> *Novate vobis novale*
> *Et nolite serere super spinas*

> Yours to drive a new furrow,
> Nor sow any longer among the briers.

Pope Francis is keenly aware of the need 'to drive a new furrow', and his demand for a reformed Church of the poor is precisely so that the sowing may bear a more abundant harvest. We are all invited to put our hands to the plough.

'From the Bishops down to the Last of the Lay Faithful'[1]

FÁINCHE RYAN

Ronan Drury became Editor of *The Furrow* in 1977, following the tragic death of the Founder-Editor J. G. McGarry on the 4 August, that same year. In a tribute to McGarry, in the first edition Drury edited, he noted:

> If the Church in Ireland is today better informed and more articulate it is chiefly because he made it so. And in other countries too. The wide world was his parish.[2]

These words summarise well the work of *The Furrow*, a work that has been continued, and well directed by its current editor in his thirty-seven years at the helm. The informing and forming of the Church in Ireland has been the work of *The Furrow*. While this can indeed be seen as the foundational vision of the publication, what has changed is the understanding of the concept 'Church in Ireland' that is in need of forming, and of informing.

The Mission of The Furrow

The Furrow has both witnessed, and contributed to, a recovery of the understanding of Church as a 'kingly people'; a 'chosen race, a royal priesthood' (1 Pet 2:9). It didn't start like this. It is interesting to read, in the first edition, an articulation by the Archbishop of Armagh, John D'Alton (1946–63), of the vision underpinning the foundation of *The Furrow*. Here we read that the programme of *The Furrow* is to be 'both wide and attractive, as it proposes to deal with the various problems which priests encounter in the course of their pastoral duties.'[3] This new publication from Maynooth was to be for priests, to help to provide them with good reading in order to make 'their preaching more effective'; so that they might help Irish Catholics 'to deepen their knowledge of Catholic belief, and of the beauty of the Liturgy; and to awaken in them a fuller consciousness of the priceless privilege that is theirs as members of the Catholic Church'.[4]

This it has done, and in doing so, it has helped to contribute to a changed understanding of the Church in Ireland. No longer regarded as a journal for priests, *The Furrow* has become an important source of information and learning for many Irish Catholics, lay and ordained – indeed even to distinguish too strongly thus, is perhaps counter to the ecclesial vision of this significant journal. The fact that lay contributions were an early feature of *The Furrow*, contributed to a change both in its style and in its programme. While originally for priests, with written contributions by priests – Archbishop D'Alton specifically asked that 'talented priests' be encouraged to write and utilise the 'vast potentialities of the apostolate of the press'[5] – this quickly changed. The first edition contained an article by 'The Architect', John J. Robinson, of Baggot Street Dublin, while no less a luminary than Lord Killanin is deemed to have been the first lay person to contribute an article to the May 1950 vision, entitled 'St Enda's, Spiddal'. So, with some speed we might say that the 'outsider status' of laity became central to the ongoing success of *The Furrow*, and in parallel we witness a transformation of the Church itself.

From 'Outsider' to 'Insider'
This is arguably the key contribution of *The Furrow* to the Church in Ireland – the recognition that the Church is a holy people of God, an informed holy people of God. Writing in the thirteenth century, Thomas Aquinas taught that just as Christ is 'anointed with the oil of holiness and gladness … This anointing also befits Christians, for they are kings and priests … all are anointed with an invisible anointing'.[6] It is this anointing that is recognised in the ecclesiological understanding of the *sensus fidelium* (sense of the faithful), so powerfully articulated in the teachings of Vatican II, in particular in *Lumen gentium*, the dogmatic constitution of the Church:

> The holy people of God shares also in Christ's prophetic office … The entire body of the faithful, anointed as they are by the Holy One, cannot err in matters of belief. They manifest this special property by means of the whole peoples' supernatural discernment in matters of faith when 'from the Bishops down to the last of the lay faithful' they show universal agreement in matters of faith and morals. (LG 12)

One of the aims of *The Furrow*, according to the Archbishop of Armagh, was that it should enlighten the minds of the priests, who might then preach and teach more effectively. The publication went further. In the summer of 1980 it began to offer a theology course for lay people. While lay people had by now become key contributors, the fact that the laity in Ireland were 'underprivileged' when it came to theological discourse was recognised as a need that required attention. As an early participant in the summer school noted, when it came to their being theologically under-privileged 'the duty of overcoming it falls, not on the underprivileged "outsiders" but on the privileged "insiders" who hold power'.[7] *Dei verbum* paragraph eight may be said to articulate a similar sentiment when it speaks of the tradition 'that comes from the apostles' making 'progress in the Church, with the help of the Holy Spirit'. It goes on:

> There is a growth in insight into the realities and words that are being passed on. This comes about in various ways. It comes through the contemplationand study of believers who ponder these things in their hearts (Lk 2:19 and 51). (DV 8)

The anointed people of God are temples of the Holy Spirit. They 'cannot err in matters of belief'. This 'supernatural discernment' of the people of God has traditionally been termed the *sensus fidei*, the sense of faith of the community of believers. The need to recognise and educate the sensus fidei of all the members of the Church, recognised by Vatican II, was made manifest and brought forward through *The Furrow*'s work. The 'contemplation and study of believers', encouraged by Vatican II, took place in Ireland in a variety of ways. This process enabled the transition of 'underprivileged outsiders' to 'insiders' … who now expect to have a share in power, and in decision making. This was an inevitable, but perhaps unseen result of the wider theological awakening of the Irish people, to which the work of *The Furrow* played no small part.

Sensus Fidelium

It is one thing to communicate the Church's teaching on contraception to someone in formation for life as a celibate priest, and quite another to seek to transmit, and indeed justify this teaching to young married people. As outsiders become insiders, new challenges are faced. This has received particular articulation in 2013 with the invitation to the Church at large to respond to questions on the 'Pastoral challenges of the family in the context of evangelisation.'[8] It was hoped that these responses would help to guide discussion at the Extraordinary General Assembly of the Synod of Bishops on the theme: 'The pastoral challenges for the family in the context of evangelisation' to be held in 2014. While this exercise has to be deemed laudable – the view of a majority of the *sensus fidelium* was being sought – the *sensus fidei* of those issuing the document and preparing for a synod on the family seems to be somewhat out of touch. Many 'outsiders' critiqued the language of the questions, while some 'insiders' sought to keep the report of the survey 'inside' by sending it to Rome, stating it was 'a matter for the Synod of Bishops and not for the local Church'.[9] Pressure from the outsider *sensus fidei* seems to have been the spur that prompted the Irish Bishops to share the results of the finding with the Church in Ireland.[10]

Today's Challenge

Once you dig a furrow, and sow a seed, chances are something will grow, and not always that which you expected. The challenge today, in Ireland, and in the 'wide world' which was identified as the parish of *The Furrow*, is to produce a Church that will give scope to the *sensus fidelium*. How is this *sensus fidelium*, which is an ever increasingly informed *sensus fidei*, to be harvested? If the process of handing on the faith is truly recognised as the work of the whole Church, and seen as a two-directional spiral process, then new methods of order and of communication are required. Augustine's phrase, cited in Vatican II: 'from the Bishops down to the last of the lay faithful', needs nuance. Communication can no longer be seen as one way. It is not for the Bishops' Conference of England and Wales to refuse to release the findings of the questionnaire on marriage and family life, whether or not as Msgr Stock understood, 'all bishops' conferences had been asked not to make the summary of the synod survey findings public.'[11] The views of the *sensus fidelium*, which includes Bishops – who have a particular role when it comes to the *sensus fidei* (in, not outside of) – needs to be shared. Rarely should such information be in need of secrecy. We are now more than fifty years from the beginning of Vatican II, and the seeds sown then, have in some instances produced fruit we did not expect.

In Catholic churches throughout the world we find female altar servers, together with lay readers, both male and female. Many dioceses and parishes today, even in Ireland, have lay ecclesial ministers, and many hospital and prison chaplains are no longer sacramentally ordained. The Spirit has indeed been active. In Ireland, more people than ever before are studying theology, or religious studies, in new places like Waterford Institute of Technology, as well as in longer established homes like St Patrick's College Maynooth. The Loyola Institute of Catholic Theological Studies, recently inaugurated in Trinity College, is another sign of the flourishing of the vision of Vatican II. The *sensus fidei* today is much more than a theory. It is a living expression of the fact that the Church's official teaching office is theologically bound to consult the faithful in its teaching process. The very nature of the Church demands it.

This of course is problematic. When one does, as John Henry Newman counselled, consult the faithful in matters of doctrine, one does not always receive the answer sought. Two areas in particular demand attention in Ireland today: that of sexual behaviour, and the question of women. When it comes to sexual behaviour, the Ireland of today is far distant from the Ireland of the fifties when *The Furrow* began to stimulate people to think. It is unbelievable for young people in Ireland to read that it was only in 1979 that the Family Planning Act, enacted by Charlie Haughey, Minister for Health, legalised contraception, with the restriction that it was only to be available on prescription for *bona fide* family planning purposes. Similarly it seems astounding now to realise that, as recently as 1993, homosexuality was decriminalised in this country. Today the question to be asked is where does the Church lie when it comes to debate in these areas. Do we currently have a theology that can distinguish between theological truths regarding human flourishing as sexual beings, and rules and regulations, indeed norms that governed life in the past? Can our theology distinguish between societal norms, and the guidance of the Holy Spirit? Have people been educated to distinguish between what is law, and what is truthful living, for a Christian?

Similar questions must be asked regarding women, and women in the Church. Pope Francis received much attention when he wrote about the need to develop a theology of 'woman'. While some read this positively, others perhaps react more like Rosemary Goldie's (an auditor from Australia at Vatican II) response to comments on the 'special nature of woman'. In the process of constructing a statement about women, during a session of the Commission on the Church in the Modern World, one of the members read

> a flowery and innocuous sentence to the commission members for their consideration. When he had finished, he noticed the women present were unimpressed. 'But, Rosemary,' he said, addressing the intelligent and able Rosemary Goldie, 'why don't you respond happily to my praise of women and what they have contributed to the church?' ... to which she replied: 'You can omit all those gratuitous flowery adjectives, the pedestals and incense, from your sentence. All women ask for is that

they be recognised as the full human persons they are, and treated accordingly.'[12]

'All women ask for is that they be recognised as the full human persons they are, and treated accordingly.' That we still need to hear these words today, in 2014, shows how far we have to go; that we could hear them said at one of the sessions of the Second Vatican Council shows that the *sensus fidei* was alive and active then. The Spirit is always working.

We could amend this statement slightly and say 'All the baptised ask for is that they be recognised as the full human persons they are, and treated accordingly.' Increasingly the baptised seek new ways to exercise the *sensus fidei* which they share with the ordained. The authority of the baptised seeks active recognition for all who have been baptised into the priestly, prophetic and kingly ministry of Christ. We have been anointed kings and priests, we are a 'chosen race, a royal priesthood' (1 Pet 2:9). Since 1950, *The Furrow* has played a pivotal role in helping people both to recognise this fact, and also in the exercise of their Christian calling, making use of the 'vast potentialities of the apostolate of the press'.[13] John D'Alton wrote these words encouraging priests to write articles for *The Furrow*, and so help form other priests, so they could in turn teach the laity. Little could he have imagined that in a short space of time *The Furrow* would have laity writing, to help form, and challenge, other laity and priests. 'For there is a growth in the understanding of the realities and the words which have been handed down … as the centuries succeed one another, the Church constantly moves forward toward the fullness of divine truth until the words of God reach their completer fulfilment' (DV 8). The people of God, '*ab Episcopis usque ad extremos laicos fideles*', 'from the bishops up to the outermost/furthest distant laity' have been anointed with the Holy Spirit.[14] All, together, participate in the journey into becoming an ever more truthful Church.

A Pope from the Global South: Redirecting Evangelisation

E AMONN C ONWAY

Introduction

It is almost fifty years since the closing of the Second Vatican Council. In the intervening period, apart from the decrees of the Council itself, hardly any other papal document has received as much attention as Pope Francis' Apostolic Exhortation, *Evangelii gaudium* ('The Joy of the Gospel'), promulgated on 24 November 2013. Part of the fascination is with the man: no Pope has achieved the celebrity status he has in such a short time. However, the document itself, which is programmatic for his pontificate, merits detailed study.[1]

A non-European Pope

We cannot underestimate the significance of the Church being led by a Pope who comes from outside of Europe.

Many of the bishops at the First Vatican Council (1869–70), though representing dioceses beyond Europe, were nonetheless European missionaries, with a European mentality and mindset. The Second Vatican Council (1962–5) was the first Council to be attended by indigenous bishops from almost every part of the world where the Church was present. This began a shift in the Church's mentality, away from being predominantly European in outlook, to being truly a world Church.

At Vatican II, the Church saw itself as having a unique role to play in the promotion of human dignity globally and in the stewardship of creation (*Gaudium et spes*). The Council also put emphasis on the Church's role as the sacrament of salvation for all humankind (*Dei verbum*). For the first time, there was also a positive evaluation of non-Christian world religions (*Nostra aetate*). The need for bishops from different cultures and contexts to collaborate closely together with the successor of Peter in leading and governing the world Church found expression in the emphasis on collegiality (*Lumen gentium*) and in establishing the custom of regular world synods of bishops. It is no surprise that each of these issues is taken up and amplified in *Evangelii gaudium*.

A Pope from the Global South

Pope Francis is not just a non-European; he also comes from the developing world, the so-called Global South. Perhaps the most distinctive aspect of what he brings to the papacy is his first-hand experience of the two-thirds world.

The last half-century has been a time of 'massive discontinuity' in world Catholicism. In 1950, almost half of the world's Catholics lived in Europe, with just over a third living in Africa and Latin America. Today, Catholicism worldwide is urban and urbanising. Just over a quarter of the world's Catholics are European, while well over half live in Africa and Latin America. The majority of Catholics in the world today live in cities or on the peripheries of cities, and in poor conditions, usually with limited access to even the basics in terms of health and education.[2]

Very often, culturally speaking, Catholics are a minority, and increasingly, along with other Christians, they face persecution. According to John Allen, it is estimated that eighty per cent of all acts of religious discrimination today are against Christians, and that from 2000–10, approximately 100,000 Christians were killed annually because of religious hatred.[3]

We need to bear these points in mind when reading *Evangelii gaudium*.

Pope Francis' election: a new epoch for the Church?

It has been suggested that Europe now belongs to an 'axis of irrelevance' for the world Church, the recognition of which it should embrace with humility.[4] On this matter, theologians have differing views.

We recall, for instance, in his famous Regensburg Address (2006), Pope Benedict XVI reiterated his long-held view that an 'inner rapprochement' took place between Biblical faith and Greek philosophical enquiry which has been of 'decisive importance', as he says, 'not only from the standpoint of the history of religions, but also from that of world history – it is an event which concerns us even today'.[5] In his view, Christianity took on its 'historically decisive character in Europe' with the result that 'the critically purified Greek heritage forms an integral part of Christian faith'. This explains Pope Benedict's preoccupation with the re-evangelisation of Europe, his choice of St Benedict, Patron of Europe, as his patron, and many of the priorities of his pontificate.

Karl Rahner took a different view. Up until Vatican II, according to Rahner, in its concrete activity, the Church resembled 'an export firm, exporting to the whole world a European religion along with other elements of this supposedly superior culture and civilisation, and not really attempting to change the commodity'.[6] The Second Vatican Council, he claimed, marks the transition from an epoch in which the Church was defined by Hellenism and by European culture and civilisation, to a new one 'in which the Church's living space is from the very outset the whole world'.[7] The potential the Church always held, since its institution to be truly a world Church, was realised in a defining way in the event of the Second Vatican Council. Those who accept Karl Rahner's analysis see in the appointment of Pope Francis a defining moment in the realisation of the Church as a world Church, and thus, in the implementation of the Second Vatican Council.

If this is so, it means that the changes Pope Francis is making in Church governance, especially efforts to make collegiality a reality; to enhance the effectiveness of the Synod of Bishops; to globalise the College of Cardinals and the Curia; are about much more than merely implementing administrative reforms in the face of corruption and scandals. They can also be read as programmatic steps in the full implementation of Vatican II.

In *Evangelii gaudium*, Pope Francis speaks specifically of the need for decentralisation (n.16) and for local Churches to take responsibility for the mission of the Church in their own particular situations and circumstances (n.30, n.33). He calls for greater collegiality (n.32, n.247), and he puts this into practice by citing texts from several bishops' conferences around the world, thus endorsing their teaching authority, the first time that this has been a key feature of a papal document.

On the specific issue we have been considering, Europe's place in global Catholicism, Pope Francis writes:

> We cannot demand that peoples of every continent, in expressing their Christian faith, imitate modes of expression which European nations developed at a particular moment of their history, because the faith cannot be constricted to the limits of understanding and expression of any one culture. It is an indisputable fact that no single culture can exhaust the mystery of our redemption in Christ (*Evangelii gaudium*, n.118).[8]

Pope Francis' distinctive approach to evangelisation

Evangelii gaudium is often referred to as a post-synodal apostolic exhortation, following on from the 2012 World Synod of Bishops. The Synod that preceded the publication of *Evangelii gaudium* took place from 7–28 October 2012 in Rome with the theme: 'The New Evangelisation for the Transmission of the Christian Faith.' It was convened by Pope Benedict XVI and was attended by almost three hundred and fifty bishops, heads of religious orders, theological experts and observers. The Synod deliberately coincided with the fiftieth anniversary of the opening of the Second Vatican Council. At its conclusion, it produced a series of propositions on evangelisation and a short statement. It also elected a committee of bishops representing each continent to support the Pope in the task of writing the post-synodal exhortation.

Significantly, Pope Francis was not at the Synod; he was not one of the three bishops nominated by the Argentinian bishops, and neither was he among Pope Benedict's nominees. He had already submitted his resignation as Archbishop of Buenos Aires, having reached seventy-five. Like Pope Francis, Pope John Paul II and Pope Benedict XVI issued exhortations following synods presided over by their predecessors. Generally, however, post-synodal exhortations reflect closely the deliberations of the synod. This is clearly less the case with *Evangelii gaudium*.

In fact, though generally referred to as *post-synodal*, significantly, the document does not describe itself as such. Officially, it is an 'Apostolic Exhortation of the Holy Father, Francis, to the Bishops, Clergy, Consecrated Persons and the Lay Faithful on the Proclamation of the Gospel in Today's World.'

According to the Argentinian journalist Paolo Rodari, in a book written with Archbishop Victor Manuel Fernandez, the term 'post-synodal' is deliberately avoided. Instead, *Evangelii gaudium* is to be read as the key programmatic document of Pope Francis' pontificate.[9]

What, then, is the provenance of Evangelii gaudium?

In writing *Evangelii gaudium*, Pope Francis is heavily influenced by the Latin American Bishops' Aparecida process.[10] There, the two key issues for renewal were identified as replenishing the vigour and enthusiasm of pastoral workers, priests and lay, and putting the entire Church on a missionary footing. These are also the two key objectives of *Evangelii gaudium*.

Pope Francis is also influenced by an earlier post-synodal exhortation, *Evangelii nuntiandi* (Paul VI, 1975), which he has described as 'the greatest pastoral document that has ever been written to this day' and as having not lost any of its timeliness.[11] It is no accident that his exhortation bears a similar name to that of Paul VI's.

The emphasis on joy (*gaudium*) is traceable to the *Aparecida document* where the word occurs with the same frequency as it does in *Evangelii gaudium*, and to another exhortation of Paul VI's, *Gaudete in Domino* (also 1975).

The key word in the subtitle of *Evangelii gaudium*, 'the proclamation of the Gospel in today's world', is proclamation. The focus is upon the joy of proclaiming the Gospel, the urgency of doing so, identification of the obstacles that prevent proclamation, and concrete proposals in regard to how these might be tackled. In *Evangelii gaudium*, joy is understood as the means of proclamation; only joyful Christians can evangelise others. Joy is also that which results from living and proclaiming the Gospel.

The 'new' evangelisation: continuity or discontinuity?

In the lead-up to the 2012 Synod, we became familiar with the term 'new evangelisation'. This had a particular technical meaning at the Synod, which it seems to have lost in *Evangelii gaudium*.

John Paul II first used the term on his first visit to his homeland in 1979. The newness was to be expressed in 'ardor, method and expressions' (1983). Gradually, the term 'new evangelisation' became focused upon those who, though baptised, had lost a sense of their faith, and 'live a life far removed from Christ and his Gospel' (*Redemptoris missio*, n.33). The decade from 1990 to 2000 was dedicated to a renewed effort at evangelisation.

As the 2012 Synod was convened, the focus of the 'new evangelisation' was specifically upon pastoral outreach to people who have discontinued practising their faith. We might think this is a specifically European problem, but it is not, and bishops from around the world were quite concerned about it. Those from Latin America, for instance, were concerned about people converting from Catholicism to attractive but often short-lived evangelical communities.

Pope Benedict XVI spoke at the Synod's opening mass of an evangelisation directed 'principally at those who, though baptised, have drifted away from the Church and live without reference to the Christian life'. The propositions issued at the end of the Synod spoke of the new evangelisation, targeting especially 'those who have become distant from the Church' (n.7).

In the *Instrumentum laboris*, the preparatory document for the Synod, the term 'new evangelisation' was used 121 times; in *Evangelii gaudium* it occurs only fourteen times, and then not really in the technical sense in which it was used at the Synod.

In contrast, Pope Francis has moved away from a specific focus on non-committed or non-practising Catholics. He tells us: 'Every form of authentic evangelisation is always "new"' (n.11). In the opening section of *Evangelii gaudium* (n.14), he identifies three principal settings for the new evangelisation: (i)

Ordinary pastoral activity, and here he includesthose who have deep faith but seldom go to mass or formal worship; (ii) Baptised people whose lives 'do not reflect the demands of Baptism' and who no longer have a meaningful relationship with the Church; His emphasis, however, clearly falls on the third when he says: (iii) 'We cannot forget that evangelisation is first and foremost directed to those who do not know Jesus Christ, or who have always rejected him', and he speaks of their 'right' to receive the Gospel.

A self-referential Church v a missionary Church

There is an important shift of ecclesiological perspective here. For Pope Francis, we cannot wait for the Church to get its own house in order so that it is in a suitable state of holiness or perfection to engage in pastoral outreach. Pope Francis frequently makes use of the image of battle. For him, there is a war going on, and in a war, one has to make do with whatever state of readiness one is in. To delay the work of mission would be an indication of self-absorption.

The Church has access to the living water that is Christ. Yet so many people are weakened by drought and thirst, and instead turn to polluted waters that only weaken them further.[12] Throughout *Evangelii gaudium* we can detect a great sense of urgency about the task of proclaiming the Gospel. This springs from knowing that through our efforts at evangelisation, Christ provides people with the living water they so deeply need and desire.

He likens the Church to a field-hospital to which the battle weary and wounded can come to experience the liberal outpouring of mercy, compassion and healing.[13] Field hospitals, of necessity, are rough and ready and have to make do; they cannot have all the 'mod-cons' of well-equipped surgical hospitals. Pope Francis is very clear that the Church is not an end in itself. The 'end' is the reign of God of which the Church is the sacrament. The Church has an urgent task to do and needs to get on with it.

There is more at play here than simply looking at the Church's problems and saying *solventur ambulando*. Pope Francis is of the view that engaging in evangelisation is in itself regenerating for the Church. He wants a Church that 'is bruised, hurting and dirty because it has been out on the streets, rather than a Church which is unhealthy from being confined and from clinging to its own security' (n.49).

This fits in with his words to the consistory before the conclave, when he reminded his brother cardinals that the Church's 'light' is like the light of the moon, in other words, it is a *reflected* light only. Quoting the Dominican theologian Henri de Lubac, Pope Francis said that when the Church forgets this, it gives way to 'that very serious evil, spiritual worldliness', a theme he returns to in *Evangelii gaudium* (nn. 93–97). The opposite to spiritual worldliness is a Church permanently prepared to leave behind securities and comfort zones and 'go forth', Abraham-like, to new lands (n.20). The theme of leaving, departing, exiting, is a common one in *Evangelii gaudium*, and explains why Pope Francis seems to prefer the language of mission to that of evangelisation.

In *Evangelii gaudium*, Pope Francis has taken on board many of the insights of the 2012 Synod. At the same time, he has, to use his own term, transposed its reflections into a distinctive 'missionary key' (n.33) along the lines we find in the *Aparecida document*. This shows that while Pope Francis wishes to promote collegiality and synodality, he still sees it as appropriate for the Bishop of Rome to give a clear sense of direction to the universal Church.

Conclusion
Paradoxically, a key message of what is a strongly directive exhortation, is that the faithful, working together with their pastors, are to take responsibility themselves for the transformation of the local Church to which they belong, beginning with a process of careful discernment of what renewal

is needed. Key to the renewal of the Church, as Pope Francis sees it, is that we should not be expecting the papal magisterium to offer 'a definitive or complete word on every question which affects the Church and the world' (n.16).

Whatever other magisterial documents emerge from Pope Francis, *Evangelii gaudium* provides a clear set of guidelines directing the Church into a new phase of evangelisation (n.17) and has 'programmatic significance and important consequences' (n.25). For this reason alone it merits careful study.

Pope Francis and the
Agenda for Pastoral Reform
EUGENE DUFFY

A Pastor from the Outset

When Cardinal Tauran stepped on to the loggia of St Peter's and announced that Jorge Bergoglio had been elected pope and was taking the name Francis, there was confusion in the crowd below: the name sounded Italian, but he was not an Italian cardinal, and no pope had previously taken the name Francis. The world was taken by surprise. But almost immediately after his appearance, Bergoglio had captivated the world with his simple style. Although his presence, words and gestures were simple, they were rich in symbolism and in retrospect one can see that the agenda for a pastoral reform was already being sketched in outline.

The fact that he was not a European was instantly significant. His election to the papacy is indicative of a shift from a euro-centric Church to one that is truly global. Europe accounts for about twenty-seven per cent of the world's Catholics, while almost forty-three per cent live in Latin America. The perspective he brings is inevitably coloured by his experience of the Latin American continent – poverty, political upheavals, popular piety and the growth of various forms of Pentecostalism. His concerns are therefore more pastoral than doctrinal.

His choice of name was both imaginative and evocative. It was a new name on the papal register and its choice suggested this was a man who was prepared to break with papal traditions. The name was a reminder of *il poverello*, whose simplicity, joy, spontaneity and poverty renewed the Church of the thirteenth century. In a dream, St Francis was told 'go and repair my church which is falling into ruin' and in his very first homily, Pope Francis addressing the cardinal-electors, spoke of building up the Church – 'with every movement in our lives let us build'. This building up of the Church involves a concern for the poor, for peace and for creation, as it did for St Francis.

His earliest words hinted that he was intent on reform. His initial greeting to the crowd in St Peter's Square was informal: *Buona Sera!* He told them that the business of the conclave had been to elect a bishop of Rome and that the cardinals had gone to the ends of the earth to find one. Behind the humour was the very serious point that he was first and foremost the bishop of Rome and, as if to reinforce the point, he avoided using any of the trappings that would have exaggerated his primatial status. He was situating himself clearly within the college of bishops and not above it. Then he invited the crowd to pray with him before he imparted his blessing. Again, aside from the humility of this gesture, he was implicitly situating himself in the midst of the People of God and not apart from them.

As the first weeks of his papacy unfolded it became obvious that his outlook and style marked a significant departure from that of his immediate predecessors. His morning homilies were more *ex tempore* than carefully scripted texts. His first visit outside of Rome was deliberately pastoral, to comfort migrants in Lampedusa and show solidarity with them. Inside Rome he visited poor parishes and celebrated Mass of the Lord's Supper in a prison and not in one of the basilicas. His style in meeting and addressing groups was informal. His willingness to give interviews and to engage with the media showed that he was conscious of the fact that his ideas communicated in this format were more likely to reach a much wider audience than any formal statements that he might issue, notwithstanding the fact that his Apostolic Exhortation, *Evangelii gaudium,* has sold more copies than any Church document since the Second Vatican Council. In a matter of months he established himself as a pastor, very much at ease with himself and ready in his actions and words to reach out to people in a very immediate, personal and non-judgemental fashion. He appeared to radiate a natural warmth and a sense of joy which he proposed as a pastoral approach for all who are ministers of the Gospel.

A Needed Reform
The election of Jorge Bergoglio followed the dramatic resignation of his predecessor, Pope Benedict XVI, whose departure followed a report from a group of senior cardinals some time earlier and which seemed to confirm the widely held view that there were elements in various curial departments whose behaviour was a cause of scandal. Furthermore, there were serious concerns among the worldwide episcopate that a growing and unnecessary centralising tendency was at work in Rome for quite some time. There was, too, the realisation that not only was there a decline in ecclesial life in Europe but the emerging churches were not without their problems as well. Therefore, when the cardinals met in preparation for the conclave in 2013, they were acutely aware that the next pope would need

to be capable of bringing about the necessary reforms within the Vatican, and also enhance the pastoral mission and credibility of the Church worldwide.

The brief but concise intervention of Bergoglio at one of the preparatory meetings in advance of the conclave resonated with the cardinals; they seemed to have found in his words the kind of approach they felt was needed if their various concerns were to be addressed. In his statement to the assembly he said:

> 1. The Church is called to come out of herself and to go to the peripheries, not only geographically, but also the existential peripheries: the mystery of sin, of pain, of injustice, of ignorance and indifference to religion, of intellectual currents, and of all misery.
>
> 2. When the Church does not come out of herself to evangelise, she becomes self-referential and then gets sick. The evils that, over time, happen in ecclesial institutions have their root in self-referentiality and a kind of theological narcissism … The self-referential Church keeps Jesus Christ within herself and does not let him out.
>
> 3. When the Church is self-referential, inadvertently, she believes she has her own light; she ceases to be the *mysterium lunae* and gives way to that very serious evil, spiritual worldliness …
>
> 4. Thinking of the next Pope: He must be a man who, from the contemplation and adoration of Jesus Christ, helps the Church to go out to the existential peripheries …[1]

He had expressed almost identical sentiments in an interview he gave to *30 Days* in 2007.[2] So these were long-held views. He was obviously influenced by his experience as a bishop and especially by the meeting of the Latin American and Caribbean bishops, CELAM, held at Aparecida in May 2007. At that meeting the bishops had elected him to chair the committee charged with drafting the final document. Incidentally, two other participants in the production of the *Aparecida document* were the

Chilean Cardinal Francisco Javier Errázuriz, co-president of CELAM, and the Honduran Cardinal Oscar Rodríguez Maradiaga, a key member of the drafting committee. Both cardinals were later to be part of the eight-member committee to advise the Pope on leading the universal church. Thus with three of the most significant members of the Aparecida conference involved in planning the reform of the Church, it is inevitable that its approach will influence how they wish to steer the reform of the universal Church. Therefore, it is important to look at the document produced by CELAM in 2007 if one is to appreciate the direction that the reform agenda is likely to take.[3]

The Aparecida Document: A Universal Application
The *Aparecida document* is a call to discipleship and mission. Christ is at the centre and the disciple is the one who has a personal encounter and relationship with him. This engagement leads to a missionary impulse which impels the disciple into a missionary mode, anxious to share the joy, love and hope that is to be found in this living relationship with Christ.

> The very nature of Christianity therefore consists of recognising the presence of Jesus Christ and following Him. That was the marvellous experience of those first disciples, who upon encountering Jesus were fascinated and astonished at the exceptional quality of the one speaking to them, especially how he treated them, satisfying the hunger and thirst for life that was in their hearts.[4]

This encounter is the 'source of life for the Church and the soul of its evangelising action.'[5] The same foundational idea is reiterated by Pope Francis in *Evangelii gaudium*: 'The primary reason for evangelising is the love of Jesus which we have received, the experience of salvation which urges us to ever greater love of him. What kind of love would not feel the need to speak of the beloved, to point him out, to make him known?'[6] This then provides a rationale for the Church and its members not being 'self-referential' or Church-centred in this case. The focus is first on Christ and then outwards in a missionary attitude, extending his proclamation and embodiment of the Kingdom of God to the whole world, bringing the compassion and mercy of Christ to all who are burdened by suffering and sin.

A second key feature of the *Aparecida document* is its endorsement of the preferential option for the poor: 'The preferential option for the poor is one of the distinguishing features of our Latin American and Caribbean church.'[7] The bishops go on to say: 'If this option is implicit in Christological faith, we Christians as disciples and missionaries are called to contemplate, in the suffering faces of our brothers and sisters, the face of Christ who calls us to serve him in them: "the suffering faces of the poor is the suffering face of Christ". They question the core of the Church's action, its ministry, and our Christian attitudes.'[8] This concern for the poor has already been demonstrated by the Pope in so many of his public activities and articulated very powerfully in *Evangelii gaudium*, where he says: 'I want a Church which is poor for the poor … We need to let ourselves be evangelised by them … We are called to find Christ in them, to lend our voices to their causes, but also to be their friends, to listen to them, to speak for them and to embrace the mysterious wisdom which God wishes to share with us through them.'[9] It is clear that the same priorities outlined by the Latin American bishops are now those of the bishop of Rome.

The third point of emphasis in the *Aparecida document* is the renewed determination of the Church to be missionary, to reach into every area of life and to every corner of the earth. 'From the cenacle of Aparecida we commit to begin a new stage in our pastoral journey, declaring ourselves in *permanent mission* (emphasis in the original). With the fire of the Spirit we will enflame our Continent with love … To be a missionary is to announce the Kingdom with creativity and boldness in every place where the Gospel has not been sufficiently announced or welcomed, especially in the difficult or forgotten environments, and beyond our borders.'[10] It was obvious in Bergoglio's address to the pre-conclave meetings that this desire to reach out to the peripheries was a passionate concern for him and one which he believed belonged to the whole Church. The same sense of urgency is expressed early in *Evangelii gaudium*: 'In fidelity to the example of the Master, it is vitally important for the Church today to go forth and preach the Gospel to all: to all places, on all occasions, without hesitation, reluctance or fear. The joy of the Gospel is for all people: no one can be excluded.'[11] More vividly he expressed the same idea in the following paragraph: 'An evangelising community gets involved by word and deed in people's daily lives; it bridges distances, it is willing to abase itself if necessary, and it embraces human life, touching the suffering flesh of Christ in others. Evangelisers thus take on the "smell of the sheep" and the sheep are willing to hear their voice.' There can be no doubt that Pope Francis wants the Church to be in a state of mission, bringing the life and light of the Gospel to bear on all human realities and in all places.

Structures for Mission

Vatican II, to some extent, corrected the over-emphasis on papal primacy that had dominated ecclesiology since Vatican I but has left a tension in how this primacy can be exercised side by side with the whole college of bishops. In practical terms this has meant that individual bishops and episcopal conferences have not either fully understood or been allowed to exercise the level of governance that belongs to them. This has hampered them in taking the kind of pastoral initiatives that are often required. Instead they have either bowed in unnecessary deference or too readily assumed that they lacked the authority to do what was required in concrete situations. The issue of the translation of the missal is a good example of undue deference by the bishops and excessive interference by the centre in the pastoral life of local churches.

Pope Francis has already given good reason to hope that this imbalance in the exercise of powers will be corrected in practice at least. His symbolic gestures, already mentioned, are indicative of that. However, even as archbishop of Buenos Aires he had shown a profound regard for the work of CELAM and referred to its *Aparecida document* as 'an act of the Magisterium of the Latin American Church' and that it 'underwent no manipulation' (from Rome). Again in *Evangelii gaudium* he says: 'It is not advisable for the Pope to take the place of the local Bishops in the discernment of every issue which arises in their territory. In this sense, I am conscious of the need to promote a sound "decentralisation".'[13] Later he says: 'Excessive centralisation, rather than proving helpful, complicates the Church's life and her missionary outreach.'[14] For him the willingness to engage with the pastoral situations in bold and creative ways is far more important than preserving structures or traditions for their own sakes. New structures, styles and methods of evangelisation must be sought to respond to current needs and situations. This new approach is offering freedom to individual bishops and episcopal conferences to be more imaginative and daring in fashioning pastoral strategies to deal with contemporary pastoral problems. Their proper pastoral responsibilities have been reasserted for them.

When Bergoglio was asked what was so special about the emergence of the agenda sketched out in the *Aparecida document* he listed three things:

i)   it emerged from the ground up;
ii)   it had the support of the people accompanying the process in prayer;
iii) it was open-ended, remaining open to change and development.[15]

Consistent with this approach, one can see in *Evangelii gaudium* his respect for the fact that the whole Church, in all its members, is Spirit-filled and gifted. 'The presence of the Spirit gives Christians a certain connaturality with divine realities, and a wisdom which enables them to grasp those realities intuitively, even when they lack the wherewithal to give them precise expression.'[16] There is here a profound respect for God's action in all of the baptised faithful and an imperative to listen to their voices.

Consistent with a comprehensive articulation of the role of the Holy Spirit in the life of the Church is the demand for all its members to engage in serious discernment. He encourages 'each particular Church to undertake a resolute process of discernment, purification and reform'.[17] The necessity for wise, evangelical and pastoral discernment is a recurring theme in his Apostolic Exhortation. It is a reminder of the freedom that the Church has to make the necessary changes or to adapt its strategies in light of new pastoral issues that arise as it makes its pilgrim journey through the world.

Conclusion
In a relatively short time, Pope Francis, by his example and words, has offered new hope to the world and to the Church. In his own pastoral style he embodies the credibility of the message that he proclaims. He has brought a fresh perspective to the universal Church from the particular experience of the Church in Latin America. He has loosened the Roman grip that seemed to be in danger of stifling the energies of other local churches around the world. He has set high and demanding ideals before all members of the Church to exercise their freedom creatively in making the presence of Christ a personal, life-giving experience for all others whose lives they touch. Most of all he has reaffirmed the teaching of Vatican II concerning the priority of the People of God and the role of the bishops as their servant leaders. There is no reason why responsibility for sound pas-

toral action be abdicated to Rome. Pope Francis has returned that to the local churches and encouraged its exercise. Even more, he has cautioned that, even a false spirituality, can be an obstacle to pastoral action: '[T]here is always the risk that some moments of prayer can become an excuse for not offering one's life in mission.'

Keeping the Door Open
OLIVER MCQUILLAN

At the fiftieth anniversary celebration recently of my Maynooth class's ordination, one of my fellow guests (now an archbishop) commented that he remembered us walking in together through the front gates back in 1957 on our way into Junior House. Fifty years afterwards, the images, the memories, of crossing that threshold from one life into another are still vivid.

I had left a boarding school, a 'minor seminary', where a bully had cast a shadow over my final two years. Passing through the front gates of Maynooth was to leave that world behind, and marked the start of one of the most fulfilling periods of my life. Some find this difficult to understand, but like so much else in life, it comes back to people.

Among the memories of early days in Maynooth which stand out was our elocution class (it wasn't yet the magnificently named Sacred Eloquence) taken by Fr Ronan Drury. This was familiar and reassuring territory unlike cosmology, logic, rubrics and other esoteric new subjects. Those elocution classes were not only thoroughly enjoyable but highly professional. Indeed, quite recently I typed up my notes of Fr Drury's lectures (from now on I'll call him Ronan) and they are used both by myself and a professional friend who teaches in Dublin (Sorry. No royalties!).

Ronan also directed the annual play which Junior House presented each year in the Aula Maxima. In first year I had the 'female' role in Agatha Christie's *The Mousetrap*, and in second year, played Teddy Roosevelt in *Arsenic and Old Lace*. These were joyous experiences.

When I left Maynooth early in my second divine year, the first person to contact me from the college was Ronan. Would I write a review of a book for *The Furrow*? I did. It was called Early Christian Art. Ronan had kept the door open to me at a time when the easy thing was to drift away.

As indeed I did in following years in terms of the practice of faith.

But the door always remained open. Part of me never left Maynooth. I hadn't been a good student in terms of study, but I enjoyed and appreciated all the interests which would accompany me throughout my life. Above all, an appreciation of the importance of friendship.

Many years later on a visit to the college, I mentioned to Ronan that I had written an article about a Presbyterian service I had attended and which had been taken by the children. He read it and suggested that I write a series of articles on Christian worship in other denominations. In this way I would open the door for his readers to as wide a range as possible of man's dialogue with his God. And so I set off on a journey that took me to thirteen different Christian Churches, with an excursion each to Jewish and Islamic worship.

I started my series in the stately surroundings of High Mass in the Pro-Cathedral, and finished in the church where I had become an altar boy at the age of seven, St Peter's, Drogheda. In between I visited the main Christian denominations, writing mostly about worship in Dublin, but also in Belfast, Cork and Mayo (Islam). Looking back, I see that in my first article I sounded a note which continues to echo in the Church today. The occasion was the celebration with Solemn Latin Mass of the centenary year of the Palestrina Choir. The celebrant was Cardinal Connell. I wrote: 'As I watched the Cardinal … I wondered if there were any other members of the congregation … with the same thoughts as myself. This is the man who has had the misfortune to embody many of the negative images which have plagued the modern Irish Church. Confronted with the scandals of clerical abuse, he has been accused of failing to respond adequately to complaints by the victims and the laity. He is seen as academic in his formation and experience, with little of the pastoral touch people long for.'

Having experienced once more (after a long lapse of time) the glory of a Solemn High Mass I wondered: 'In throwing out the bath water of Gregorian chant, polyphony, and Latin, did the Church lose the baby of respect, awe and spirituality? Was account taken of the profound difference between what is popular and what is merely populist?' I answered this question when I attended the most beautiful service in the whole series: the celebration of the Candlemas Eucharist and Procession in Dublin's Christchurch Cathedral, the Feast of the Purification. On the service I commented: 'I found prayerfulness, reverence, a total level of congregational participation, beauty, mystery and drama in this worship in Christ Church. It provided context to the despair of the Protestant Churches at the official Catholic Church's rejection of Anglican and other Protestant Orders and what is seen as a benignly intransigent attitude to ecumenism – "Of course we desire Unity, but you'll first have to accept that your Orders and your Sacraments are invalid' – all the more painful."'

I have been at other services in Dublin's two Church of Ireland cathedrals, including ordinations, and there is more than just ceremony.

The Church of Ireland has both married male and women priests. There is self-assurance, the visible strength and pride of their ministers in their marriages, and warm acceptance by colleagues and congregation for women ordained to the ministry.

No greater contrast to the splendour of the worship in the Pro-Cathedral and Christchurch could be found than that which I came across when I attended the Easter Sunday Family Mass in the Church of Our Lady of Lourdes, more commonly known as the Matt Talbot Church, on Sean McDermott Street. This is at the heart of the inner city. The service was a dialogue between the young celebrant and the children of the parish, a priest fully in tune with his congregation:

'How did Jesus feel this week?' he asks them. A child answers: 'Sad.'

'How did his mother feel?': 'Sad.'

'What happened on Sunday morning?': 'He rise from the dead.'
'Rose,' the correction comes gently. 'Did Jesus say what was going to happen?': 'Yes.'

'Did his friends believe him?': 'No.'
'Why?': 'Cause they didn't.'

'How did he rise?': 'He was a holy man.'

'He was more than a holy man. What was he?': 'The son of God.'

The priest gestures to the basket in front of the altar. 'What do Easter eggs symbolise?': 'Chocolate.'

'What do real eggs mean?' 'Babies.'
'Yes. Life.'

Throughout, the noisy children of the parish performed the drama of the Resurrection story from the Gospel with simple homemade costumes, improvised props. I wrote afterwards: 'This was Sunday worship without music, without singing. But there was the music which Christ would have loved most, the sound of children's voices, raised not in pain as around so much of the world but in joy.'

My second article for the series dealt with the Presbyterian service taken by the children. It was full of delight, but followed fully and seriously the Presbyterian system of prayer, praise (hymn-singing) and Bible study. In my final article of the series I would note: 'On a Sunday morning recently the Minister in the same church (a woman) performed the early Communion Service, but unexpectedly was unable to preside at the 11 o'clock service. No problem. Another woman, an elder of the Church, conducted this with total effectiveness in her place, and yet another (female) elder delivered the sermon which the Minister is in the habit of writing out fully.'

My visit to the Ardfallen Methodist Church in Cork city prompted a different set of thoughts on children and the family. On arrival I was warmly welcomed and told: 'Today's will not be a normal Service. There is to be a baptism, so it's a family day, and there will be visitors, friends of the family, coming from various parts of Cork.' Indeed, throughout I was to be moved by 'the sense of community and participation, the joy, the simple prayerfulness, the shared sense of fun, the noise even, the pleasure of being present with other people … The congregation forms a happy community here, and the visitor is made to feel at home with them … The Minister is unfazed by the continuous babble of children's voices.' I would record in my final article of the series: 'The warmest memory I carry with me from the series is that of the family worship around a baptism in Cork's Methodist Church. The young minister, in the presence of his wife and two young children, walked wreathed in smiles among his parishioners with the newly baptised Christian in his arms. An infectiously happy occasion. Would that an Irish Catholic congregation could experience this joy.'

Of course there are more tangible lessons to be learned from Methodism. Like the Catholic Church today, the Anglican Church of Wesley's time faced the challenge of irrelevance. Through social changes a generation had evolved whom the Church wasn't reaching. His chosen method (the word is deliberate) was Revival, Evangelical zeal. He also saw that there would never be enough ordained ministers to fulfil this mission, and so a system of itinerant lay-preachers was established. He also developed a system which allowed the plain people to manage the affairs of their local churches/societies. Lay leaders (note, *Leaders*) have always played an important role in the life of Methodism.

Several themes of relevance to the Catholic Church today recur throughout all the articles: clerical celibacy, a married priesthood, women priests, inter-faith communion, communion in both kinds, the role of the Holy Spirit. And *Humanae vitae*.

Clerical celibacy

The Orthodox Churches see themselves as direct descendants of the early Christian communities. Two things stand out. Authority belongs to the ecumenical councils, and they retain a married priesthood, the exception being monks from whose ranks bishops are chosen.

In my article on the Lutheran service I noted that the pastor was a woman. Later in the article I describe how the 'Sunday school teacher', a man, then spoke to the children. He proved to be the husband of the woman pastor, and is also a pastor. Of course Luther was reviled (in our early version of Church history) as 'the heretic monk who married a nun'. The full humanity of Luther's teaching has now come to be appreciated. In my article I wrote: 'It is one of history's great ironies that Luther did not want to leave the Church. He wanted to reform it.' Today in the Irish Church we are still seeing priests who are working for renewal and reform being silenced and excluded.

At the Lutheran Service the faithful, including visitors, were invited to receive Communion. Luther insisted (following Jan Hus, and in defiance of the Council of Constance) on serving communion in both bread and wine for all the faithful. This was a central point of his theology. I wrote: 'I have always found it strange at Mass in my own church to have the priest administering both bread and wine to the "helpers", who then serve only the host to the rest of the congregation.' In his article 'Giving or Sharing' (*The Furrow*, May 2014) Professor O'Loughlin writes: 'Long before fast-food restaurants had worked out the processing of people through their "fast-food" systems ... our liturgy had adopted remarkably similar processes.'

Inter-faith Communion is a separate issue. For many the defining moment of Mary McAleese's presidency was when she received Holy Communion at a service in St Patrick's Cathedral, earning for herself a strong episcopal rebuke.

In my article on the Seventh Day Adventists I wrote of their commitment to the belief, 'The body is the temple of the Holy Ghost.' I brought up the painful subject of child abuse in this context. But abuse by priests and religious, while an enormous problem, was/is not a systemic problem. 'The systemic problem was and still is in the Church itself, its organisation with all its defence mechanisms, which stretch from the Pope down to his local vicars. It is an axiom that we should always solve the right problem, not the wrong one. But if the Church cannot see what the problem is then it cannot solve it.'

When I attended a service of the Religious Society of Friends – the Quakers – I understood their claim that the famous silence of their worship is not the dead absence of sound but the active listening for the voice of God. My only regret looking back on my Maynooth years is I did not understand the practice of meditation. Was it too early in the morning? Was it taken seriously? When one considers today the explosion of interest in mindfulness, centering prayer meditation, consciousness levels, and the revival of interest in mysticism, one has to ask, did we miss something which could have been of value, not just spiritual but psychological, emotional – and even physical – in our lives?

One of the strongest memories I have of my time in Maynooth is of the singing of *Veni Creator Spiritus* at the opening of each retreat. In an article I asked how is the working of the Holy Spirit understood in the worship of the Catholic Church today? How often is the Spirit called to be present among worshippers?

As I write this article, two items have appeared in today's newspaper. The first shows former president Mary McAleese in the news again. Again rebuked by an archbishop. This time for describing Pope Francis's plan to ask '150 male celibates' to review the Church's teaching on marriage and family life as 'bonkers'. At a meeting in UCD she had said there was 'just something profoundly wrong and skewed' about the nature of church consultation of the family.

The second story is of the death of a fellow student in Maynooth whom we considered at the time to be brilliant in many ways. My own particular memory is the (in retrospect) rather amusing one of my playing possibly the most unlikely Ophelia in theatre history to his Hamlet. That was Paul Surlis. The Irish Times carries his obituary. It describes him as 'an outstanding example of that generous, outreaching generation of Catholic priests fired by the bright vision of the Second Vatican Council, but who were to witness it being actively obscured in subsequent decades'. The obituary records him as describing *Humanae vitae* as 'a major mistake from which we Catholics are still suffering.'

I was invited to review Fr Brendan Hoban's *Where do we go from here? The Crisis in Irish Catholicism* for *The Furrow*. Both book and review raise too many issues to revisit here. I have been married over forty years now, and many of my friends, even those of the same vintage as myself, live in a state of suspension between belief and disbelief, between dutiful religious practice and the avoidance of it.

There are many causes of disaffection. An obvious one is the succession of scandals of sexual abuse and the institutional failure to deal with them. But overarching all is the Church's teaching on contraception. The effect of *Humanae vitae* since its publication cannot be exaggerated. In my review of Fr Hoban's book I wrote:

> No efforts by the Church … will ever again persuade or convince the great majority of Catholics that contraception is wrong. All the efforts to do so will be wasted, the frustration will turn – has already turned – to a patient but sullen acceptance that the Church is not going to yield and will therefore have to be tolerated, the Church's teaching parked in some parallel mental plane … The tragedy is that no matter what excellent initiatives (are mounted) to restore Vatican II, this stumbling block will remain as an unbridgeable divide between the majority of the faithful and the upholders of the Magisterium.

The theme of this article has been, 'Keeping the Door Open'. One might have thought that *The Furrow*, at the ripe age celebrated in The Beatles's song 'When I'm Sixty-Four', might have grown tired. But no. A glance through issues even of this year alone will show an extraordinary openness to a wide range of topics. Let's imagine we're setting an exam paper. Traditional format of statement and invitation to discuss. The topics:

> 'Catholic morality should not directly be reflected in state law' (p.265). *Discuss.*

> 'It is time that the mystical life, which has been nurtured in the cloisters for so many hundreds of years, comes alive among the laity' (p.314). *Discuss.*

> 'Perhaps fundamental changes are needed to the concept of priesthood including the unthinkable such as ordaining women and ending compulsory celibacy for priests' (p.291). *Discuss.*

'If Jesus, to whom the average pope claims to have total loyalty, was infallible, he forgot to mention it' (p.289). *Discuss.*

'The publication and promulgation of *Humanae vitae* contributed greatly to a loss of relevance of any formal teaching by a celibate Church around human sexuality' (p.200). *Discuss.*

'In the past, major errors of judgement have been made by those who have held positions of leadership and authority in the Irish Church' (p.3). *Discuss.*

'Go into a room full of contemporary women and explain to them that a priest must have male genitalia in order to represent Christ as groom to the Church as bride' (p.161). *Discuss.*

That should keep us going for a while.

Fr Ronan Drury has kept a door open for me personally for over fifty years, firstly to the college which was a major influence on my life, and secondly to the pages of *The Furrow*. More importantly, in a Church that is struggling to retain (or regain) its relevance, through his editorship of *The Furrow* he has kept a door open to a range of voices and viewpoints which members of our own and of other Churches have been enriched by sharing.

The Future Church: John Allen

AIDAN RYAN

One of the most respected and influential journalists commenting on Church affairs in the English-speaking world is John L. Allen Jnr, an American who formerly worked with the National Catholic Reporter and is currently an associate editor with the Boston Globe. His online column 'All things Catholic' is very widely read by other journalists, and indeed by church leaders, as a source both of information and of unbiased comment on the unfolding life of the Catholic Church worldwide.

In 2009, he published a book called *The Future Church* in which he outlined a global vision of the major trends in Catholic life in the early twenty-first century and of how he thought these trends might unfold as the century unfolds.

This article is not so much a review as an attempt to convey something of the content and flavour of this book to people who may not have read it, and to offer some personal reflections on it. The trends Allen identifies are ten in number, as follows:

1. The church is becoming truly a world church, with a shift of the centre of gravity increasingly to the southern hemisphere;
2. Catholicism is becoming increasingly evangelical, with a clearer sense of Catholic identity and an increased commitment to evangelisation;
3. The Islamic faith is also increasing its influence in the world and this is a major challenge to Catholicism;
4. The new demographics, affecting firstly the developed world, but increasingly the developing world, suggest that population trends are towards an ageing population with longer life expectancy;
5. Expanding roles for lay people in the church, which is becoming less clerical and more participative, with much more lay involvement in ministry, especially by women;
6. The biotech revolution, with the advances in genetics and the possibilities these contain for e.g. human cloning, artificial prolongation of life, and the ethical dilemmas which will arise from genetic manipulation;
7. Globalisation of culture, of international finance and commerce, made possible by the explosion in the means of mass communication and the social media, making the world in a real sense a global village;

8. Ecology – the increasing awareness of the fragility of life on the planet and the responsibility to make decisions based on this awareness;

9. Multipolarism – the fact that there are not just two superpowers, but many centres of influence and change in the world, e.g. the rise of China, and the Tiger economies of the Far East, of India and Brazil;

10. Pentecostalism – the growth of the pentecostal, charismatic groups and movements, especially in the mega-cities of the world, and the influence this has both as a challenge and an invitation to the mainline churches.

There is one chapter devoted to each of these trends, in which the author addresses the topic in a very methodical manner. First, he introduces the topic under the heading 'What's happening' which outlines the manner in which each trend has emerged and is currently manifesting itself. The next sub-heading is 'What it means' which indicates how the trend will affect the church (a) almost certainly, (b) probably, (c) possibly or (d) 'long shot'. For example, interestingly, in a book written in 2009, he suggests, in the chapter on 'A World Church', that the election of a pope from the global South was 'probable' at some stage during the twenty-first century. Only four years later, it happened, and it now seems at least a strong possibility that both Asia and Africa will provide a pope for the church at some stage during this century.

The second 'trend' – towards a more evangelical church, with a clearer sense of Catholic identity and a stronger commitment to evangelisation, was a clear priority for Pope John Paul II during his long pontificate. Pope Francis seems to emphasise more the core message of the Gospel, but is if anything even more enthusiastic about the proclamation of the message of Jesus to the world today.

Regarding Islam, there is the urgent need for greater dialogue with the more mainstream and moderate currents of this major world religion, but there is also the threat posed to the lives and safety of Christians by the more extreme currents and elements within Islam.

The chapter on demographics is particularly interesting. It claims that the world population generally is ageing, not just in the West, but worldwide. Longer lifespans will mean greater availability of older people for active involvement in the ministry of the church, but also that the ministry to older people will have a higher profile than heretofore. The ministry of the parish nurse may assume an importance similar to that of the parish catechist.

Greater involvement of lay-people, especially women, has been for many decades now a feature of church life. This trend will continue and probably accelerate. Allen explains near the end of the book why he did not include 'Women' as a separate trend. Much of what he has to say about this topic is included under this heading of lay involvement.

The bio-tech revolution poses many ethical-moral dilemmas for church teaching. Particularly controversial are issues like human cloning and the artificial prolongation of life. There will be greater need than ever for religious traditions of all kinds to present a common understanding of what it means to be truly human in offering guidance in these areas.

The world is becoming increasingly globalised, especially in the manner in which the resources of the world are shared, not shared, or shared unjustly. Aspects of this reality include the widening gap between rich and poor; global conflict and the arms trade; human trafficking; political corruption; and the rapidly increasing numbers of migrants and refugees. All of this means that the Catholic church will increasingly be committed to the defence of universal human rights and the promotion of the dignity of the human person and of social solidarity at all levels. Another aspect of globalisation is the dramatic development of the Internet, and the spread of social media in a manner that has profound implications for communication at all levels.

There is a steadily growing awareness of the fragility of planet Earth and of the dangers posed to it by human economic activity and lifestyles. The challenge to the church in this context is to provide leadership, both by word and by example, in addressing this looming threat to the very existence of the human race.

The penultimate 'trend' is what the author describes as 'multipolarism' – the fact that we live no longer in a world with one or two 'superpowers', but one which has a larger number of centres of influence – e.g. the tiger economies of Asia, the rise of Brazil as an economic giant. This reality, too, offers both challenges and opportunities for the church.

The tenth 'trend' is Pentcostalism, which some see as a major threat to the church, especially in the megacities of the world. However, it can also be seen as something from which the church can learn valuable lessons in lay leadership, more spontaneous worship and a greater sense of face-to-face community.

Towards the end of the book, the author describes how he went about devising his list of trends – mainly by means of publishing draft lists in his online column and by engaging with the audiences at over two hundred speaking engagements over several years. As one might expect, he received a huge number of suggestions from all points on the theological spectrum – from the illegitimacy of all the popes since Pius XII to the ordination of women by rogue bishops. Some of the more mainline suggestions were – the priest shortage, fundamentalism, pets replacing children, homosexuality, the permanent diaconate, Catholic TV, dissolution of the family, and cyber-spirituality. He lists five major issues that surfaced constantly, but which he decided not to categorise as a trend for a variety of reasons. These were – women, the sexual abuse crisis, polarisation, the ecclesial movements, and the legacy of Pope John Paul II. His reasons for not including any of these as a trend stem from the criteria he decided to use in determining what constitutes a 'trend' for the purposes of his book. These were, firstly, it had to be global, not just a feature of one part of the church. Secondly, it had to have a significant impact on Catholic grassroots, i.e. ordinary Catholics in parishes, not just theologians, activists or even journalists. Thirdly, it had to be something that church leadership was engaged with, not something that they would rule out on principle. Fourthly, to be a trend, the reality described had to be likely to be lasting over time, not just a passing phase. Fifthly, it should not be ideologically driven, i.e. it should be a factual reality rather than a judgement. Lastly, it may be one part of the wider ten trends.

There are several notable features of this book. When read by an Irish person in a present-day Irish cultural setting, it greatly broadens the ecclesial context in which we live. There is a constant temptation to be excessively local – even parochial – in our outlook. Allen has a truly global view of Catholicism which can greatly enrich our reflection on the issues facing the worldwide church at this time and on the responses to those issues emerging in various parts of the world.

That said, the trends outlined have their implications for Ireland too. Among the features of church life in Ireland at present is the increasing number of people who are called (rather unsatisfactorily), non-nationals. Many are from other EU member states, but there are also a growing number of non-Europeans – especially Filipinos, Nigerians, and Brazilians. It is interesting to note that, among the as yet very small number of permanent deacons in Ireland, there are several non-Europeans. However, it would be great mistake to think of the burgeoning churches of the developing world as a source of personnel to 'bolster up' the church in Ireland in its present form. If they come as missionaries, they will bring fresh ideas, methods and priorities. They will not 'prop up' decaying structures, but will build from the ground up.

The demographic trend is already evident in Ireland also, though perhaps not as evident as in other European countries. Again, the permanent diaconate is a case in point. The majority of those who have been ordained for this ministry, and of the candidates at present in formation for it, are in the second half of life and many of them are already retired, or nearing retirement, from their secular occupations or professions.

It seems to me that a major challenge for the church in Ireland is to foster and expand non-ordained ministries and roles that are open to men who do not wish to be ordained, and to women. In the trend regarding the expansion of lay ministry, John Allen describes how this trend manifests itself in the US, where many parishes have lay administrators, mostly women. There are possibilities for Ireland in this trend also.

A further trend that is present also in Ireland is the 'charismatic/pentecostal' trend – not necessarily confined to prayer-groups where a 'charismatic' style of prayer predominates. In a wider sense it can be seen also in the various ecclesial movements. These are not, at least as yet, as prominent a feature in church life as they are in some other countries. But the desire for face-to-face community and for a more spontaneous style of prayer is an increasingly felt need here too.

An admirable feature of the book is that it is factual and unbiased. It simply states facts as they are and presents various ways of interpreting these facts without favouring or giving undue emphasis to any one viewpoint. There is a form of 'religious affairs' journalism, not unknown in Ireland, that has a thinly disguised ideological position – one that has been described as 'the last acceptable prejudice' – anti-Catholicism. Allen is a good example of religious affairs journalism at its best – well-informed, theologically literate, unbiased, and clear in presentation. This is not to say that the book is completely without flaws. There are sections that tend to be repetitive of other sections and at times the American origin and outlook of the author is more evident than one might wish for. But, all things considered, this book provides a comprehensive overview of the major features of Catholic life at the beginning of the twenty-first century and a very readable account of the trends that are likely to influence the Catholic church in the decades ahead. From an Irish perspective, it can give us at least some clues about the way forward for the Catholic church in this country, as we seek to discern where God might be calling us in the coming years.

III. CHURCH AND CULTURE

According to Lydia
JOHN F. DEANE

COCK-CROW

It was soon after dawn and he was out already,
raw and impatient, for we could hear his axe
splitting wood, the first dull dunts, then the quick
rupturing sound, echoing against the roosters' calls;
there was a strength and such assurance in the sound
the village came to itself with a morning confidence;
the thousand-year-old olive stumps resisted stanchly,
but he would later polish the wood to a perfection
smooth to the thumb. By noon he'd pause, listening
to the laughter of young girls busying themselves
among the olive trees; in the afternoon loafing-hours
he would slip away to some small wilderness
alone, as if the fruits of earth and toil were slight, a shadow
darkening the woman's face watching from the doorway:

BEDROCK

Wilderness. We heard first about locusts and wild
honey; then, demons and wild beasts. The absences, no
water. The sun so fiery that the low hills
shimmer like a mirage. There are cool, sheltering places,
occupied. Easy to believe in demons, so little sound
there the mind hums. By day the burning, by night
the crackle of frost; thudding stillness of the heart, admitting
wisdom, the cosmic dust; immured in desert nothingness
and the struggle with the mind. Opening to loneliness,
to the holiness of the unresponding; garnering strength
against the worst that noon can do, or the trailing moon;
dying to flesh-hungers, earning a certainty
that washed him through with tenderness, that raked
spirit and flesh to wild uncompromising love:

The Binding

The lake's edge – generation after generation
depending, shallow at the shores, bronzewater, gold;
millennia of shells, patterned dull and gay, becoming grit –
profound, a harvest, what's left of innumerable deaths;
they have drawn the boats up onto the grass, and sit
examining the nets; the human heart, they know, is forged
out of such bindings, such husks, at the very lip
of wilderness. This day, out of a sky so bright
it chafes like silver, they hear the high-pitched cry
of a swooping sea-eagle ripping the air. The man –
in mulberry-coloured robe and leathern sandals – has passed
down along the margins towards the boats; at once
there is disturbance, a sharp kerfuffle at the lake's edge
and the brothers, without a backward glance, forsake the shore:

Kfar Nahum

Beyond the village, willows, scrub grass, small waves
frivolously fingering the shore; warm breeze under grey,
scarce shifting, clouds; the day lifeless, and everyday
ordinary; a fishing-boat drawn up onto stones,
no shore-birds visible; noon, as if the world had
paused, uncertain, waiting. In the crumbling synagogue
craftsmen and fishermen sat, bemused, the stranger
standing before them, reading, and expounding; as if he bore
quietness in his bones in spite of the earthed resonance
in his voice; the authority, the unaccountable wisdom
that had been concealed somewhere in the Torah scrolls,
the mourners, the merciful, the hungry. Puzzlement
among them, here and there a muttering anger. Words,
as ours, but new, and other. A man like us. Unlike. But like:

Disturbances

By sunset, in Kfar Nahum, he had drawn to himself
many of the broken, crazed and trodden-down,
the undesirables, the pariahs, the freaks;
the space between gate and lake was a market-field

of clamour, pleading, incredulity and tears. Soon
he was exhausted. A yellow moon
hoisted itself slowly above the village, and a crow,
lifting in dudgeon out of the roost, called a loud
craw! to the clouds. By now, we were unsure of it,
what had happened, for something difficult
was insinuating itself within the stepped-out limits
of our life, but we knew there would be consequences,
grave. It was owl-night, the bird calling out 'who? who?';
can what is broken be whole again, what's crooked straight:

THE FLOWERING

That night we lit lamps everywhere, outside, within,
on grass and pathway, down to the shore; he sat on,
all light and shadow, his words gathering radiance
and darkness into their texture; we lived a while in an island
of being, apart, and unmanageable; and oh! the strangeness:
birdsong, a cock crowing, bright-winged moths singeing
                    themselves
against the flames; smoke from the oils sometimes
itched the eyes but we stayed, startled when he said: your
sins are forgiven! and no-one, there and then, doubted it –
we thought of our blessed YHWH; we thought of the stone
heads and torsos of gods in the city set on their shaky
pedestals, and the night swelled; as if the raw green stem
of the Pentateuch were about, latterly, to open into
a great red wound, like the high and blossoming amaryllis:

DEMONS

It takes a lifetime to cast demons out;
you struggle with them, you, demoniac, you, unclean,
they throw you down, you howl inside, you get
up again, you have to. Lest they destroy you. He
touched them, lepers, too, their sores, their bandages,
their dead eyes. He would take all burdens on himself.
Thirsted and hungered have we, for such as he, to enter
into the soul's holding. I have found, down in my heart,
there is a sphere so still, so silent and untouched

it is pure as the snow-topped summit of Hermon
glistening in the distance. He, gathering them all, to table,
the manic, the castaways, the hobbled (we thought him mad)
and there was laughter, and quiet and – I tell you this –
peace where never there was peace, nor laughter ever:

TABLE

I need to tell of this, I need to set it down – how he brought them in with
him, and how they grinned at the shaken host; servants, with disdain,
offered water for their hands and feet but the stranger knelt and helped
them: the beggars, the bedraggled, and the whores;
they reclined on cushions at the rich man's table: who did not
eject them, offering lamb and artichokes and goat's cheese,
wine and pickled fish and pastries soused in honey; they
asked for barley bread and barley beer. The stranger broke
and dipped the bread and passed it to them, told them jokes
and stories of lost sheep and prodigals and wheat seeds scattered
against the wind. It was, the host adjured, a ghostly meal, touched him
with joy and bitterness, this kingdom rife with casualties –
but it was I, he said, who found I was immured in poverty:

SAMARIA

Jacob's well, Shechem, route of nomads, revolt, crusade . . .
of people toiling down valleys of silence into exile: she drawing near –
heart torn by love-failures – to the source now,
the sustenance. The stranger, waiting; out of exodus and genesis
with demanding words. Between them, issues of time, of history,
the depths of the iced-over, petrified heart. 'I thirst': who, then,
is keeper of the soul in need: he, or she? Between them, between
past and future, the clarity of water in the moment of its
giving, words echoing beyond the sound of words, beyond clanging
of consonant, bird-call of vowel, how the heart, in its taut holding,
wants to yield, to the presence, the immediacy. She, later,
returning home, stumbles, her pitchers full. He
stays, on the ridge of stone, staring down into the deep
till the moon brightens, down there, in the uttermost darkness:

PAPYRUS

The word, I have discovered, is food for my surviving,
this need to lay down words on strong papyrus, in strait
and patterned lines, hints of love and yearning, and now
this penchant towards sorrowing, for memory is uncertain, inaccurate, and, like waters, fluid. Words of Yeshua
who sought to slip away, before dawn, to a desert place, to touch
his source and sustenance. For after all, after that mid hour,
my life will not be what it was; what, then, had happened? The word
existence seemed to shift, as boulders shift in a quake, the straight
line of living twisted back upon itself in a kind of anguish,
what we had accomplished suddenly became undone, the
comfortable dark was now backlit by a more aggressive fire –
for he had stood, tears on his cheeks, before the sealed tomb;
he called: and there was a death silence: I heard a hum
of insects, somewhere the faint cry of a jackal, an echo
out of Lethe and in the heat of noon my body chilled:
slowly, they unsealed the tomb, stood at its gaping mouth
mute with darkness; the sisters clutched each other, terrified;
he emerged, slow, slow, shrouded in white cotton, like a great
woodcock with folded wings, body camouflaged in snow,
and it was I who called, out of a living hope within me,
fly high! Lazarus, fly! But he stood still: perplexed, perhaps
blinded by the sun, when the sisters moved to him, and the crowd
astounded, cried with a shrill ululation, like flocks of startled
shore-birds until he stood, freed, and moved towards Yeshua
like a lover stepping out in exaltation. I understood there is no such thing
as the ordinary world, that words themselves are not
transparent, and world became, just then, afraid of this man of men:

MEDITERRANEAN

Came that day on the beach; Yeshua stood a long while
and spoke, of love, of mercy, of tenderness; my spirit
sang. We grew hungry. And there he was, frying fish over stones,
with garlic, oil, fresh bread, and I could not figure
from where came all that food; there were sea winds, and each
morsel that we ate spoke benevolence while the ocean, out behind us,
murmured its assent. He had his place now in my heart, no, it was
even deeper than the heart; we had come for pleasure, what we took

was the scent of the sea, a sense of comfort mixed with dread,
the sunset pink of flamingos flying over. I remember the new port,
breakwaters, the Roman galleys, new economies; the stranger –
Yeshua – had taken spittle on his fingers and touched the eyes
of a blind man; but Yeshua had mentioned death and we saw,
beyond the grasses and wild flowers a small group, hostile, gathering:

THE GARDEN

Dusk – the sun going down – threw long shadows across
the ground; he appeared, coming in from the valley, and collapsed
on the hard earth; somewhere a bird sang, though the word
'snickered' came to mind. I remembered Genesis: the Lord God
walking in the garden, time of the evening breezes. An hour
passed; the world darkened further; up in the city
lights flared. I thought I heard sobbing, even a scarcely
suppressed cry; he rose, and moved, stumblingly, back
towards the wall; I heard voices, protestations. Then he came
to fall again, scrambling on earth as if his bones were fire
and though I sensed rather than saw his body, he was distorted
like limbs of the olive trees. I heard weeping; I heard fingers
scrabbling against ground. Weakness, and failure; embarrassing.
Relief to see the flare of torches coming this way from the city:

THE VIEWING

When he was harried out to be jeered at, blood-
ugly, rag-scraggly, filthy with sores, I knew
he must be guilty and I was ashamed. He could
scarcely hold himself erect, they jostled him,
there was blood congealing on his face, his
fingers, even on his naked, blistering feet. He had no
hope, he was already stooped amongst the dead.
Like a fool he stayed silent, stubbornly so, though
words could not save him now. This was public
degradation, his agonies watched and mocked, death
the ultimate humiliation, for even rats
will creep away to die, in private, in a dark
corner. We knew now that his name would be
forgotten, left with his corpse in merciful oblivion:

HILL OF SKULLS

(i)

I stood on the slope, at a distance from the other women;
it was done on the Hill of Skulls, dread place, to discourage
thought; high posts planted, waiting for the cross-
branches, the flower, and the fruit, where the dead earth
was rusted over with spilled blood; a little aside –
though within eye-shot – from the city's bustle and indifference;
Miryam, for it must be she, stood propped between strength
and failure, determined mother to the last. I had dreamed
he would put an end to violence. The big iron nails
were not the worst, though the heavy hammer-blows
shuddered the earth and shuddered my heart – it was the body
writhing in agony, chest strained beyond the possible at each
in-breath, out-breath, it was how humankind spits hatred
against its own, the tender-hearted, innocent, the children – but

(ii)

it's how things are, the soldier said, and will always be.
The moments passed, each one heavy as an hour; I tried
prayer, but to whom, or to what? The sky darkening, the groans
lengthening, the screams … He was burning. Near us the cackling
magpies. In the sky, the vultures. The way, he had said,
the truth, the life – is the way death, then? Life, the urgencies
only of the body? And truth, what is truth? His blood
mingling on the earth with blood of the contemned. Love
the final casualty. Clouds blackened; hot winds
blew in across the hill, shadows were dancing wildly
amongst confused noises. He cried out, though rarely. My
tears were silent, copious. I heard a distant, drawn-out
thunder. After such hours he screamed out, died; as if
he had exhaled, with his last breath, all the light and

(iii)

life of the world. It was all thunderstorms as they
took him down and as I hurried through the streets
people were staggering by, like ghosts. I never felt
so much alone. That was the most silent evening,
night was black and long and I armed myself about

with fires of spitting olive-wood; the laneways crawled
with furtive shapes; I clung, desperately, to the supposed
mercy of time; words had lost essence and would spill
like hot grease; how could the world know he had lived, how
could the word love be redefined? Everything unfinished, all
undone. But I had inks, formed out of soot and oil and tears
and would carve deep in the papyrus. I remember –
the mountainside – he said: those of singleness of heart
will be blessed, for it is they who will see God :

SUNRISE

So clear we had not seen it: in the giving away of your life
you find it. Soon after dawn I was leaning on the stone walls
of the vineyard out beyond the city; there was a well, timbers
covering it; I heard the wood rattling; there was a man
stooping over, reaching for a drink; he saw me, called out
something, waved, and was gone. Tricks of the light, I thought,
the sudden wing-claps of doves distracting. I stayed, fingers
worrying the clay between the stones. I had not even
waved back. Bright this early and I imagined the valley
singing softly. The intimacy of grape-flesh, I thought, the skin
peeled off, the dark wine waiting. The mind can find itself
so foolish, hoping for too much. The quickening of the heart
urgent against grief. Or urgent towards unspeakable
joy. And I stood there, baffled again by this one life:

THE TURNING

After the killing, there was no hope left, nowhere
to turn. We abandoned the city, wondering if we might
get somewhere. Sat, disconsolate, by the river, knowing
how goodness appears and is vanquished before it is
grasped. Wondering if there is a way for mortal beings
to start over. Someone, walking the same path, may offer
wisdom, and insight. Becomes, in the nonce, mediator
between place and non-place, life not-life, death and
not-death. The day advancing, our steps more sprightly,
we would hold to light against the nightfall. Logs
blown to flames in the hearth; dried fish and olives, figs

and honeyed wine; the ready warmth of love, the torn hands
blessing and breaking bread. What the blood had known
known now in spirit and for truth. And so we turned:

LYDIA

I fear onslaughts of foolishness before the end,
the loss of wonder when the mind cools, the wine
ordinary, the bread bread. Do not fear, he said, only
believe. I work to keep the heart open, to hold to the blessing
that made me aware, then, I was blessed; glory in the once-fire
that will be ash, in reason beyond reason. I work to cherish
the variegated birdsong, the damson flowers blossoming
when they will. That I may ever overflow with Yeshua,
as a jug will overbrim with a wine both sweet and bitter;
for I know I will meet him again, the raw wounds of humanity
on his flesh. I remember the sea's edge, when, late evening,
he spoke from the fishing-boat anchored just off-shore: See
and hear as a child, he said, that the deaf hear and the blind
have their eyes opened, the lame walk and the dead rise again
and blessed is the one who does not lose faith in me.

I Wonder

PÁDRAIG MCCARTHY

Not like
A lone beautiful bird
These poems now rise in great white flocks
Against my mind's vast hills
Startled by God
Breaking a branch
When his foot
Touches
Earth
Near
Me

(14th Century Persian Mystic, Hafiz;
translated by Daniel Ladinsky)

Wonder. Astonishment. Awe.
How often do words like these crop up in our vocabulary as members of a church? Not in the really BIG ideas like eternity and infinity, or the reality of the cosmos or the Big Bang, but in the everyday minutiae?

How often could these words describe the source and summit of Christian life in the liturgy? Not in doing extraordinary theatrics to astound, but in the extraordinary reality of the sacred in the everyday, of Emmanuel who is with us all days? In the wonder that we are here at all, and gathering, and reflecting, and celebrating it? Where the words of a gifted poet can express what goes beyond our words, and leads us into where our only possible way to exist is in an even deeper listening silence? No matter how enveloping the surrounding noise.

Think not a place where it is we who find something however deep; rather a place where we realise that we are the ones who have been found.

We can be sprung free from what Wilbur Reese described:

I would like to buy $3 worth of God, please.
Not enough to explode my soul or disturb my sleep,
but just enough to equal a cup of warm milk
or a snooze in the sunshine.
I don't want enough of God to make me love a black man
or pick beets with a migrant.

> I want ecstasy, not transformation.
> I want warmth of the womb, not a new birth.
> I want a pound of the Eternal in a paper sack.
> I would like to buy $3 worth of God, please.

That foot of God in the image of Hafiz touches earth in my front garden each time I go out this July, and see the red flame of crocosmia (or *mont-bretia* if you prefer; *Feileastram dearg*) 'Lucifer' ('light bearer') standing and blazing their blooms shoulder high. Echoes of West Cork hedgerows ablaze with the orange-coloured variety. Immigrants from South Africa. I am startled each time; struck with wonder. Not wonder *why*, or *what*, or *how*, or *who*; just wonder *at*. That startling wonder seems to have broken in, or out, more frequently in recent times. Wonder seems such a vital element of faith that I'd like to call it a theological virtue! (*Wonder*, and along with it, *Fun*.) It is an essential component of Mystery. I don't have a thesis to prove here; my purpose is just to share a short eclectic personal reflection of some perhaps insignificant experiences of Wonder which startle me. Perhaps it may echo or awaken your wonder.

I like how Gilbert Keith Chesterton wrote of such a realisation on a basic level in *How to be a Lunatic*, chapter four of his autobiography. He offers a blend of rational and intuitive. Be ready for the last three words of this extract:

> But as I was still thinking the thing out by myself, with little help from philosophy and no real help from religion, I invented a rudimentary and makeshift mystical theory of my own. It was substantially this: that even mere existence, reduced to its most primary limits, was extraordinary enough to be exciting. Anything was magnificent as compared with nothing ...
>
> At the back of our brains, so to speak, there was a forgotten blaze or burst of astonishment at our own existence. The object of the artistic and spiritual life was to dig for this submerged sunrise of wonder.

No, he didn't write '*wonder of sunrise*'; he wrote, '*sunrise of wonder*'. Feel the power of the image, of the words. See the sun from any location of your choice, rising from the sea-horizon on any ordinary or extraordinary morning, and let yourself be filled not just with sunlight, but even more marvellously with wonder, framed by the early morning breeze. The fact that it is an everyday reality does not make it less extraordinary, but more so. The mission is not so much to summon the sunrise of wonder from the vasty submerged deep. Rather, the object is to throw open the shutters to let the sunrise of wonder in, and then even to widen the cracks in the earthen jars which we are to let the wonder out.

The wonder in the experience of communicating calls for a burst of astonishment. The fact that you can make sounds, or put strange marks on paper or on a computer screen, and lo and behold! I can partake of what you want to get across – often imperfectly, but yet it happens. George Bernard Shaw was too pessimistic: *The single biggest problem in communication is the illusion that it has taken place.* Sometimes true, but his own words communicate and give the lie to making it a general rule.

It can transcend time: I can go to the Chester Beatty Library in Dublin Castle and look at manuscript P45: the earliest manuscript known (from around AD250) containing four gospels and the Acts of Apostles; and I can even decipher some words (pardon my Greek!). I can see the celebration of the Word in the gospels in the Book of Kells in Trinity College, Dublin, from around AD800, and ask what great wonder must have possessed those scribes to value the word so highly. It seems miraculous to me that I can look at such writing and process it seemingly instantaneously and effortlessly into sounds in the air to share them with so many others. It tends to be when I come across communication in characters or symbols or sounds I don't understand, that I am reminded of the wonder of it.

What was it that inspired the writer of the psalm? What experience gave the writer such a sense of trust in a loving God that he could sing, 'The Lord is my shepherd; I shall not want', even in the valley of darkness and death? Can I let myself be immersed in the wonder of that? What kind of divine playfulness was there in those who formed the alphabetical psalms, each verse beginning with the successive letters of the Hebrew alphabet? This is crowned by the longest of our psalms, 119, where it is not just one verse per letter, but eight verses per letter. Think of the blessed fun, echoing the blessed fun of chaos to creation. That achievement is again the foot of God touching the earth of my life.

Perhaps it was a passing moment of enthusiasm, or perhaps it was a lasting conviction, when the writer of Psalm 139 tells us: 'You knit me together in my mother's womb: I am wonderful, and all your works are wonderful!' Where did all that arise from? To be able to say it now is a sunrise of wonder.

The experience of deep grief too can bring wonder in a new way. When some good friends of mine lost their daughter Maria to a brain tumour at the age of twelve, the depth of grief for me was totally unexpected. I never knew I could experience something like that. Kahlil Gibran caught it with his words in *The Prophet*:

> Your joy is your sorrow unmasked. And the selfsame well from which your laughter rises was oftentimes filled with your tears.
> And how else can it be? The deeper that sorrow carves into your being, the more joy you can contain.

> Not in any theoretical way, but in the anguish that revealed more clearly the depth of love, I found wonder: a wonder which must have been the gateway to the wonder of knowing both that I could love, and that Maria could simply love me. A *mysterium tremendum*, a *mysterium fascinans*, as Rudolph Otto might have said. A mystery so strong that one trembles, and yet is fascinated and captivated.

It is so easy to use the word 'God'. We can sing, '*He's got the whole world in his hands*'. But given the power disparity, when one party has all the power, we can fall into fear of loss of control. God, in Christ, takes the initiative to change the power equation and joins us in mutuality and vulnerability, even to the experience of death, but we can still find it difficult to relinquish the fear and control impulses. Enter another wonder: the crazy image, that God is a God who dances with joy over me! What a loss of dignity on God's part! Let wonder break into the equation, and we can be startled to read what Zephaniah the prophet (3:17) wrote:

> He will rejoice over you with happy song,
> he will renew you by his love,
> He will dance with shouts of joy for you
> as on a day of festival.

This is not the kind of Cloud of Unknowing that I would have expected to enter, but it's there. What can I do about one who dances with joy over me? I can only let myself be absorbed by a reality I do not control, and join in the dance. Even more, BE the dance, where dancer and dance are distinct and at the same time inseparable. God's foot touches the earth near me as earthily as does mine. Jesus and the Father are one (Jn 10:30). *May they all be one, just as you, Father, are in me and I am in you, so that they also may be in us, so that the world may believe it was you who sent me* (Jn 17:21).

But surely I'm not ready for that? There's so much yet to sort out. Then I hear the story of the weeds in the wheat, and recall yet again that I don't have to get it all sorted; if I wait until all that is done, then nothing will bear fruit; I am encouraged to go ahead anyway, trusting in the one who is better qualified for the sorting than I will ever be.

Julian of Norwich tried to figure out the problem:

> In my folly, before this time I often wondered why, by the great foreseeing wisdom of God, the onset of sin was not prevented: for then, I thought, all should have been well. This impulse [of thought] was much to be avoided, but nevertheless I mourned and sorrowed because of it, without reason and discretion.
>
> But Jesus, who in this vision informed me of all that is needed by me, answered with these words and said: 'It behoved that there should be sin [sin plays a needful part]; but all shall be well, and all shall be well, and all manner of thing shall be well.' These words were said most tenderly, showing no manner of blame to me nor to any who shall be saved.
>
> (*Revelations of Divine Love*: Ch. 27)

Even when prayer fails (with me, it's usually into sleeping!), there's the wonder of what Paul wrote in Romans 8:26–27 on the Spirit (breath) praying beyond words within us when we know not how. We hum along, awake or asleep. The mystic Muslim Hafiz reflects an echo of what Paul wrote:

> I am a hole in a flute that the Christ's breath moves through,
> listen to this music.
> I am the concert from the mouth of every creature,
> singing with the myriad chorus.
> I am a hole in a flute that the Christ's breath moves through,
> listen to this music.

Remember the majesty of Handel's Hallelujah chorus? Leonard Cohen has his own low-key way of spreading the message. This is one of his versions. Hear the music; or sing along as you read it.

I did my best, it wasn't much.
I couldn't feel, so I tried to touch.
I've told the truth, I didn't come to fool you.
And even though it all went wrong
I'll stand before the Lord of Song
With nothing on my tongue but Hallelujah.

God's foot which Hafiz evoked also touched the earth unexpectedly at my first diocesan retreat at All Hallows College in 1968, as a very young priest. I remember wondering at all those other priests, few of whom I had met before, many of whom seemed ancient beyond belief, who were also on retreat after countless years in the diocese. I wondered what it must be like to live in their world, but it was ahead of me (and now I've arrived!). What kept them at it after forty, fifty, sixty years or more? And here they were, listening (well, maybe) to the retreat director (I've no idea who it was). What would keep me at it? The only answer I can offer is faithfulness. With all our quirks and gifts, our achievements and failings, it can only be God's faithfulness first, and then ours.

It still causes me wonder now where it has led me. But *wonder* without *ponder* is likely to evaporate. If I don't take the time to ponder on the wonder, there is danger I will not be wonder-full. The pondering has been helped by a cloud of witnesses. For example, *The Furrow* has been one of the vehicles (pardon the mixed metaphor – a cloud doesn't need a vehicle!).

I was beginning to learn the ropes of the wonder of new furrows in the exhilarating years following Vatican II: *Novate vobis novale*, 'Drive a new furrow', the motif of *The Furrow* from Jeremiah 4:3. Much sowing among thorns. What was a new Furrow preparing the way in 1950 for J.G. McGarry and Ronan Drury is still, for me at least, a fresh Furrow allowing new shoots of hope, nourishing wonder.

We can be startled with new wonder as the foot of God touches the earth and breaks the branch. T.S. Eliot wrote at the end of 'Little Gidding':

We shall not cease from exploration
And the end of all our exploring
Will be to arrive where we started
And know the place for the first time
Through the unknown, unremembered gate
When the last of earth left to discover
Is that which was the beginning …

Quick now, here, now, always—
A condition of complete simplicity
(Costing not less than everything)
And all shall be well and
All manner of thing shall be well
When the tongues of flames are in-folded
Into the crowned knot of fire
And the fire and the rose are one.

The fire and the crocosmia in my front garden are one. So much reason for Wonder. And Awe. And Astonishment. And may this essay cause you the reader to wonder anew!

Poets, Theologians and God
DERMOT A. LANE

The purpose of this paper is to scan very briefly what is being said about the mystery of God by some poets and theologians. It is a theme that has been well-served by the discerning eye of the editor of *The Furrow* over a period of nearly forty years. The Irish Church and society owe a great debt of gratitude to Ronan Drury for this particular service among his many other services in Maynooth.

This paper will present a short account of what some poets and theologians have to say about the question of God. I will then outline how *not* to respond to some of the issues raised by our poets and theologians. The paper will conclude with a few theological principles to guide the way forward. When you find poets and theologians echoing each other, then it is time to sit up.

Poets on the Question of God
The untimely death of Dennis O'Driscoll on 24 December 2012, fittingly and beautifully mourned in the pages of *The Furrow* in February 2013 by Anne Thurston, has left the Irish Church and society bereft of an astute observer of shifts within culture. What is presented here is only a flavour of his musings on the mystery of God.

In a well-known poem in 2002 on 'Missing God', he lists some sixteen different occasions when he would like to have heard reference to God, but nothing was forthcoming:

> Miss Him during the civil wedding
> when ...
>   ... we wait in vain
> to be fed a line containing words
> like 'everlasting' and 'divine'
> Miss Him when the TV scientist
> explains the cosmos through equations ...
> Miss Him when a choked voice at
> the crematorium recites the poem
> about fearing no more the heat of the sun ...
> Miss Him when we stumble on the breast lump
> for the first time and an involuntary prayer
> escapes our lips.[1]

Five years later, O'Driscoll writes about 'Intercession':

> God and humankind meet on uncommon ground.
> They just don't speak the same language.
> He plays hard to get.
> They try to smoke him out from his lair with incense …
> Both sides operate to incompatible agendas
> Priestly meditation fails to close the widening rift.[2]

Susan Millar DuMars, an American poet living in Ireland, published a short collection entitled *The God Thing*,[3] reviewed empathetically by Conall O'Cuinn SJ in *The Furrow*.[4] She writes with extraordinary feeling about illness, death and grief. She is searching, like O'Driscoll, in many places for the sacred; she captures the often disappointed soul-filled sentiments of many. One poem in particular stands out as striking a chord familiar to many. She is describing the death of a friend. The poem is entitled 'Undiscovered':

> We lie together quietly
> in our big boat of a bed …
> the familiar soft spell
> of his voice. *Now that I've seen death,*
> *I don't know how anyone*
> *can think there's a God.*
>
> I see what he is seeing:
> the final clench of jaw, the last
> mute struggle, the leak of colour
> starting at the hairline …
> *We're machines, we break down*
> *Nothing more. Nothing else …*
>
> Something had gone. Though we can't
> see the breeze, we know when
> it stops blowing. Something had gone.
> I only want to know what it was.[5]

DuMars captures the quest of many for the meaning of death, the significance of bodily existence, and the source of life.

The third poet is the well-known T. S. Eliot who was deeply concerned about what was happening to our understanding of God. Over seventy years ago, he perceptively and prophetically pointed out in 'The Choruses of the Rock':

> But it seems that something has happened
> that has never happened before:
> though we know not just when,
> or why, or how, or where.
> Men have left GOD not for
> other gods they say, but for
> no gods; and this has never happened before.

Theological Voices

What Eliot said in eight lines, Charles Taylor expanded in eight hundred pages in an important work entitled *A Secular Age*.[6] Taylor answers Eliot's 'when' and 'why' and 'how' and 'where' this loss of faith has happened: in the year AD1500 most people believed in God and now in AD2000 most find it difficult to believe in God. We have moved gradually, via the Enlightenment and modernity, from a situation of belief to a new situation in which un-belief has become the default position. Taylor rejects simplistic theories of secularism, like the falling off of numbers attending church or the removal of God from the public square. Something deeper is happening which could be summed up, very inadequately, in a number of shifts: from an enchanted to a disenchanted universe, from *kairos* time to *chronos* time, from theism to deism, from deism to an impersonal order, from transcendence to an immanent frame of reference, from a hierarchical social order to a levelled, self-sufficient society, from a relational, 'porous' self to an independent, 'buffered' self, from a moral order with transcendent roots to an order of exclusive humanism.

Something similar has been on the mind of Benedict XVI for a number of years. In a letter to the Catholic Bishops of the World in 2009, he noted:

> In our days, when in vast areas of the world the faith is in danger of dying out like a flame which no longer has fuel, the overriding priority is to make God present in the world ... The real problem at this moment in history is that God is disappearing from the human horizon.

This theme was raised also by Benedict at the 2012 Synod of Bishops in Rome and he also alluded to it in his resignation speech in March 2013.

A third commentator is Jim Sweeney who highlights the disconnect between contemporary culture and the proclamation of the Gospel. Sweeney says we are living in 'a new situation' in which 'for the first time life without God is a realistic cultural option for whole societies'. The reason for this startling statement is that 'at the societal level the old myths, the old narratives, drawn from the scriptures, no longer hold power; they no longer stir the imagination across generations, they've lost cultural resonance and died'.[7] The major point in Sweeney's account of what is happening is to point up the absence of any living relationship between traditional expressions of the Gospel and contemporary culture.

There is a view that the world may be going through 'an axial period', that is, a time of revolutionary change that constitutes a turning point in global history. The concept of an 'axial age' was first introduced by Karl Jaspers in the 1950s to describe how world history, cosmological viewpoints and world religions were founded on a concept of 'transcendence' that emerged somewhere between 600–200BCE and that this view of transcendence has been foundational for civilisations globally up to the present time. It is now believed, in the light of the new cosmologies, the new technologies, and global shifts that something similar is taking place and that a real change of consciousness is occurring at global, religious and cosmic levels, affecting our understanding of transcendence. A changed vision of transcendence is impacting on the way we see God, for some negatively and for others positively, for some as a threat to faith, and for others as an opportunity to deepen our limited grasp of the mystery of God.

It is noted that most of the faith stories we have today were born in the first axial age which knew nothing about the theories of evolutionary biology or the new cosmologies. Further, many Christian doctrines were forged in the crucible of a Christendom-Christianity and depend on Hellenistic concepts that no longer have the philosophical power that they had in the first thousand years of Christianity. The experience of God today frequently takes place away from organised religion in other places like the so-called 'secular' contexts of the arts, music and film. The language of traditional Christianity has become too formulaic for many and for others 'the words are sodden with overuse and imprecision'.[8]

How NOT to Respond to These Shifts

It is far easier to indicate how we should not react to these developments than it is to say how we should respond. There is a natural temptation to resist changes that impact negatively on deeply-cherished beliefs, especially when they challenge existential faith commitments. This natural reaction forgets, however, that the 'object' of these deeply held commitments is, and has been, and will be, greater than anything we will ever be able to grasp or understand or imagine in this life. If we really believe that God is incomprehensible and is the great 'known unknown' in our lives, then these radical changes might be opportunities to get to know more personally and prayerfully this intimate and unutterable presence, lest the traditional forms lose all power to hold us.

In reaction to this current state of affairs, one should stop scapegoating secularism. Demonising the secular by way of response to this crisis of faith unwittingly ends up alienating large sections of society who live out their lives in the secular world, without necessarily giving up on faith. We do well to remember that Vatican II through *Gaudium et spes* speaks positively about the autonomy of earthy affairs and secular culture (a. 36, 41, 56, 76). Further, secularisation and some forms of secularism can protect faith from lapsing into superstition, idolatry, and ideology. To be sure, there are forms of secularism that are aggressively anti-religious and should be taken seriously and engaged with in dialogue.

In struggling with secularism, we should remember that there is a variety of secularisms, just as there is a variety of Christianities. Distinctions must be made before critiquing secularism. In particular, we need to distinguish between an open and closed secularism,[9] between what some call procedural secularism and programmatic secularism, and others call the social process of secularisation and the ideology of secularism. Not everything secular is anaemic to faith, and therefore simply opposing the secular is often bad theology.

A second way *not* to respond to the contemporary crisis of faith is to blame the culture. Christians should stop blaming contemporary culture for the decline of faith, especially popular culture and the communications culture. We need to understand what is going on in contemporary culture through critical analysis. Much of the content of popular culture and the communications culture is concerned with issues that are also of deep concern to Christian faith: life and death, pain and suffering, love and infidelity, hopes and dreams, memory and imagination, trust and betrayal.

Faith does not exist without cultural expression: a faith that is not enculturated in contemporary forms is not a living faith. Christians need to distinguish, without separating, the ongoing interaction between faith and culture.

Again, the issue of faith and culture, the disconnect between the good news and contemporary culture, is by no means clear-cut. There are aspects of contemporary culture that are alien to Christian values, such as the cult of violence, the dehumanisation of humans, the assault on the dignity of the individual, the objectification of sex, and the exploitation of the female form. Equally there are aspects of contemporary culture that resonate with faith, such as its portrayal of beauty, its fascination with difference and otherness, its concern for human rights, and its passion for social and ecological justice.

A third way to *not* respond to the current crisis of faith is to condemn the rise of individualism. Once again, people of faith should stop blaming individualism for the loss of faith. There is nothing wrong with individualism. Everyone is called to develop his or her potential to be a unique individual. More than ever, the individual feels the need to express herself so as to avoid becoming 'a mere cog in the machine' and to resist being swept away on a tide of globalisation where one size fits all. Becoming an individual, sometimes called the process of individualisation, should be cultivated and supported by Christian communities. Where individualism can become problematic is when it takes place at the expense of other individuals, ignoring the common good of society and the flourishing of all in community. Equally problematic for individualism is when the individual refuses the call of self-surrender in the service of others. Some forms of individualism refuse to accept that it is in the service of others that the individual comes to be and to know himself.

Theological Principles
If we are to face honestly the questions raised by our poets and theologians concerning the mystery of God in the twenty-first century, and if we are to accept that we are living through an axial age concerning transcendence, then we must be guided by some underlying theological principles. It may be helpful, by way of conclusion, to intimate some theological principles that might guide us in this time of deep transitions and radical transformations.

First, it must be recognised that God is not an object alongside other objects, not an item of information alongside other items of information, not an explanation alongside other explanations. If God were merely any one of these, then people would lose interest very quickly and this may well be the reason why so many are losing interest so quickly.

Secondly, it needs to be noted that the God of contemporary faith does not, in the normal course of events, intervene externally from time to time in the natural processes of biological evolution and the development of human history. Instead, the God of the Judaeo–Christian tradition is a God already actively involved through the gift of the Spirit poured out on creation and on all flesh.[10] This gift of the Spirit continues to be active intrinsically in the world in surprising ways: in creation and history, in prophets and holy persons, in cultures and religions, in the creative arts and healing insights of modern science, in the awakening of the inner life and the experience of transcendence, and in the churches as messianic communities endowed and empowered by the particular gift of the Spirit of Jesus Christ.

Thirdly, we need to be clear that faith in God is not a blind leap in the dark; instead it is a reasoned response of the whole person embracing experience, trust, joy, emotions, desire, moral sensibilities, imagination and interpretation. This experience of God is more about God finding us than us finding God. To this extent, the revelation of God in human experience is not a projection but a discovery of what is already there; is not a human construct but the unravelling of a gift already given in life; and not a human creation but a making explicit of what we are already vaguely familiar with. Further, this experience of God is not some kind of exotic, out-of-the-body experience; instead it is often an experience of the most ordinary kind that takes on extraordinary, even mystical, signification.

And finally, we need to learn how to approach the mystery of God with humility. This means discovering that the more we say about God, the more likely it is that we will get God wrong. Loose talk about God often ends up, not edifying people, but generating, unwittingly, new forms of atheism, incredulity, and alienation. We must acknowledge, with humility, that we know very little about God, and that more often than not, 'less is more' when it comes to talking about the mystery of God. We need a new appreciation of the value of learned ignorance (*docta ignorantia*) as a form of knowledge and begin to realise that such ignorance is the beginning of theological wisdom. At the same time, however, before we can arrive at this learned ignorance, we must have plumbed the depths of the historical and personal revelation of God in Jesus Christ. The originality of that revelation is that 'God is love'(1 Jn 4:8, 16), an insight that unfolded in the New Testament and the early centuries in terms of understanding the one God as Father, Son and Spirit *and* as Spirit, Son and Father. Communicating the uniqueness of the Christ-event in the twenty-first century will require an expansion of the theological imagination in a way that is able to engage with other religions as intimated by Vatican II. Only then can we move to the cultivation of a fully informed learned ignorance. In the meantime, however, it needs to be noted there is nothing more destructive of good theology than a premature negative theology.

The Furrow on Film
MARK PATRICK HEDERMAN

The advantage of living in a monastery is that there are monks who are even older than Ronan Drury and a library which contains every issue of *The Furrow* from the first one in February 1950. Fr Placid Murray, of our community here at Glenstal Abbey, remembers the meeting in which J.G. McGarry launched the idea of such a journal. All present threw five pound notes on the table without having a clue what they were undertaking. They didn't even realise that in such a journal one was expected to extend pagination throughout a whole volume. Vol. I, No. 2, therefore, begins again at page one, and so Vol. I, No. 3 has to take up at page 117. In that third number, April 1950, Ronan Drury reviews Seamus Murphy's book *Stone Mad*. Murphy had done his apprenticeship as a stone carver in the 1920s and his book, now regarded as a classic, celebrated the work of all those 'stonies' whose craft was beginning to die out in the 1940s. Ronan quotes one of these stalwarts as an epitaph for the stone carver: 'People aren't building for the future generations any more, them days are gone … that trade's wiped out. 'Twas nice work but slow.'[1] Let's hope it doesn't become an epitaph also for *The Furrow* in an age of digital editions and online printing.

In this article I would like to examine the unique and invaluable contribution which *The Furrow* has made towards appreciation of cinema in Ireland, at a time when that very particular form of twentieth century art was getting a hard time and many powerful people in our society were fearful of it and hostile towards it.

Cinema's arrival in Ireland was broadly contemporaneous with the establishment of a number of organisations whose most explicit goal was the encouragement and development of a distinctively Irish identity.[2] Most ideologies behind political regimes of the twentieth century were opposed to modern art of every kind, which they saw as decadent. Ireland in the twentieth century, at the official level, was neglectful and suspicious of the arts. Artists and intellectuals were feared and suppressed by politicians, church leaders and society at large. Few artists felt welcome or safe to express themselves in any but the most traditional and righteous fashion. Ireland in the twentieth century became a 'Nanny State', if we accept that to mean a country where the government or its policies are overprotective, or interfere unduly with individual freedom and personal choice of its citizens. Far from the kind of dialogue between our society and the arts, which would have been both salutary and invigorating, there developed an atmosphere of fear and suspicion which was expressed and enshrined in the 1923 Censorship of Films Act, and the 1929 Censorship of Publications Act. Such censorship legislation, in the words of Joe Lee, 'served the materialistic values of the propertied classes by fostering the illusion that Ireland was a haven of virtue surrounded by a sea of vice'.[3] Ciarán Benson[4] puts it this way: 'If the state had a responsibility for arts and culture ... its self-understanding required that it defend itself against what it understood to be the dangers of the arts rather than incorporate them as ways in which national self-understanding might develop.'

In 1961, a Scandinavian report on Design in Ireland stated baldly: 'The Irish schoolchild is visually and artistically among the most undereducated in Europe'; an indictment re-echoed in 1965 by The Irish Council of Design which described education in this country as 'a tradition in which art as a whole has been gravely undervalued'. Over ten years later, after welcome reforms had been introduced into the education system, a report commissioned by the Arts Council of Ireland recognised that the 1970s were years of enlightened reform at every other level of the education system but 'the peripheral role which the arts have traditionally played in Irish education has been perpetuated in the recent changes'. The same report warned that 'Ireland may be faced with a future public which, far from fruitfully exploiting the opportunities available to it, may be characterised by a uniform mediocrity of taste controlled by commercial interests.'[5]

Attitudes towards cinema, the art form invented in the twentieth century, provide an interesting litmus test, an indicator of attitude and intent. The twentieth century with all its technological invention and cultural fashions was pitted against an almost racist view of Irish purity.

During the course of the Dáil debate on the Censorship of Films Bill in the early 1920s, William Magennis, Professor of Metaphysics at University College Dublin, and Cumann na nGaedheal TD, expounded at some length on the evils of cinema: 'Purity of mind and sanity of outlook upon life were long ago regarded as characteristic of our people. The loose views and the vile lowering of values that belong to other races and other peoples were being forced upon our people through the popularity of the cinematograph.'

The Censorship of Films Act in 1923 provided for the appointment of an Official Film Censor and a nine-person unpaid Censorship of Films Appeal Board. Magennis was worried about the effect that cinema would have even on those chosen representatives who would guard the rest of us from obscenity. For him, cinema was equivalent to a deadly plague, what Ebola might represent for us today. The ordinary person did not have the defences or immunity required for viewing films. Only medical doctors, who had built up this immunity, through their work in combating diseases, would be capable of dealing with the pestilence of cinema.

Five of these officially appointed censors spanned the fifty-year period from 1923 to 1972. James Montgomery and Richard Hayes, the first two, held the office between them for more than thirty years. The first of these set the tone. Guided by theological certainty, he set a strict moral blueprint that lasted for half the twentieth century. Richard Hayes, the medical doctor who came after him, was a friend of de Valera, having grown up with him in Bruree, Co. Limerick. American movies became enemy number one: the Harlotry of Hollywood. As James Montgomery put it: 'one of the greatest dangers of films is not the Anglicisation of Ireland, but its Los Angeles-ation.'

Just as the censors felt they had begun to get a grip on all the films entering the country, they were faced with an even greater enemy in the arrival of television. Every home in the country could have a traitor in the sitting room spewing forth filth in every direction. Their situation became impossible to supervise when the so-called 'spill-over signals' from British and Northern Ireland TV channels were available to forty per cent of the Irish population by the end of the 1950s. When ITV entered the lists in 1956, official opinion was that this channel was 'governed by ideas that are wholly alien to the ordinary Irish home'. This was the date and the atmosphere in which *The Furrow* entered the scene.

As far as I can tell, the first reference to film or cinema occurs in the August 1950 edition in the review section. Gerard Herbert is reviewing *Focus*, a monthly film review and *International Film Review*, a quarterly publication of The International Catholic Cinema Office (OCIC). This reviewer concludes, quoting *Vigilanti cura* of Pius XI[6] to support his views: 'we need not only good films but a film public educated to appreciate good films'.[7] He suggests that 'nearly every young person goes to the cinema nowadays. The country lad regularly cycles to the pictures in the local town … the cinema is the continuation school for most of our young Irish workers, and what is learned there should interest us enormously.'[8]

An article called 'Art in the Cinema' is featured in the second year of *The Furrow*. John F. McPhillips suggests that cinema 'has suffered painfully through lack of serious discussion and by the neglect of those intelligent and culturally privileged people who might have saved it from some of its vulgarity and fatuity'. His question about cinema as art is twofold: a film is the product of a group, many of whom are essentially technicians, the result of the efforts of many minds and many skills; 'can one have a work of art that does not bear the signature of one creative mind, a mind using a particular medium to convey its vision of life and truth and beauty and to express its experience of living?' McPhillips gives the perceptive answer, and is one of the first to recognise, that the real artist behind the film is the director, 'even though the name of the director is seldom noted by the public'.

He also makes two other important points which remain relevant: 'There is a real need for more critical discussion in this country, where the cinema habit is becoming part of the life of the countryside, before the natural good taste of our people is confounded. If discussion of films were started in schools and continued in youth clubs, the level of critical appreciation would be raised.'[9]

In 1954, the editor engaged John K. Dempsey to dialogue with readers about cinema. In the January edition he quotes 'an extract from today's paper' saying that 965,000 people in the twenty-six counties attend the cinema every week and spend £3.5 million per annum on cinema tickets. He calculates that the population of Southern Ireland at this time would be about two and a half million, of whom some are making fifty million visits to the cinema per annum. He asks whether cinema is no more than a menace, a drug, or pure trash. He presents it rather for what it is, an entertainment industry which can be divided into two categories, helpful for both classification and assessment: propaganda and art.

For the next decade, *The Furrow* was serviced by two exceptionally enlightened and open-minded commentators who provided perspicacious critiques of films being shown in cinemas around the country: Fr Peter Connolly [1956–8], Professor of English Literature at Maynooth,[10] and Fr John C. Kelly SJ [1960–5].

Kelly was asked to become part of the newly restructured censorship board in 1965, but only remained there for nine months as he was eventually sent to Rome. He was one of the most informed advocates of cinema at the time and even now his views are pertinent as guides to our approach to the overwhelming reality of modern communications technology. Interviewed by John Horgan in January 1965, before he took up his new position on the censorship board, he advised that:[11] 'Film-makers should not stop making films in which sexual matters were treated properly just because some people in the audiences, because of their own improper dispositions, might make improper use of his film.' He warned his colleagues on the censorship board: 'To condemn a film which deals with sex properly and is not intrinsically evil is possibly to commit an injustice which could be grave. Instead of censoring films we should be preventing those who might be harmed by them from gaining access. The job of education is to prepare people for such adult viewing: It should be said that the principles stated here should be grasped substantially by everyone who has reached the age of puberty; otherwise his sexual education is gravely defective and the blame must he laid not on the film makers but on parents, educators and religious teachers.'

The debate between those who favoured a 'blanket' system of censor-ship and those who preferred a system of grading was reopened by Kelly in his last article on films in *The Furrow*.[12] 'The very young or, those too young to have completed their sexual education and training, should be excluded from serious and sincere films dealing with sexual matters: excluded either by parental control or by the use of a limited certificate for showing. We should be 'educated' before we view certain films, which, in themselves, are serious explorations of important aspects of our life as human beings.' With regard to his duties as a member of the new board he suggested that: 'the negative duties of a film censor are clear: he has to keep out pornography, for instance. But he can also fulfil a very constructive role. He should think of the weaker members of the community and should try to see that they are helped towards a greater understanding of the films they see.'

Such help was certainly provided by *The Furrow* in the critical years since its foundation. Obviously its critiques and commentaries were confined to the films which the very strict censorship procedures in place in Ireland allowed to filter through to our cinema screens. Later commentators in its pages were Fr Michael Sweetman SJ [1965–7]; Desmond Forristal, who looked after the section 'Stage and Screen' from 1970–8 and David O'Grady from 1980–4.

For the last thirty years, with the proliferation of possibility for viewing films of every kind, from videos to DVDs, from those shown on TV channels to those screened in cinemas, it has not been possible to cover so wide a spectrum. The programme for *The Furrow* in 1985 announced a change. No longer would there be a reviewer of films specifically. Instead a whole new section was introduced called 'The Arts, the Media and the Christian'. This amalgam would appear quarterly and include 'surveys of important events in the arts and the media in Ireland'.

However, for the crucial years between 1950 and 1985, *The Furrow* provided its readers with measured, insightful and intelligent guidance with regard to one of the most important cultural phenomena of our times. Here are some of the valuable lessons learned from *The Furrow* over the years, which can also guide us today in the quandaries we face even more pressingly: We should certainly be filtering whatever reaches us via the internet, which in itself is a blessing, but which can be used for many evil and devastating purposes; for instance, we should not allow either ourselves or our children to become victims of highly organised and ever more sophisticated pornography industries. But we must avoid the errors of infantilism: treating the public as if they were children. We must train ourselves and our children to become discerning and judicious in both our choice and our evaluation of the fare we allow ourselves to ingest. And here, advice from *The Furrow* in the 1950s echoes even the most up-to-date research in media studies: 'Subjects such as film or media studies too often only begin to be taught within second-level education where they are treated as an offshoot of English instead of being treated as independent subjects … available from early primary grades. Essentially, it is yet another instance of the old struggle for children's hearts, minds, souls and sexual bodies, that is always best won when there is openness and dialogue.' Whatever the society's decision will be, and whatever steps we take or precautions we provide, 'irresponsible indifference and unsubstantiated moral panic are the greatest enemies to ensuring that vulnerable users are adequately protected'.[13]

Fógairt an tSoiscéil i gCultúr Briste
(Ar Chothrom Caoga Bliain Gaudium et Spes)
BREANDÁN Ó DOIBHLIN

Bunriachtanas is ea é le haghaidh an Soiscéal a fhógairt, dar leis an doiciméad *Gaudium et spes* de chuid Chomhairle na Vatacáine, go mbeadh an Eaglais ag síorscrúdú 'comharthaí na linne' agus á léirmhíniú faoi léas an tSoiscéil d'fhonn a bheith in ann freagra a thabhairt ar na ceisteanna a chuireann an cine daonna orthu féin mar le brí na beatha. Cad iad féin mar sin na 'comharthaí seo na linne'? Cá fhad de radhairc siar sa stair a ba ghá dúinn a iniúchadh chun conclúidí ar bith a aimsiú a mbeadh brí nó muinín ag baint leo? Cad é an comhthéacs cultúrtha ina n-iarrtar orainn an daonnacht seo againn a bhreathnú ina haontacht agus ina hiomláine? Cad iad na gnéithe de chuimhne na staire is féidir dúinn a shonrú a bhainfeadh le hábhar?

Chun an raon radhairc a chúngú agus a chruinniú mar sin d'fhonn téama nó iomas éigin a shonrú a mbeadh fiúntas ann, b'fheidir go bhfaighfí treoir éigin tríd an rogha sin a bhunú ar nadúr an phróiséas daonna lena ndéantar luachanna a sheachadú (luachanna reiligiúnda ina measc), tríd na gnéithe sóisialta agus síceolaíocha a bhaineann leis a scrúdú agus, go háirithe inár gcás féin, i dtaithí na staire.

An próiséas daonna trína ndéantar luachanna a sheachadadh, 'traidisiún' mar is féidir a thabhairt air, is é a chruthaíonn an timpeallacht phearsanta agus stairiúil a saolaítear cách isteach ann agus as a ndiúrnann sé na luachanna a chomhdhéanann féiniúlacht dó. Cé gur trí mheán an teaghlaigh, an oideachais agus ilmheáin na cumarsáide a thagann, d'fhéadfaí an feiniméan seo a chur i láthair ina scéim mar ghníomhaíocht a bhfuil dhá mhol nó dhá phearsa i gceist ann, ceann amháin ag seachadadh go gníomhach agus an ceann eile ag glacadh chuige (i dtús báire ar aon nós). Ní gá gur beirt phearsana indibhidiúla a bheadh i gceist ach ionadaithe mar a déarfá ó dhá ghlúin i ndiaidh a chéile, tuismitheoir agus leanbh i dteaghlach, abair, ach ina theannta sin instititiúid nó cleachtadh nósmhar d'aon chineál sa chomhluadar, múinteoir agus mac léinn, ceardaí agus printíseach, cainteoir teilifíse agus seallach, nó fiú córas giúláin sóisialta agus an duine aonair a chleachtann é.

Ó thaobh síceolaíochta de, níl an dá eilimint seo ar an leibhéal céanna, tá ceann amháin acu ag cur in iúl, tá an dara ceann ag iarraidh a thabhairt leis. Agus fiú amháin an méid sin éilíonn sé dhá ghné eile de phróiséas an traidisiúin, leanúnacht gan bhriseadh agus iontamhlú pearsanta ag an té a ghlacann. Is é an t-iontamhlú sin a chuidíonn le féiniúlacht a chomh-dhéanamh dó agus, an ghné is tábhachtaí, is é neart na muiníne atá aige as fiúntas an méid atá á sheachadadh a chinntíonn beocht agus cumas téarnaimh an traidisiúin agus téagar na féiniúlachta a chruthaíonn sé. B'fhéidir gurb é an chuid is luachmhaire de thraidisiún beo den chineál sin feasacht na buaine a spreagann sé sa duine aonair ar cosaint é in éadan cásúlacht agus soleontacht na beatha daonna. Ní bhacann sé sin substaint an méid atá a sheachadadh a bheith á athscrúdú nó á scagadh níos faide anonn, ach beidh de bhuntáiste ag athscrúdú den chineál sin go ndéanfar é laistigh d'aigne chinnte i leith na todhchaí.

An uirlís nach bhfuil scaradh leis ón phróiséas fíordhaonna seo is í an teanga labhartha í, an fhoirm is éifeachtaí agus is solúbtha den chumarsáid idir daoine. Dá thairbhe sin, an córas luachanna agus an coimpléasc síceolaíoch a ghabhann leis, brathann siad cuid mhór ar an teanga dhúchais trína súitear isteach iad i dtús báire. Suim na taithí, na gcleachtaí agus na gclaonta chun nithe a ghlacadh nó a dhiúltú, tá siad mar bheadh siad arna n-ionchollú i gcomhréir na teanga agus de réir a cheile déantar díobh an athartha orgánach ar comhartha sóirt í ar chomhluadar neamhthuilleamaíoch. Ar ndóigh, an ghné dhaonna de sheachadadh an chreidimh reiligiúnda, ní haon eisceacht do ghnáthriail sheachadadh an chultúir é agus ar toradh moille déantar ionchollú air agus crann taca dó den oidhreacht chultúrtha i gcoitinne.

An mbeimis ag dul ar bhéalaibh na hargóna mar sin dá molaimis mar shanas, agus sinn ag léamh ar 'chomharthaí na linne' ón am a tháinig bunadh Caitliceach na tíre amach as ré na bPéindlithe, dá molaimis nach bhfuil feiniméan staire ar bith inchomparáid, mar lena thábhacht do neart na leanúnachta cultúrtha, (an reiligiún san áireamh), ná ollaistriú teanga na naoú aoise déag a mhalartaigh traidisiún cultúrtha ársa ar choinsiastacht nua a súdh isteach go duamhar faoi bhrú ó fórsaí as traidisiúin andúchasacha?

Ba é seo an gníomh deireanach i ndráma an chóilíneachais sin a raibh pobal dúchasach na tíre faoina smacht leis na céadta bliain. Torthaí tubaisteacha an chóilíneachais ó thaobh síceolaíochta agus sochaí de, is minic agus is forleathan ríofa iad; polasaithe a b'ea iad a raibh gá leo chun an t-ionsaí ar phobal eile a dhí-urchóidiú tríd an mhuintir a léiriú mar fódhaoine agus a dtoil chun frithsheasaimh a lagú trína meas orthu féin a chur ar ceal. B'fhéidir nar mhiste iarmhairtí na straitéise sin a lorg i síceolaíocht agus igcomhluadar Caitliceach ár linne fein, fiú amháin.

B'fhada, ar ndóigh, na hÉireannaigh dulta i dtaithí ar an smacht polaitiúil agus míleata, ar an éagóir eacnomaíoch agus ar a dteanga agus a dtraidisiún cultúrtha a bheith faoi thoirmeasc dlí. Ina dhiaidh sin, agus d'ainneoin ar a laighead ceathrú milliúin seadaitheoirí Sasanacha agus Albanacha a theacht isteach sa tír tar éis Cogadh an Dá Rí, bhí an pobal dúchais beo go fóill san ochtú aois déag i saol détheangach, nó b'fhearr a rá in diglossia[1] san áit nach raibh rogha eile acu ach Béarla a labhairt lena máistrí cóilíneacha ach mar ar fhan an Ghaeilge ina hurlabhra inmheánach agus ina sainfhriotal eatarthu féin.

Cé gur lean creimeadh mall an chultúir sin i riocht détheangach na naou aoise déag, tharla ollathrú ó lár na haoise sin amach. Ollsuaitheadh an Ghorta Mhóir agus na milliúin marbh nó ar imirce, tá an chuma air gur athraigh sé próiséas malltriallach an détheangachais ina dhiongbháilteacht bhuile chun fáil réidh le teanga na sinsear agus iompú amach ina phobal aonteangach amháin. Pe cúis a bhí leis nó pé tosca a mhíníonn an scéal, ní féidir aon rud amháin a cheilt agus sin gur athrú réabhlóideach a bhí ann nach bhféadfá ach féinmharú cultúrtha a thabhairt air, ó laghdaíodh na ceithre milliúin cainteoirí Gaeilge in 1840 go níos lú ná milliún laistigh de dhá ghlúin daoine.

B'fheidir nár mhiste a chur ina luí orainn féin cad ba chiall don méid seo i gcúrsaí creidimh. B'fhada Gaeil na hÉireann dulta i dtaithí le glúnta anuas ar Eaglais faoi cheilt agus a gcrábhadh féin a chothú agus a chur i bhfriotal laistigh de chultúr príobháideach pearsanta nach bhféadfadh a bheith ag brath ar chultas poiblí. Dá thairbhe sin, bhíodh gnáthimeachtaí an lae á síortionlacan leis an urnaí nárbh fhéidir a chleachtadh go poiblí, agus bhí taisce d'íogaireacht chreidimh lonnaithe i bhfriotal na teanga Gaeilge go príomha. Ba é toradh a bhí air sin go raibh gach a ndearna siad ar maos i gcéadfaíocht chreidimh, rud a chruthaigh taisce ollmhór de bheannachtaí, de phaidreacha agus d'amhráin agus véarsaíocht chráifeach.

Arna seachadadh ó ghlúin go glúin mar bhí, bhí fuinneamh neamhchoitianta inti ó thaobh céadfaíochta agus údaráis, agus b'amhlaidh a ba mhóide sin gur fás nádúrtha a b'ea í ar shaol agus modh beatha na ndaoine seachas í a bheith á cur rompu ón taobh amuigh ag institiúid eaglasta. Nuair atá an coimhthíos seo á thionlacan i measc na cléire le diagacht nár saothraíodh as an nua as taithí agus stair na sochaí dúchais, féadann an chuma a bheith air gur rud aisciúil agus andúchasach é an deabhóideachas úr atá á bhrú orthu ón taobh amuigh. Agus nuair a thagann an crudh ar an tairne, féadann an chuma choimhthíoch seo deighilt a a chruthú de réir a chéile idir cúrsaí creidimh agus féiniúlacht an duine agus na sochaí, agus go háirithe idir iad agus aon chiall do chinniúint ar leith a bheith acu.

Torthaí an Aistriú Teanga in Éirinn
Aithnítear coitianta go raibh sainghnéithe ag baint leis an aistriú teanga, *language shift* (mar a deirtear leis), in Éirinn. Bhí an claonadh ann mar shampla gur tharla sé thar dhá ghlúin daoine in ionad na dtrí cinn ar a dtarlaíonn go hiondúil. Abair go dtéann lánúin as an tSicil ar imirce go Nua-Eabhrach gan de theanga labhartha acu ach a gcanúint féin. Maireann siad i ngeiteo Sicileach gan a fhoghlaim ach stór focal Béarla an-chúng le gnó a dhéanamh lasmuigh de. Is í an chanúint Sicileach teanga an teallaigh agus labhraíonn an chlann an chanúint Sicileach mar chéad teanga, gan Béarla Mheiricea a fhoghlaim go dtí go dtéann siad ar scoil, ach iad ar a suaimhneas i gcónaí sa gheiteo Shicileach. A gclann siúd, fásann siad aníos ag labhairt Béarla lena dtuismitheoirí; seans go mbíonn mear-eolas agus cion áirithe ar chanúint na seanlánúna ach tagann siad féin in inmhe trí mheán an Bhéarla agus ó thaobh síceolaíochta de déanann siad iad féin a iontamhlú le Béarla a dtuismitheoirí agus na sochaí Meiriceánaí. In Éirinn tharlódh an próiséas seo thar dhá ghlúin daoine mar gur chuir glúin tuismitheoirí áirithe rompu d'aon turas 'an Ghaeilge a cheilt' ar a gclann agus chrois ar na seantuismitheoirí Gaeilge ar bith a labhairt leo, rud a spreag drochmheas agus tarcaisne sa ghlúin óg i leith ar chuaigh rompu.

Is drámatúla go mór an toradh sa phróiséas Éireannach mar gur chruthaigh sé briseadh iomlán i seachadadh na hoidhreachta cultúrtha. Rinneadh Meiriceánaigh ó thaobh cultúir de de pháistí Sicileacha na tríú glúine go deimhin, ach páistí na dara glúine in Éirinn chaill siad a n-oidhreacht agus ní bhfuair ina hionad ach an méid a d'fhéadfadh an scoil a mhúineadh dóibh de thraidisiún Béarla. An saol iomlán timpeall orthu a sonraíodh riamh sa Ghaeilge, ceileadh orthu é: an domhan fisiciúil ar ndóigh lena chuid ainmneacha traidisiúnta ar *flora* agus *fauna* agus a raibh de scéalaíocht ag gabháil leo; an téarmaíocht ar a staideanna síceolaíocha agus an coimpléasc de bhéaloideas agus de chrábhadh a bhain leo, fiú chomh fada le logainmneacha a bhfearann dúchais nach raibh iontu feasta ach gibiris gan chiall ina gcluasa.

Nuair a cuireadh an díobháil seo i gcomhar leis na scoileanna 'náisiúnta' nua nach raibh ceadaithe iontu ach Béarla agus é de pholasaí acu an deighilt a chur i bhfeidhm le díspeagadh na Gaeilge agus nós cruálach an *bhata scóir*, tugadh cailliúint beagnach iomlán de shubstaint chultúrtha an traidisiúin chun críche. Mar aon le tionchar na cléire a bhí ag teacht as Coláiste Mhá Nuad, a raibh a n-oideachas faighte acu trí mheán an Bhéarla go heisiatach agus iad curtha as seilbh ar aon tuiscint dá n-oidhreacht chreidimh dúchais, ní fhéadfadh a bheith d'iarmhairt air ach míthreoir agus coimhthios a chruthaigh sna glúnta óga drochmheas agus fiú fuath nimhneach do sheansaol na Gaeilge. Ardchigire na scoileanna 'náisiúnta' féin, níor mhiste leis a rá i dtuarascáil chuig na huachtaráin sa bhliain 1855: 'We are quietly but certainly destroying the national legend ... of the country.'

Glúin nua seo an Bhéarla, baineadh a chiall de gach rud a ba dhúchas dóibh, go fiú a n-ainmneacha pearsanta féin. Na sloinnte Gaelacha a chinntigh dóibh a n-ionad sa seanchóras sóisialta, cuireadh as a riocht iad de réir mar a thograigh tiarna talún éigin nó oifigeach stáit nó mar a shocraigh duine de na múinteoirí nua sna scoileanna 'naisiunta'. Samhlaímis dúinn féin an méid a ba thoradh ar an rud is pearsanta dá bhfuil agat, d'ainm, á chur ar ceal go deo le 'haistriúchán' nach bhfuil ann ach caracatúr: Ó Coinneáin ag teacht amach ina Rabbitte, Ó Leocháin ina Ducke, Mac Con Alla ina Swann, agus Ó Gormlaigh bocht iompaithe ina Grimes, Grimshaw, Grimley agus fiú Bloomer (tar éis an tsaoil nach ionann 'gorm' agus 'blue'). An bhfuil fianaise ar bith ann is soiléire a leiríonn caillteanas iomlán an féinmheasa ná an géilleadh seo do d'ainm féin fiú a ligean uait?

Go fiú sna hainmneacha baiste, rinneadh an briseadh leis an rud a bhí ann, agus bhí cuid suntasach ag an chléir sa méid sin leis na cláracha baiste. Cuireadh deireadh leis an seanchleachtadh Gaelach ainmneacha baiste na seantuismitheoirí a chur ar aghaidh trína n-ainmneacha Gaelacha a 'aistriú' go rud eigin is fearr a d'oirfeadh don dearcadh nua, ainm Clasaiceach, b'fhéidir, nó ainm as an Tiomna Nua. Dá bharr sin ar fud dheisceart na hÉireann ar fad, an seanathair a raibh Conchúr air, fuair sé garmhac darbh ainm Cornelius; garmhac Thaidhg, tugadh Timothy nó Thaddeus air; iompaíodh Donncha ina Denis, Dónall ina Daniel agus mar sin dó. Sa

Tuaisceart d'iompaigh Feilimí ina Felix, Art ina Arthur, Eochaí ina Atty. Níor imigh ainmneacha ban slán ach oiread: naomh álainn Iarthar Chorcaí, Gobnait, rinneadh Abigail di; iompaíodh Síle ina Julia, Siobhán ina Susan agus an rud is áiféisí ar fad, an banphátrún náisiúnta, Bríd, fuair sí ainm as úrscéilín grá de chuid na linne, Bedelia; atá anois ina Delia, cé gur annamh duine de mhná an ainm seo anois a mbeadh a fhios acu gur Bríd a bhí ar a sinsear.

Maidir leis an ghlúin páistí sin ar imríodh an chaill orthu, seans maith go mba cheist leo cén mhungailt chainte a bhí ar siúl ag Grandma agus í ag cur síos tine ar an teallach ar maidin in onóir do Naomh Bríd no i láthair aingle Dé, nó cén nathán a bhí i mbéal Grandad agus é ag teacht isteach an doras ag deireadh an lae. Agus gan amhras ligeadh na seandaoine osna chiúin astu agus iad ag iarraidh coinneáil suas le Paidrín an Bhéarla a bhí ina riail docht sa teach feasta seachas an 'Sé do bheatha, a Mhuire', a ba nós agus a ba chion leo féin riamh. Tá cuimhne fágtha againn ó dhuine de chead 'timirí' Chonradh na Gaeilge go bhfeiceadh sé 'a household on their knees saying the Rosary, the old folk saying it with understanding and devotion in their own language, the children answering in a language unknown to the rest of the household ... frequently tricking and belittling the old people ...'

Seans maith anois nach mbainfidh an méid seo as an léitheoir ach gáire Sheáin Dóite. Ach níl sé á riomh ach mar chomhartha a léiríonn coimhthios fíor-urchóideach ón chóras luachanna atá ceangailte go dlúth le friotal agus focail na teanga a tréigeadh. Na páistí bochta a d'fhág fanaiceacht a dtuismitheoiri ag brath ar aonteangachas Béarla iad, tuismitheoirí nach raibh acu féin ach Béarla briotach agus blas aisteach air, fuair na páistí seo iad féin beo i ndomhan fisiciúil, síceolaíoch, cultúrtha agus reiligiúnda nach raibh gléas teanga imleor acu lena chur in iúl. Bhí a lorg sin orthu (mar a tuairiscíodh go minic) sa chuthach feirge, sa searbhas agus sa chiontacht i leith a gcuid sinsear, mar aon le coimpléasc ísleachta buanleanúnach, an rud a dtugann muintir na hAstráile 'cultural cringe' air. Níor rith sé le haonduine de réir dealraimh gur féidir dhá theanga a choinneáil i do cheann le chéile, nó go bhféadfaí oidhreacht na teanga amháin a chaomhnú le linn do bhuntáiste pragmatach na teanga eile a chur leis.

Ar aon nós, is chuige seo atáimid gur fágadh bearna ann nár chuaigh mórán trasna air, briseadh iomlán sa seachadadh cultúrtha a chuir críoch laistigh d'achar goirid le cultúr reiligiúnda ársa. Dá éifeachtaí an chaiticéis sna scoileanna, nó dá dhúthrachtaí na deabhóidí agus na cleachtaí nua in Eaglais an Bhéarla, is deacair gan creidiúint gur cailleadh rud éigin a raibh tabhacht bhunúsach leis. Is ait an rud é agus sinn ag breathnú siar ar an athrú seo, go bhfuil an chuma ar an scéal gur tharla sé gan glór ar bith a ardú ach ar éigin chun an chiall a bhí leis a cheistiú, go háirithe i measc na cléire san am. Is iontaí fós é go bhféadfadh sé seo titim amach sa naoí aois déag nuair a mhúscail an Rómánsachas tuiscint dá gcuid fréamhacha san oiread sin de mhionchultúir na hEorpa. Theip go hiomlán ar an chliarcholáiste náisiúnta i Má Nuad maidir leis an scéal, nár bhreathnaigh chuige fiú amháin go mbeadh léamh agus scríobh na Gaeilge ag sagairt a bhí ag dul amach a fhreastal ar pharóistí arbh í an Ghaeilge a dteanga labhartha san am. Is fianaise fós don méid sin an oiread sin seanmóirí atá le fáil i gcartlanna deoiseacha a scríobhadh i bhfoghraíocht ghránna as siocair nár múineadh riamh do na seanmóirithe scríobh na teanga a bhí á labhairt acu.

An díobháil a rinneadh, ba dhomlasta i gceart é sa réimse sin is príobháidí agus is pearsanta le linn a bheith chomh hilghnéitheach agus chomh leitheadach agus atá, cúrsaí creidimh. Duine ar bith ar ndóigh a bhfuil cur-amach aige ar an chúpla cnuasach de phaidreacha traidisiúnta na Gaeilge atá ar fáil (agus níl aon rud againn atá ionchurtha le sé imleabhar *Charmina Gadelica* na hAlban le Carmichael), is léir dó gur amharcadh ansin ar an saol daonna ar fad ó phointe radhairc reiligiúnda. Dá ainneoin sin, níor tugadh riamh faoi staidéar diagachta dáiríre a dhéanamh ar mheon reiligiúnda na nGael. Cén aigne a chuireann sé in iúl maidir le Dia, leis an Chruthaíocht, le coibhneas Dé le daoine, leis an bhFuascailt, peaca agus olc, aithreachas agus athmhuintearas, obair agus ceiliúradh, nádúr sacraimintiúil an domhain timpeall orainn? Agus cad a mheasfaí de i gcomparáid leis an deabhóideachas tairteolach a cuireadh ina ionad? Cén cion ná dáimh a d'fhéadfadh na fíréin a mhothú leis na naomhphátrúin úd a ndearnadh ciorrú barbartha ar a n-ainmneacha ag aineolas na naoú aoise déag agus a bualadh anuas ar na heaglaisí caiteadrálta Caitliceacha: Munchin in ionad Mainchín, Muredach agus Jarlath ar Muiríoch agus Iarla, Canice agus Eugene ar Chainneach agus Eoghan?

An conamar bocht de liotúirge na ndaoine a tháinig slán trí ré na bpéindlíthe, chuaigh cléir aimsir Victoria go nimhneach sa tóir air, ar fhaitíos go mbeadh bodaigh mhóra an Chinsil ag magadh fúthu. Laethanta pátrúin, tipiciúil de gach tír Chaitliceach san Eoraip, cuireadh teir orthu mar nach mbeadh iontu ach údar le meisce agus le drabhlás. Níor mhiste b'fhéidir breathnú arís inniu ar an bheart creidimh a imríonn an *festa* no *fiesta* in Eaglaisí eile nár loiteadh mar a loiteadh sinne.

An urraim shaonta shimplí a tugadh go háitiúil don uisce i bhfoirm an tobair bheannaithe, déantar neamhshuim de nó lochtú air le linn seanmóiríthe a bheith ag iarraidh tuiscint a mhúscailt do chiall shacráilte shacraimintiúil uisce an Bhaiste. (Leis an bhfírinne a dhéanamh, bhíodh feachtais den chineál ceanna ar siúl ag sionaid na n-easpag sa bhFrainc sa 17ú agus san 18ú aois i gcoinne a leithéid d'iarsmaí na 'págántachta'.) Ach duine ar bith a bhfuil aigne oscailte aige a bhreathnaíonn ar cheann de na fuaráin sacráilte seo ag brúchtadh amach as faoin charraig, de chineál abair Tobar Chiaráin in aice le Carn na Ros i gCo. na Mí, feicfidh sé an t-áimear atá ann chun ciall don tsacráilteacht agus don tsacraimintiúlacht a mhúscailt in ionad céadfaíocht reiligiúnda den sórt a ligean i ndearmad.

D'fhonn an fhadhb a shainléiriú
Níl na ráite scáinte seo ach ag iarraidh teacht ar an ghá ata ann, ar mhaithe leis an soiscéal a fhógairt, le staidéar a dhéanamh ar an ábhar a d'fhéadfaí 'antropolaíocht' an chrábhaidh ag daoine sa tír seo a thabhairt air. Má chreidimid, mar is dual don Chaitliceach creidmheach, gur tabhartas saorálach ó Dhia í suáilce an chreidimh, ní féidir mar sin aon aidhm eile a bheith leis an 'Soiscéalú' ach an ithir a ullmhú a bhféadfadh síol an chreidimh fréamhacha a chur síos inti. Agus is ar éigin is freagra imleor ar an fhadhb ár n-iarrachtaí ar fad a chruinniú ar an seomra ranga chun fírinní agus aigne dhiagachta an Chreidimh Chaitlicí a mhúineadh. Óir cé a d'fhéadfadh a rá, dá éifeachtaí ár modhanna teagaisc nó dá tharraingtí a chuirimid an teachtaireacht i láthair go n-aimseoidh sé, *ipso facto*, an chréafóg is gá, nó nach mbeidh ann i ndeireadh na dála ach foclaíocht?

Seo an áit a mbeidh riachtanas le staidéar agus machnamh leanúnach ar mheanma an chreidimh ionainn, idir chultúr agus síceolaíocht, agus ar stair na creidiúna ag na glúnta a chuaigh romhainn. Is réidh againn sólás a bhaint as cuimhní na misinéirí móra san 'aois órga' nó dílseacht na gcéadta bliain de fhorlámhas cóilíneach nó an fuinneamh agus an fhlaithiúlacht lena ndearnadh an Eaglais scriosta a atógáil sa naoú aois déag. Ach is bocht an comhshólás na cuimhní seo, a bhfuil a sciar fein de rómánsachas na naoú aoise déag ag roinnt leo, i láthair na dtosca nach foláir apostátacht náisiúnta a thabhairt orthu ag deireadh na fichiú aoise. Pé cúiseanna a d'fhéadfaimis a thagairt leis, cléir údarásúil, rómhuinín sa deabhóideachas, níor mhiste b'fhéidir é a chur i gcomparáid leis an olldiúltú den chineál céanna a tugadh do cheann de na rudaí a rinne meabhair náisiunta dúinn riamh, teanga agus cultúr na Gaeilge, ach a caitheadh i leataobh go toilghnústa céad bliain roimhe sin, agus a raibh torthaí air nár measadh i gceart go fóill ná nár baineadh ceacht ar bith astu.

An chaoi a bhfuil staid na ceiste sin faoi láthair, ní féidir ach buille-faoi-thuairim a thabhairt fá dtaobh de na hiarmhairtí sin, ach ar éigin a bheimis ag dul thar fóir agus a rá nach foláir ná go raibh siad domhain, bunúsach fiú amháin, agus b'fhéidir díobhálach go deo d'aon chiall de chinniúint chomónta a bheith i ndán dúinn. Mar le rud amháin, nílimid gan fianaise ó thraidisiún na Gaeilge ar shlad an chóilíneachais agus ar an lagachar a bhí ina thoradh air. Nílimid gan ráitis ardghlóracha ach oiread ar thurnamh agus titim ó chultúir eile a sriosadh ag ansmacht cóilíneach, leithéidí abair dúchasaigh Thuaisceart Mheiricea.

An t-athrú d'aonturas ó ghnáthchúrsa an détheangachais go staid an aonteangachais, is follas go raibh tionchar aige ar phróiséas an tseachadadh cultúir atá luaite againn cheana. Ach páistí a fhágáil d'aonturas ag brath ar an aon teanga amháin as lár an détheangachais, chruthaigh sin iontu *ipso facto* drochmheas ar gach ar bhain lena sinsir, noch a léiríodh dóibh mar ábhar nárbh fhiú a chaomhnú ná a sheachadadh, go háirithe an teanga ina raibh na luachanna sin seadaithe.

Ina theannta sin, chinntigh an briseadh seo i leanúnacht an chomhluadair dhaonna go gcaillfí ceann de na nithe is luachmhaire in aon traidisiún beo, an tionchar cumhachtach chun seasmhachta agus chun féinmhuiníne a ghineann oidhreacht a bhfuil cion agus meas air. An cumas chun cloí le creideamh nó cinnteacht de chineál ar bith agus é a admháil go forimeallach (nílimid ag caint ar ghalamaisíocht!), brathann sé, seachas cabhair Dé, ar chóráiste morálta. Tá sé sin ar a sheal ag brath ar dhiongbháltacht agus ar chiall do gach is sinn agus do gach ar de sinn, aigne ar a dtugaimid féiniúlacht.

Os a choinne sin, an tuiscint do bhuaine agus slándáil an chomhluadair, an chiall don athartha agus don chinniúint atá ag an chomhluadar sin, ach iad a laghdú agus gintear neamhchinnteacht agus féin-amhras, ag lagú an chomhartha sóirt eile sin a bhaineann le féiniúlacht mhuiníneach, an cumas chun fórsaí a chuireann an leanúnacht i mbaol a mheas go criticiúil agus a eiteach más gá. An ghlúin a mbeadh an oidhreacht le glacadh acu, níor cuireadh iad i seilbh ar oidhreacht urramach ach ar shamhailt den saol a fuair a luach ó chomhluadar andúchasach marsantach, ó chóras scolaíochta namhdach, ó eagraíochtaí polaitiúla nua agus ó Eaglais a múnlaíodh i gcleachtadh na Fraince agus na Róimhe. Arbh iomarcach a mhaíomh go bhfuil torthaí an phróiséis sin le feiceáil go fóill sa dúil atá ag ár muintir sa rud nuálach, ina n-easpa tuisceana do na fórsaí stairiúla a chruthaigh agus a chuir ó chríoch iad, sa chlaonadh atá acu luachanna a mheas de réir breithiúnais anall agus aithris a dhéanamh ar chomhluadair eile.

Ní gá go mbeadh drámatúlacht ar bith ag roinnt leis an chreimeadh cultúir agus creidimh sin. Ná ní gá go mbeadh sé teoranta do thosca staire sealadacha áirithe. Tá sé ag leanúint ar aghaidh i gcónaí ar bhealaí nach sonraítear. Ní lú é mar shampla i dTuaisceart Éireann áit a bhféadann an ghráin a d'fhág eachtraí áirithe sna 'Troubles' ar dhaoine flosc a ghiniúint chun fáil réidh le gach aon sórt deighilte, agus eiteach dá bharr d'aon difríochtaí cultúir agus creidimh in ainm an 'le-chéileachais'. Is féidir próiséas den chineál sin a thabhairt faoi deara san iarracht chun dul suas sa saol a dhéanann Caitlicigh a chumascadh sa mheánaicme Phrotastúnach agus i ndomhan an Bhéarla agus na Breataine: meadú ar líon na n-óganach Caitliceach ag freastal ar scoileanna 'Protastúnacha' ardnósacha, Caitlicigh ag bogadh isteach i gceantair chónaithe mheasúla, iad ina mbaill de na clubanna 'cearta' golf nó rugbaí nó cricéid, ina dhiadh sin céilí pósta 'fiúntacha' acu agus turnamh dá thairbhe sna luachanna ba bhun leis an phobal Caitliceach traidisiúnta. Chun an creideamh a bhuanú i dtoscaí mar sin, éilíonn sé múnlú ar leith chun féinmhuiníne sa phobal Caitliceach mura bhfuil sé le dul ar ceal, idir chultúr agus chreideamh, ag feo sa saecláirachas agus sa chailliúnt chreidimh is toradh air sin.

Is pobal a raibh an dúshlán céanna rompu a tháinig amach as sclábhaíocht, gorta agus bochtaineacht sa naoú aois déag chun aghaidh a thabhairt ar dheacrachtaí agus ar bhrú na fichiú aoise, pobal arbh iad a gcomharthaí sóirt an rud ar ar thug socheolaí Francach 'le catholicisme du type irlandais' – 'Caitliceachas den chineál Éireannach' – tugtha don deabhóid, frith-intleachtúil, géilliúil do nósanna beatha, údarásúil, cléireachúlach, cineál d'arm in íona catha, a múnlaíodh amhlaidh (ní foláir a admháil) ag an dearg-ghá chun teacht slán; cineál a mhairfeadh anuas go dtí Dara Comhairle na Vatacáine. Is anuas ar an Eaglais chreapallta sin a thit ó 1968 ar aghaidh, réabhlóid a ba bhunúsaí go mór ná aon rud a bhí an Chomhairle a chur chun tosaigh, 'comhartha eile de chuid na linne'.

Cuma cén tuairim atá againn de réabhlóid 1968, cé acu a bhreathnaímid é mar an t-intleactúlach Francach Raymond Aron ina *'croisade sans croix, une lutte sans objet'* – 'crosáid gan chros, troid gan chuspóir' – nó ar nós *Jean-Marie Domenach san iris Esprit 'l'expression d'un besoin de spiritual sans référence au spiritual'* – 'friotal ar an ghá leis an spioradálta gan tagairt don spioradálta' – is féidir a rá gurbh iad is mó a bhí thíos leis sa bhFrainc na hinstitiúidí sin a raibh beart bunúsach á imirt ag an údarás iontu, an Ollscoil, an Páirti Cumannach agus go háirithe an Eaglais Chaitliceach. Mar a deir René Rémond: *'Le catholicisme fut alors visé à la fois comme culture, comme système intellectuel, comme institiúid'* – Ionsaíodh an Caitliceachas mar chultúr, mar chóras intleachtúil agus mar institiúid, an triúr le chéile. Is ar éigin is ábhar iontais é, nuair a leath an galar chomh fada le saol intleachtúil na hÉireann a ba lú a neart, go raibh na torthaí a bhí air lán chomh bunúsach.

Bhí an t-atmaisféar nua ar maos i ndímheas ar gach norm óraice, agus eiteach d'aon institiúid nó maorlathas a gcuirfí ina leith gur srian a bhí ann le saoirse féin-fhriotail, rud a cuireadh i suim go gonta sa sluaghairm mhillteanach: *'Il est interdit d'interdire'* – toirmeasc ar aon toirmeasc. Is é a chuir an réabhlóid roimhe cultúr an phléisiúir agus na féinspéise nach mbeadh i gceist ann ach tóraíocht gan acht ar an sonas príobháideach agus pearsanta. Bhí sé mar bheadh samhailt sin na daonnachta a milleadh in Auschwitz, ag Hiroshima agus sa Ghúlag, go mbeadh sé tar éis milleadh faoi bhunsraith na réasúnaíochta agus cinnteacht an chreidimh araon in intinn na glúine sin ar fad, agus an bealach a oscailt chun gach sort cúistiúnachta, dúshláin agus míthreorach.

Éigeandáil a b'ea é feasta do gach struchtúr cumhachta a raibh céimse laistiar de, agus níorbh aon eisceacht an Eaglais. Ní cheadófaí d'aonduine feasta a rá: 'Is é seo an buntraidisiún; seo í an fhírinne.' Óir bhí athrú treo ar fad ar bhealach na fírinne; níorbh aon tóraíocht a bhí ann feasta ar fhírinne oibiachtúil a mholfaí ó aon údarás nó aon chóras anuas. As sin amach, beidh gach rud bunaithe ar an indibhidiúlach a shocraíonn dó féin cad is údar céille dar leis féin, a dhéanann a chuid turgnamhaíochta dó féin agus a chuireann a chuspóirí féin in iúl.

Ar measadh a bheith cinnte i réimse an chreidimh, breathnaíonn sé, bíodh sin ceart nó mícheart, as dáta agus ina bhagairt ar shaoirse an duine. Cuirtear suas do gach gné den údarás seachtrach, go fiú an teaghlach, an scoil, an córas polaitíochta, má fheachann siad le teorainn a mholadh nó a leagan síos leis an rogha indibhidiúil. Ina leithéid sin de chás, eagar iomlán an Chaitliceachais idir intleacht, údarás agus seachadadh, milltear faoi le mórathrú cultúrtha. Agus níl áit ar bith is túisce a léirigh sé a thorthaí ná in Éirinn, i bpobal a raibh próiséas an chultúr dúchais tar éis cuid mhór dá fhuinneamh a chailliúint thar an chéad go leith bliain roimhe sin.

Cad is féidir a dhéanamh?
Pé anailís a dhéanfaimis ar 'chomharthaí cultúrtha na linne' atá dulta i bhfeidhm ar mheanmanra na haimsire seo, is deacra fós aon mholadh praiticiúil a dhéanamh mar le fógairt an tSoiscéil sna tosca seo, ach amháin an méid seo a rá: Má tá fiúntas ar bith sa scagadh atá déanta againn go dtí seo, ní foláir an fhógairt sin a bheith bunaithe ar phróiséas leasaithe de chineál éigin, iarracht chun seachadadh an chultúir a chóiriú arís ina ghléas óraice de chuid stair an chine dhaonna. B'fhéidir go mba chúis misnigh dúinn áfach an moladh a rinne *Gaudium et spes* gur cheart a bheith de bhunaidhm ag aon anailís chultúrtha forbairt agus slánchóiriú phearsa an duine chomh maith le leas an phobail agus an chine dhaonna ar fad a dhéanamh. Dhealródh sé mar sin go mbeadh mar thoradh ar an anailís seo i láthair ár n-aird a threorú i leith coimhthios síceolaíoch agus sóisialta na sochaí seo a leigheas, an coimhthios atá ina iarmhairt ar an chiorrú coiscritheach a rinneadh orainn le céad go leith bliain anuas. Léireodh sé, cheapfá, an gá atá le hiarracht chun na gnéithe sin den seachadadh cultúrtha a athchóiriú a ndearnadh dochar nó díobháil orthu: an tuiscint do leanúnacht ár n-oidhreachta; tionchar, mura ndéarfaimis údarás, na hoidhreachta cádhasaí sin; agus an mhuinín sin as a sinsir sna glúnta óga a dhéanfadh oidhrí toilteanacha agus díograiseacha díobh orthu.

D'fhonn réimse an phlé a chúngú agus a dhéanamh ionláimhsithe, d'fhéadfaí, b'fheidir, an phróiséacht seo a fheiceáil mar thionscnamh chun cuimhne na sochaí a athghabháil, chun ár ndíchuimhne chultúrtha a leigheas agus an seachadadh a briseadh a chneasú. Ní leor chuige seo léann na leabhar amháin nó fachtanna na staire a bheith ar eolas. Baineann an t-eolas stairiúil sin lenar tharla do dhaoine eile; an chuimhne atá i gceist anseo, baineann sé lena bhfuil ag tarlú dúinn féin, leis an méid is cúis le sinn a bheith mar atáimid. Is minic múinteoirí staire sa tír seo ag gearán go bhfuil an t-aos léinn atá acu 'ar easpa chiall don stair'; ní de bharr iad a bheith aineolach ach gan a bheith ar a gcumas ceangal beo a fheiceáil idir a gcinniúint phearsanta féin agus stair an am atá caite. Míníonn an méid sin freisin an teip chun aon ionad buan sa ghnáthshaol a ghnóthú don Ghaeilge a fhoghlaimítear ar scoil.

An chuimhne a athghabháil sa chiall atáimid a rá, éilíonn sé taithí an am atá caite a athchruthú sa duine féin. I gcomhthéacs an oideachais bíonn tábhacht ar leith leis an litríocht náisiúnta a athshealbhú, mar gurb í an friotal ealaíonta í idir fhilíocht agus phrós ar aisfhreagra na nglúnta a d'imigh romhainn ar a dtosca stairiúla féin. Arís, ní hé atá i gceist eolas na bhfachtanna amháin a fhoghlaim; is é is mó atá ann féiniúlacht a athghaibhniú i ndialóg leis na glúnta a chuaigh romhainn: briseadh croí an díshealbhaithe agus na deoraíochta le Fearghal Mac an Bhaird, ampla agus mírún na gcóilíneach nua le Dáibhí Ó Bruadair agus le haoir fhíochmhar Aogan Ó Rathaille, an chumha i ndiaidh dínit na filíochta a cailleadh á ríomh ag Art Mac Cumhaigh.

Ag an phointe seo, má tá romhainn an Soiscéal a fhógairt as an nua, éilíonn sin go nglacfaimis dáiríre leis an bheart síceolaíoch a d'imir an teanga shinsearach i stair an phobail, d'ainneoin í a bheith beagnach imithe mar ghléas cumarsáide. Ní hé atá i gceist anseo polasaí nó propaganda na hAthbheochana ach an teanga a bheith ina finné agus ina córas iompair do leanúnacht chultúrtha na sochaí san am atá thart agus ina héarlais den rud céanna sa todhchaí. Níor mhiste dár scotaicmí cultúrtha, an chléir san áireamh, machnamh domhain dáiríre a dhéanamh ar an iarmhairt a d'fhéadfadh a bheith ar an bhfuarchúis chomh fada agus a bhaineann le seasmhacht an chomhluadair náisiúnta agus lena acmhainn spioradálta. Ar leibhéal níos cúinge, ar ndóigh, ach seo scéal thairis, níor mhiste don Eaglais oifigiúil dearcadh pastúireach ionraic a fhorbairt i leith an mionramh arb í an Ghaeilge a rogha teanga, agus ar dóibh is dual an leanúnacht sin a ionchollú lenár linn féin.

An Chríostaíocht in Éirinn, tá sí fréamhaithe i stair agus i sibhialtacht ar leith agus níl sé thar ár gcumas, d'ainneoin tubaistí an dá chéad bliain a ghabh tharainn, iad a athghabháil ina n-eisint trí leas a bhaint as an leanúnacht a mhair beo. Toise stairiúil an chultúir sin, féadann sé beocht úr a spreagadh i gcomhluadar na gcreidmheach agus creatlach a dhéanamh do choimpléasc eaglasta nua. Na tobair bheannaithe a rinne na chéad misnéirí a atiomnú chun an Baisteadh a dhéanamh iontu, féadann siad a bheith ina mball íogair le haghaidh ciall nua don tsacraimint sin, díreach mar a d'fhéadfaí tuiscint an chomhluadair do thábhacht na hEocairiste a athbhunú ar charraigeacha Aifrinn agus ar fhothracha eaglasta an tseansaoil, nó toraíocht an phobail ar Dhia a léiriú go drámatúil ar ulaí na dturas crábhaidh traidisiúnta. Theastódh breathnú ar an oidhreacht Ghaelach idir stair, naomhsheanchas agus bhéaloideas mar thaisce de chéadfaíocht chreidimh i lár saol an tsaeclárachais agus na neamhchúise, go háirithe chomh fada agus a bhaineann lena dtuiscint don tsacráilteacht a ghabhann le háiteanna nó le pearsana nó le traidisiúin áirithe agus an chaoi a gcuireann se rúndiamhra na cinniúna daonna in iúl.

I ndeireadh báire, d'fhéadfadh feachtas fógartha an tSoiscéil a ghlacadh de chuspóir an Creideamh Caitliceach a shuíomh ina dhlúthchuid d'fhéiniúlacht na bpearsana agus an phobail. Ní foláir dá bharr sin é a shamhlú i gcomhthéacs na bhfachtóirí sin a bhfuil an fhéiniúlacht fréamhaithe iontu agus a chumann an chaoi a fhorbraíonn sé. Ní foláir toisí an ama agus an spáis a maireann an cine daonna iontu a naomhú ina gciall don spás sacráilte agus do rúndiamhair na heisceatolaíochta Críostaí.

Chun an chéadfaíocht chreidmheach sin a chruthú mar ithir don spioradáltacht agus mar dhlúthchuid den phearsantacht, ní leor an t-eolas intleachtúil; éilíonn sé go nglacfaí an mheanmanra seo mar shealúchas pearsanta agus mar chomhdhamhna den phearsantacht. D'aonfhocal amháin, ní foláir é a shúrac isteach le grá agus le dáimh. Is sa chomhthéacs seo freisin is gá fealsúnacht na scolaíochta Caitlicí a shuíomh – mar shás cruthaithe pobail seachas mar *ethos* doiléir domhínithe éigin.

Á luaithe a chuireann aigne den chineál sin fréamhacha síos sa phearsantacht óg, is amhlaidh is seasmhaí a iompaíonn sí amach go hiondúil. I gcás cultúir a bhfuil cumas ann, bíonn sí súite isteach ina heisint sa teaghlach i rith an aois linbh agus (cé nach cuí a leithéid seo a lua na saoltaí seo), bíonn sé de chomhartha sóirt i gcultúr dá leithéid é a bheith in ann scrúdú criticiúil a dhéanamh, agus más gá an diúltú a thabhairt do na fórsai sin a bheadh ina mbagairt ar a bhunluachanna. Ar ndóigh, i gcultúr a bhfuil cumas téarnaimh óraice ann, déantar neartú ar na luachanna sin trí theanga phobail a ndealraíonn fiú an fhoclaíocht agus an chomhréir inti a bheith ina mbábhún cosanta forimeallach don iontamhlú inmheánach sin. Ní hé atá i gceist cúrsaí propaganda nó níochán intinne an aos óig trí bhrú teaghlaigh nó sochaí. Is mó is cóir an próiséas seo a bheith ina fhianaise fhorimeallach ar dhlúthchaidreamh agus dáimh, é mar chuspóir aige i gcónaí féinmheas agus féinmhuinín a athchruthú sa duine agus sa phobal.

Ní eisceacht ar bith sa chomhthéacs seo luachanna agus cultúr an chreidimh. Is é atá sa tuairisc seo i láthair an cur-síos teoiriciúil idéalta ar thoscaí a seachadta, ach mar ábhar comparáide léiríonn sé éiginnteacht agus guagacht an chultúir in Éirinn sa lá atá inniu ann. Níl ach gur móide sin a chuireann sé ina luí orainn chomh leochaileach agus atá leagan cultúrtha na sochaí seo agus chomh haibrisc agus atá an bunús sóisialta a mbeadh aon fheachtas fógartha creidimh ag brath air.

D'ainneoin na n-ainneoin, is é ár ndualgas tabhairt faoin iarracht, óir, mar a deir an diagaire Francach: '(Urlabhra na críostaíochta), ní mór í a bheith iompaithe go toiliúil agus go nithiúil i dtreo an duine dhaonna agus an chine dhaonna, á mbreathnú i gcomhthéacs imeacht na staire agus chomhlíonadh forásach na gairme a fuair siad, d'fhonn an dínit is dual dóibh a bhunú ar Chríost. Sin samhailt na críostaíochta don duine agus foinse an daonnachais chríostaí.'[2]

Nó chun an coibhneas idir creideamh agus cultúr a chur ar bhealach eile, i bhfocail an Phápa nach maireann: 'An creideamh nach dtéarnaíonn ina chultúr, is creideamh é nach bhfuil glacadh leis go hiomlán, nach bhfuil tuigthe sa smaoineamh istigh, nach bhfuil tugtha in éifeacht go dílis sa saol.'[3]

[Gluais Ar Leathanach, 299.]

A Dualistic Theophany: Nature as Source of Fear and Love in Wordsworth

BRIAN COSGROVE

An early poem of Wordsworth's, published in the 1798 *Lyrical Ballads*, provides a representative example of what might be called a (specifically) Romantic pastoralism. In 'To My Sister', the speaker invites his sibling, on 'the first mild day of March', to 'Come forth and feel the sun'. This is not, however, a simple escape from the confinement of the domicile into the fresh air and open spaces of nature. A significant Romantic intensification is evident in the second stanza:

> There is a blessing in the air,
> Which seems a sense of joy to yield
> To the bare trees and the mountains bare
> And grass in the green field.

True, the wilfully simple language in the last two lines points to a traditional pastoralism in which sophistication and the possibly attendant corruption of innocence are to be held at bay. But in that second stanza, we must still pause to evaluate the precise force of the striking word, 'blessing' – however muted the word may be by the next line, telling us that such a blessing only 'seems' to yield 'a sense of joy'. For the larger claim for the sanative and restorative power of Nature is not to be denied, and emerges with some *éclat* in stanza six:

> Love, now a universal birth,
> From heart to heart is stealing,
> From earth to man, from man to earth;
> – It is the hour of feeling …

The harmony to be found in Nature is not simply a tranquil alternative to 'the din/Of towns and cities' ('Tintern Abbey', ll. 25–6). Rather, nature provides an occasion for the deep perception of an ultimate harmony here called 'Love': a love, moreover, that in the penultimate stanza is referred to

the blessed power that rolls
About, below, above ...

So in this intensely Romantic pastoralism, Nature is not just an aesthetic or soothing end in itself, but also mediates that deeper reality which is not, on the strictest empirical evidence, actually *there*.

We used to refer at moments such as these to Romantic 'pantheism'; there has emerged a reluctance, however, to use the term because it is less than accurate. Pantheism, according to dictionary definition, is the 'belief or philosophical theory that God and the universe are identical (implying a denial of the ... transcendence of God)', which is theologically too precise for Romanticism. The tendency now is to refer to panvitalism, a word suggesting, more neutrally, the life or energy in the whole of creation; and it can suggest a *universal (possibly divine) immanence*, while leaving open the question of transcendence. Thus in 'To My Sister' the positive life or energy called Love is indeed universal, 'stealing' from 'earth to man, from man to earth' in a grand, sustaining symbiosis. This, in short, is the Romantic belief in the 'One Life', which is given one of its most articulate formulations in a letter written by Coleridge to W. Sotheby on 10 September 1802. Referring to the poetry of William Bowles, Coleridge advocates an engagement with nature which, he feels, is missing in Bowles:

> Nature has her proper interest; & he will know what it is, who believes & feels, that every Thing has a Life of it's [sic] own, & that we are all *one Life*.
>
> (Letters, ed. Griggs, II, 864)

The letter in question later observes that in the Hebrew tradition it is in God that all things 'move & live, & *have* their being' – 'not *had* ... but *have*', Coleridge emphatically adds, in a rejection of the absentee God implicit in much eighteenth-century thinking (*ibid.*, 866). So here Coleridge does clearly make the 'One Life' dependent on the Judaeo–Christian Godhead – a position which, in fairness, Wordsworth would not necessarily have endorsed (prior, at least, to his turning to Christian belief after 1805).

There is a great climactic passage at the core of 'Tintern Abbey' which makes abundantly clear the centrality of panvitalism to Wordsworth's thought, and the possible theological implications of that panvitalism. This is the passage (ll. 94–102) where the poet tells us how, in his maturity, having left behind 'The coarser pleasures of my boyhood days', he has been privileged to sense in Nature:

> A presence that disturbs me with the joy
> Of elevated thoughts; a sense sublime
> Of something far more deeply interfused,
> Whose dwelling is the light of setting suns,
> And the round ocean and the living air,
> And the blue sky, and in the mind of man:
> A motion and a spirit, that impels
> All living things, all objects of all thought,
> And rolls through all things.

With the recognition that the energy which is diffused throughout nature likewise resides 'in the mind of man' the way is open for a creative interaction between Nature and the human Imagination. Thus the Imagination confronts what is (however mysterious) no longer an alien but an interpretable nature and can on occasion, at least, see (as 'Tintern Abbey' has it, l. 49) 'into the life of things'. And it is of great general significance that man can be emphatically 'at home' in this nature to which he is so intimately linked.

*

It is 'Tintern Abbey' that provides us with one of the central master-narratives in Wordsworth. In returning, in imaginatively re-created memory, to his earlier experiences with Nature, the poet establishes a principle of continuity between past and present, and, by extension, a basis on which to project an envisaged future. This means that Wordsworth's childhood is important to him, not primarily because of some archetypal notion of primal innocence, but because it was (he believed) in his childhood that the crucial, formative experiences occurred. 'The Child', as stated in the 'Rainbow' lyric, is 'father of the Man'. The most elaborate version of this master-narrative (which affirms continuity) is to be found in Wordsworth's subjective epic (and masterpiece), *The Prelude*. What threatens to fracture that sense of continuity is the crisis faced by the emerging adult, namely, the high hopes, followed by extreme confusion and disappointment, over the development and outcome of the French

Revolution. That crisis is resolved when the young man in his early twenties re-establishes organic connection with a former, more stable self, that has been nurtured by nature.

In 'Tintern Abbey', Nature in retrospect is unequivocally hailed as

> the nurse,
> The guide, the guardian of my heart, and soul
> Of all my moral being
>
> (ll. 109–111)

In Book I of *The Prelude*, the young Wordsworth is likewise seen to be subject to the 'ministry' of a Nature which, 'through many a year', haunted him among his 'boyish sports'. We have now, however, to deal with a significant shift of emphasis. We have seen how intimately in 'To My Sister' Nature is associated with harmony and tranquillity; and Book I of *The Prelude* does in fact retain this sense of Nature as a source of massive calm, conveying the essential stillness of Nature's 'high objects' and 'enduring things' (I, 409). But Nature also functions – and in the most telling way – as radical challenge or disturbance: even if the disturbance is finally interpreted in positive terms, as creative and (perhaps morally) educative. Yet one must acknowledge that there remains an undeniable sense of stress in such experience, a stress indicated in the simple four-letter word, 'fear'.

In Book I, following a lengthy preamble, the poet finally gets to grips with the highly disturbing personal experiences of Nature in his past:

> Fair seed-time had my soul, and I grew up
> Fostered alike by beauty and by fear …
>
> (ll. 301–302)

There follow three episodes recalling imaginative experience of a kind that is repeated throughout *The Prelude*. The most detailed of these in Book I is the third. The young boy one evening takes a boat (a 'pinnace') that is not his, and rows across the lake, fixing his eye 'Upon the summit of a craggy ridge' (l. 370). As he rows, the angle of his vision alters with his movement, and he is in effect subjected to an optical delusion:

> lustily
> I dipped my oars into the silent lake.

And, as I rose upon the stroke, my boat
Went heaving through the water like a swan;
When, from behind that craggy steep till then
The horizon's bound, a huge peak, black and huge,
As if with voluntary power instinct,[1]
Upreared its head. I struck and struck again,
And growing still in stature the grim shape
Towered up between me and the stars, and still,
For so it seemed, with purpose of its own
And measured motion like a living thing
Strode after me. With trembling oars I turned,
And through the silent water stole my way
Back to the covert of the willow tree;
There in her mooring-place I left my bark, –
And through the meadows homeward went, in grave
And serious mood ...

The aftermath is equally disturbing, as the boy's psyche struggles to cope with 'a dim and undetermined sense / Of unknown modes of being':

No familiar shapes
Remained, no pleasant images of trees,
Of sea or sky, no colours of green fields;
But huge and mighty forms, that do not live
Like living men, moved slowly through the mind
By day, and were a trouble to my dreams.

(ll. 373–400)

Since the boy has in effect stolen the boat, the experience might be interpreted as a salutary provocation of appropriate guilt; but such a trite formula fails to accommodate the poetic multidimensionality of the passage. More to the point, we have here a memorable example of what Frederick Garber identified as Wordsworth's 'manifold terror of otherness' (Garber, p.137). Nature, at times a calm source of nurturance, in intimate relation with man, can also manifest itself as sinister threat, and there is real panic in the passage ('I struck and struck again ...' refers to the oars beating the water, but it evokes the sense of struggle against an assailant). We may in any case recall that the word 'panic' derives from the nature-god Pan, whose awesome power might be felt in lonely natural places. No wonder that the preamble (ll. 301–2) speaks of the way the young boy was fostered by 'fear'.

One way of treating this type of experience is to refer to the Romantic sense of the sublime, the representative spokesman for which is Immanuel Kant. What appears to happen in the stolen boat episode is that the mind is shocked out of its perceptual complacency. So Kant sees the encounter with the sublime as the moment when the mind becomes aware of its own perceptual limitations and, in addition, is thereby humbled before *transcendent* possibilities. As Thomas Weiskel puts it: 'the defeat of the [merely] sensible imagination accomplishes subjectively the end of the natural order' (Weiskel, p.42). In the intense subjective experience of the sublime, the empirical world seems to disappear (Wordsworth might simply say 'disappears'), overwhelmed by an alternative perception. The end of the natural order of which Weiskel speaks is a source of a frightening sense of disorientation, but is also a prelude to an 'awesome', or even, in Kant's word, a 'devout' (Weiskel, p.42) acknowledgement of an order of reality *beyond the senses*. Weiskel, as a late twentieth-century sceptic, is less inclined than Kant to speak of pure transcendence, or to use such a term as 'devout'. We should note, however, that in a fragmentary prose work on *The Sublime and the Beautiful*, Wordsworth's suggestion that the experience of the sublime arises from an awareness of an 'external power, to a union with which we feel we can make no approximation, while it produces humiliation and submission, *reverence or adoration* ...' (italics added: *Prose Works*, II, 355). We are close here to Rudolf Otto's gloss on the 'mystical' character of 'the wrath of God' (Otto, p.100), which he relates to the *mysterium tremendum*: it is, he adds, 'an entirely non-[natural] or supernatural, that is, numinous quality' (ibid., p.13).

Weiskel summarises as follows: the sublime experience begins when the conventional 'readings of landscape', break down, and 'in that very collapse' is discovered 'another order of meaning' (p.22). We are then disposed to feel 'that behind the newly significant absence lurks a newly discovered presence ...' (p.28). In the boating-episode in *The Prelude*, the 'significant absence' of familiar objects ('No familiar shapes / Remained ...', ll. 394–5) heralds the entry into 'another order of meaning' ('huge and mighty forms that do not live / Like living men ...', ll. 398–9).

If the perceiving mind, empirically anchored, has been confounded, then that humbling of the habitual mind allows for the empowerment of the alternative mode of perception that the Romantics hail as the Imagination (or, *simpliciter*, vision). It is precisely in seeking a kind of fulfilment that ordinary 'reality' cannot provide that the Imagination declares its special status; and Weiskel rightly speaks (p.63) of the 'thirst for totality', for absolute fulfilment, awakened by the sense of the sublime. It is on some such basis that Wordsworth can declare as his credo: 'Our destiny, our being's heart and home, / Is with infinitude, and only there ...' (*The Prelude*, VI, 604–5).

*

By the time Wordsworth died in 1850, attitudes to nature had already begun to undergo a radical change. Such change is associated with the name of Darwin; but the fact is that *The Origin of Species* appeared in 1859 and that even before Darwinism proper, many of the ideas that we think of as Darwinian were already being explored by scientific thinkers. Such 'pre-Darwinians' included Sir Charles Lyell, a close and influential friend of Darwin (though he was never an enthusiast for the idea of evolution), whose three-volume *Principles of Geology* appeared in 1830–3; and Robert Chambers, who, in his *Vestiges of the Natural History of Creation* (1844), was in fact a powerful influence in popularising an evolutionary view of nature. For students of literature, the impact of their ideas is fully registered in Tennyson's *In Memoriam*, an elegy for his close friend Arthur Henry Hallam who died young in 1833. *In Memoriam* was published in the same year as Wordsworth's death, 1850; though it had been composed over many years prior to publication.

One of the most disturbing suggestions in these writers who so influenced Tennyson was that nature, and by extension the Author of nature, are indifferent to the welfare of all living things. Nature is seen as a blind or random process in which neither gifted individuals (such as Hallam was, especially for Tennyson) nor entire species (plural) have any special claim on a loving Creator. 'It is clear,' wrote Chambers (p.377), 'that the individual ... is to the Author of Nature a consideration of inferior moment.' Chambers proceeds to compare whatever 'system' can be found in nature to 'a lottery, in which every one has the like chance of drawing the prize' – or, we might add, the like chance of survival (see Ricks's annotation, *The Poems of Tennyson*, II, 371). Lyell had anticipated this radical lack of confidence in the so-called natural order when extending such scepticism from the individual to the species. Thus his second volume has this quotation on its title-page: 'It is not only the individual that perishes, but whole species' (see *The Poems of Tennyson*, II, 372n.). Subsequently the emergent science of palaeontology would confirm, in its discovery of fossils, the reality of mass extinctions.

In Tennyson the traditional plaint of elegy that neither nature nor the gods could save the lost loved one is raised to new pitch of intensity, with painfully explicit rebuttals of a wholly alien nature as a source of sustenance. Nature is seen as a 'phantom', a 'hollow form with empty hands' (*In Memoriam*, section 3); moreover, far from being in any sense 'theophanic', nature even in its apparent design carries no guaranteed revelation: 'I found Him not in world or sun, / Or eagle's wing, or insect's eye …' (section 124). The God that Tennyson continues, with difficulty, to believe in is more purely transcendent; or if immanent, immanent in the human heart, not in nature. At the end of section 124, he compares his lamentations to those of a child who still 'knows his father near', but his conclusion suggests a more remote deity: 'And out of darkness came the hands / That reach thro' nature, moulding men'. The 'darkness' is striking; but even more significant is the immense shift in emphasis indicated by the preposition 'through'. It is entirely inconceivable that Tennyson could say, as Wordsworth does in 'Tintern Abbey', 'I have felt / A presence …' whose 'dwelling' is in both nature and man.

The Contemplative Christian Lawyer

MARY REDMOND

My first piece for *The Furrow* appeared in 1978, while I was still in my twenties. It was part of a series on Christianity and my title was 'The Lawyer as a Christian'. Fr Ronan Drury, Professor of Homiletics at Maynooth, had recently succeeded the first editor of *The Furrow* after the latter's tragic death. The length and first class quality of Ronan's editorship is remarkable in journal publishing in any subject. I am delighted to record my appreciation for him and for *The Furrow*, which I anticipate eagerly every month.

For this *Festschrift* I decided to revisit the article. It was not until the mid-1980s that I traded my academic gown for practice and started a real 'apprenticeship'. The first thing that struck me on rereading it was how much the lawyer's landscape in Ireland has changed in less than forty years. I believe 'contemplative law' is an idea whose time has come for serious consideration in this country. I say 'serious' as not long ago this suggestion might have appeared 'wacky,' today it might be seen as trendy. In fact it is neither.

The contemplative lawyer is someone who will have taken meditation instruction and who incorporates it into her daily life. I am not advocating a choice between contemporary or contemplative law. Not unlike the way an experienced lawyer-mediator might, the contemplative lawyer would leverage contemporary law but in a new way. Lawyer and client would be mindful of each other, the nature of the client's problem would not change, the appropriate solutions might be different[1] and how to deal with them certainly would. The changes the lawyer would experience within herself over time would not only be beneficial, but pivotal. And her work would likely encompass all of her subject, the ethics of it as well as its reform.

There is a growing literature on the contemplative lawyer, particularly in the US. Several lawyers from major law firms and students from Yale, Columbia, Denver, Hastings, Miami, Missouri-Columbia, North Carolina, Stanford and Suffolk have taken (in most cases, 'mindfulness') meditation instruction on campus. This is sometimes part of law school courses. They join thousands in the corporate sector, in athletics, in health-care settings, those connected with particular groups, or activities, such as environmental organisations, philanthropists and other leaders, prisoners, and the homeless.[2] In recent times phrases such as *therapeutic jurisprudence, holistic lawyering, collaborative law, transformative mediation* have become commonplace in other jurisdictions and they are making an appearance here as well.[3]

Little known but significant is the growing success of 'contemplative medicine' in Ireland.[4] The Royal College of Physicians started a twelve-day accredited course in 2013 called, *Meditation: Healing from the Centre*, with Laurence Freeman OSB. A second course is now available. The course offers the gift of attention at all levels of life, personal and professional. By the end of their training, 'participants will have improved self-awareness and knowledge, greater resilience and ability to handle stress, developed a regular practice that trains the mind, received benefits in [their] personal relationships, confidence in sharing meditation practice and skills to teach meditation.'

Laurence Freeman is a Benedictine monk, and Director of The World Community for Christian Meditation[5] (WCCM) a contemporary, contemplative community now in more than a hundred countries. The form of meditation to which I was introduced over five years ago was Christian Meditation, which is a 'mantra meditation'. John Main,[6] who founded what is now the WCCM in 1975, described meditation as a discipline, and it is a discipline that we are not used to. Sitting upright is a first step. Secondly, a person must learn to say their word. The word he recommended was *maranatha – ma-ra-na-tha*, an Aramaic word, the language that Jesus spoke, and it means *Come, Lord*.

Other contemplative practices may produce some of the same or similar outcomes to those produced by Christian meditation. 'Mindfulness' meditation, best known perhaps, may be distinguished from concentration meditation, where the meditator focusses attention exclusively on a mantra (as in Christian meditation), or an image or a mental state. The many types of contemplative or spiritual practices are beyond the scope of this article.

To illustrate the potential differences meditation might make, picture the following in the law offices of a private practitioner. An employer client has come for advice having received a letter of resignation from a senior manager who has been on sick leave for almost a year. The client's fear is that the company is looking down the barrel of a smoking gun: a claim for constructive dismissal. The senior manager writes that the work-related stress he is and has been under rules out any prospect of a return to work.

The lawyer hears two important words in what the client is saying, 'resignation' and 'stress'. She quickly transforms what might be a complex human situation into dry facts that fit legal rules bearing on those words. The lawyer will ask about the senior manager's contract of employment, its notice requirements and grievance procedures. She will ask whether the senior manager invoked the company's grievance procedures. No? First hint of dissatisfaction was the resignation letter? Tick, a point in the client's favour. What about the sick leave, when did it start, and crucially, what reason was given for the illness by the senior manager's doctor? The client will produce all medical certificates received. If there is no reference to 'work related' stress that will likely mean another tick for the client. A claim for stress might be started in the civil courts, further questions will probe details there.

The lawyer is doing what she is trained to do, namely, applying to the facts general principles of law enacted by Parliament or decided by judges. The client may venture regret at having received the senior manager's resignation. He may even be experiencing anger or remorse or emotional pain at having to consult the lawyer in the first place. The lawyer's task is to judge whether there might be liabilities for her client and, if so, what protection or remedies the law prescribes. She herself may be stressed, perhaps this is the first meeting in a day full of 'back to backs' or she has not yet received an affidavit in another case which must be served by close of business that day. She makes a note on her attendance pad to chase up the barrister. She jots down other matters requiring her attention that have nothing to do with the client before her.

Apart from the fact that the lawyer is not always present to her client, she is thinking about external, not internal, sources of satisfaction for him: what does the law say about the relevant facts. Granted the client may be less interested in internal sources of satisfaction but the lawyer is assuming that he and the senior manager are or are likely to be adversaries, in other words, that there may be an ensuing claim where one disputant will win and one will lose. Victory for the winning employer/employee respectively is either a judgement of no liability or a money judgement. Excluded from the money rules are non-material values such as loyalty, love, compassion, dignity which very rarely transmute into justification for money damages.

Imagine the lawyer, while not abandoning her training to put people and events into categories that are legally consistent, focussing on persons as well as acts. In practice this would require a reversal of the present concentration on the lawyer's cognitive capabilities, and a cultivation of emotional facilities. Research elsewhere shows a business case for this: it helps avoid excessive adversarialism, delays, soaring costs, solutions that may be less than best, client as well as lawyer dissatisfaction. In the scenario just described, with a deeper connection and a quest for her client's real needs, the lawyer would have picked up on any positive statements about the senior manager and the client's regret at seeing the manager leave. This would have presented the client with the possibility of an entirely different route within a revisioned lawyer–client relationship, collaborative and participatory.

At present there is a drive to introduce mediation into legal disputes. The Mediation Bill before the Oireachtas is an example, and one objective in the reform of Ireland's employment laws is to persuade parties to settle their differences closer to the workplace. But for as long as the lawyer's traditional approach, illustrated above, dominates, mediation is unlikely to be the lawyer's first choice, even where it may be the most appropriate solution for the parties. In Justice Janine Geske's article, footnote three, she describes how Marquette Law School, where she is Distinguished Professor of Law, looks at restorative justice through the specific study of that subject as well as by studying skills in other forms of the alternative dispute resolution curriculum such as mediation. 'The listening skills, the techniques of ensuring that someone knows they have been truly heard and understood, and the designing of a process that can best address the conflict … Future lawyers should understand the importance of those skills …'

One Yale law graduate, who attended a meditation retreat, reflected afterwards that, as lawyers see themselves as master strategists and problem solvers, they should realise that a contemplative approach is the key to solving 'our own chief problem: the meaning, purpose and manner of our lives'. Any revision of the lawyer/client relationship has to begin with the lawyer seeking this key. Most of us, during and after our education, have been taught to forget that inner treasure some call Soul. Although often allied to a religious tradition or belief, Soul is not necessarily so. Meditation facilitates the journey inwards, thus inevitably bringing us to consider 'the meaning, purpose and manner of our lives'.

Often, the manner of our lives requires attention; all too often it remains unattended to. There are no statistics in Ireland about lawyers' stress or anxiety levels, their divorce rates, or substance abuse, although the pressures here are little different from other countries where statistics attest to the degree to which all of these exist. Law Care is an advisory and support service offered to lawyers in Ireland and the UK, funded by professional bodies, designed to help lawyers, their families and staff to deal with such issues. Undoubtedly some would prefer approaches such as counselling, psychotherapy or Prozac and these may be entirely appropriate in many cases. But meditation is a daily practice, hence *a way of life* and, as such, it seems to me to command a place on any list.

Looking back, it seems that the concept of the contemplative Christian lawyer resonates with 'The Lawyer as a Christian' and joins up some of the dots in my article of 1978. Back then, quoting Thomas Merton, I lamented the imminence of 'an age of technological barbarism', of people adoring the machine and of engaging in a cult of work for its own sake although the machine had not yet taken over law practice in Ireland. That could not be said today, a fact self-evident on the desktop of any lawyer, with its browsers and emails, icons and folders about client work, practice management, 'knowledge' (precedents and documents), house styles, billing hours, and so on. It is ever more important today to 'awaken and develop the personal dimension in this technological world' as Professor Enda McDonagh has written,[7] to counteract an ever-increasing focus on end-products and results. Meditation is one way to awaken and develop the personal dimension in this technological age, with its emphasis on presence of and awareness to, oneself and others.

John Main quotes St Peter (1 Pet 4:7–11) in *The Way of Unknowing*:[8] 'Above all keep your love for one another at full strength … Do you give service? Give it in the strength which God supplies.' Translated, speak out about your discipline and give the best service you can for others. This encompasses what is on your desk and surely, too, law reform, and legal ethics.

In 1978, I cannot say what degree of trust the public had in lawyers but without doubt it was a great deal higher than today. Yet even then, it seemed to me, legal ethics was important, as if a moral sense is missing among lawyers, the spirit of the law is gone. This means, among other things, for the lawyer not to be a pure technician of law 'in whose hands justice suffers immensely'. The pure technician lawyer is the professional fluent with section this and that but who does not or can not stand back and ask the simple question: what is an appropriate solution here for the client, let alone the parties? Such a solution may not consist merely in the lawyer's answering questions put by the client; often that is only part of the service. It is fair to say that 'justice under law' is not a tea-room topic for lawyers. But it is unfair to criticise this when, still, legal ethics consists in the main of professional norms for law practice[9] and is not taught as a discrete course to law students.

A lawyer once commented to me that he feared meditation would somehow make him compassionate. How could he conduct an effective cross-examination in the interests of his client if he were *compassionate*? I responded that I thought precisely the opposite, is true. Compassion enables us to recognise injustice, to name it with courage, and to act with strong skill (not ever, of course, to 'fillet the witness'). Many of us as law students were motivated by such feelings.

Does meditation make a person think only of himself? John Main, echoing St Paul's 'The love of Christ urges us on' (2 Cor 5–14) says 'If our life is rooted in Christ ... then we need have no anxiety about regulating our action. Our action will always spring from and be informed and shaped by that love. Indeed, the more active we are, the more important it is that our action springs from and is grounded in contemplation. And contemplation means deep, silent, communion; knowing who we are. Knowing who we are by being who we are' (*The Way of Unknowing*, footnote eight above).

In 1978, I started my article by saying that the lawyer as Christian is more important for what he is than for what he *does*. For every Christian 'being' takes precedence over 'doing' or 'having'. I did not understand as clearly then what 'being' might involve. Not forgetting about judging, acting and doing, of course, but 'being', journeying into the quiet in stillness, and as a result feeling and performing better, deriving more job satisfaction, being present to oneself and to the client, seeing things as they actually are, having the balance to make fully informed decisions, moving away from the lawyer's win/lose paradigm.

Might Law Care, or one or both of the professional bodies in Ireland consider helping lawyers to *be* as well as to *do*?

Living the Questions

CATHERINE TWOMEY

I have come so that they may have life and have it to the full – Jn 10:10

> ... the point is to live everything. Live the questions now. Perhaps then,
> someday far in the future, you will gradually, without even noticing it,
> live your way into the answer.
> – Rainer Maria Rilke in *Letters to a Young Poet*, 1903

When asked to contribute to this Festschrift for the redoubtable Ronan Drury, I cast around for a fitting theme for this inadequate token. *The Furrow* has been a small but significant presence in my life for the best part of forty years – and the ground it has broken open has brought stimulation, spiritual sustenance and perhaps above all, validation of my own experience that faith is not always nor often, simple. Therefore, I offer little more than a questioning piece.

To be a young Catholic primary school teacher in the 1970s and 1980s was to be expected to wear a uniform of conformity in religious thought and action. In my time in college, in the early seventies, the message to students was unequivocal and stark – failing Religion (or Irish) in end-of-year exams resulted in expulsion. No mercy was shown as these subjects were considered to be of such fundamental importance that anyone who failed them was simply not worthy of a second chance. That said, my all-too-brief two years at St Patrick's College, Drumcondra was a roller-coaster ride through an education that was headily more liberal than anything I had encountered during secondary school. Shocked by the philosophy lecturer's positive portrayal of Karl Marx, I wondered, leaving the lecture hall, how this man would continue to be employed in a Catholic college? Marx, after all, from the little we studied in secondary school, was just about the devil incarnate! As I waited for him to be fired, I was mystified by his equally enthusiastic lecture the following week on St Thomas Aquinas! What was this man about? He wasn't afraid to examine the elements of atheism and belief, and place them before us. This was my first exposure to objectivity and as the scales fell from my eyes, I realised how much of our schooling had been indoctrination and how indoctrination results in infantilised thinking.

Gradually, a sense of incipient new freedoms dawned. After all, I was among the first female students to be admitted (and welcomed) into that all-male bastion. I became an atheist briefly, then agnostic (there are times when I wonder if I still am) and my worried parents urged me to 'talk to a priest'. I had several chats with the chaplain of the house to which I was assigned, during which he, wisely, said little, listened a lot and seemed more interested in the poetry I had started to write and how I was getting along socially, than in setting me on the right track vis-à-vis God and the Church! I continued to go to Mass because I didn't want to upset my family and, of course, studied the Religious Education module, passed my exams and got my first job in my old school.

Once out of college and in the system charged with catechising successive classes of children, a teacher's deeply felt questions about God or morality or even religious practice were precluded. If they were voiced at all, many questions were never properly heard because they were dismissed as only 'doubts' which even the saints had but they always came around in the end (why else would they have been canonised?). The 'simple faith' was commended to us all and held up as the ideal. There was little or no acknowledgement of the existence of a spirit of enquiry. At best, lip service was paid to questioning, and answers were not so much given as respectful, honest responses in the course of a dialogue but rather, with the aim of reining in the questioner and preventing him or her from straying any further from the fold.

There is a method currently popular for growing carrots to give them a healthy start. Sow the seed in a length of guttering filled with a layer of soil. When the young plants' leafy tops are a few inches high, ease the carrot plants, soil and all into a drill made in the ground where the tap roots are allowed to develop by reaching deep into the soil. If the carrots are left too long in the guttering, the tops will look similar to the ones in the ground but the roots will be stunted. So it was with we teachers, many of whom, in a repressive climate where fear of genuine exploration was rampant, learned to keep our beliefs and practices, or lack of same, to ourselves, but outwardly conformed to the expected role and image.

A glaring paradox was that the then 'new' curriculum of 1971 urged teachers to 'arouse and stimulate the child's interest ... to cultivate an enquiring attitude of mind' thus ensuring exploration, understanding and real learning. Questioning was seen as integral to the learning process and learning itself was to be more democratic with the teacher as co-learner, rather than the expert with all the answers. Yet there remained a deep and ingrained fear of questioning among school authorities at the time. Once, some years later, after a Board of Management meeting, I and another Board member, a local businessman, were standing next to the Reverend Chairman, over the customary cup of tea, when the latter gloomily pronounced that 'the trouble with young people nowadays is that they are being taught to question'. He blamed it on the aforementioned 'discovery methods'. Summoning my courage and idealism, I replied 'But surely, Father, that's the point of education?' He shot me a withering look, promptly turned his back on me and continued to talk to the businessman, cutting me out of the conversation.

I was interested to discover, recently, that in the same year of the publication of that primary school curriculum, Gabriel Daly wrote in *The Furrow*:

> A serious obligation lies on the shoulders of us priests and religious in this matter. We have to see to it that our preaching and teaching does not unwittingly promote unbelief by our failure to deal with the questions that people are asking. We have obligations, serious obligations, towards those members of our congregations and classes *who are asking searching questions*. [My italics] To regard such questions as an attack on the Church's authority would be a serious misreading of the situation. These questions go far deeper than that. We can, of course, continue to preach only to those of untroubled faith. It will save us a lot of trouble.[1]

It was assumed that the nation's primary teachers were universally of one mind, and if they weren't, they should be, of the institutional one, that is. Why was it that the spirit of enquiry aspired to in the secular curriculum was never considered important for the ongoing education of teachers of the religion programme? In fact, at the time Fr Daly offered an answer, but was anyone reading him?

> … for we may unconsciously suspect that attending to the unbelief of others *will stir up in our own hearts and minds an answering chord of unbelief from which we intuitively shy away*. [My italics] The fact may well be that we do not really want to face the possibility that belief, real belief, involves a lot more than the acceptance of a list of doctrines. It is possible to accept the Church's teaching as one would the membership rules of a club, but this would not be faith.[2]

How often in the years that have passed have I heard from podium, pulpit, discussion group and staffroom extended metaphors of club, football or hurling team used to describe and circumscribe the people of God, from lay and religious alike, phrases like 'when you sign up, you play by the rules'.

I noticed often a sort of resentment that sometimes prevailed amongst those who went to Mass every Sunday towards those who didn't, when they came to present their children for the sacraments. I believe this is partly what lies behind the feeling amongst many primary teachers and some clergy, that schools should not be involved in sacramental preparation any more – The cry goes up: 'What's the point? The parents aren't bringing them to Mass. Then, when they do, they don't know what it's about.'

But what is it about, really? Pádraig Daly reflects on the words of Fr Herbert McCabe: 'The whole of our faith is the belief that God loves us: I mean there just isn't anything else', which he uses as an epigraph to his poem:

FIRST COMMUNIONS

Can it matter,
In God's enormity,
That few who watch
Aglow in the light of a child,

Know the why of the bread,
Have any prayer but, 'Thanks'?[3]

As I said earlier in this article, there have been times in my life when I could not, in all honesty, say an unqualified 'yes' to the question of whether or not I believed in God and I am sure I am not alone in this. However, during those times, I was often surprised by a need to give thanks to some entity for the many blessings in my life, for the love of family and friends, for the privileges and opportunities I had been given, for my health, for the myriad small delights in days or weeks. Call it positive thinking, but could I have stumbled into prayer?

If someone who doesn't normally attend church, presents their child for the sacraments, they are sometimes asked if they believe in God. For many people, faith in God is not simple and if, as we say, God is Love, how can the parent of that child be refused or asked to leave? If questions must be asked, ones closer to the heart of the matter might be: 'Do you love your child? Do you want the best for him or her?' Most of us are not able to express the complexity and scope of our deepest feelings adequately when it comes to each other, so how can we attempt to account for our relationship with God, tentative or otherwise, with the blunt tools of yes/no answers?

'The priest may have to dig deep in order to find the energy and gentle humanity which can enable him to enter into the joy of the family and lead them imaginatively through the rich experience of baptism' wrote Michael Olden in *The Furrow* (February 2011) during which he suggested that truly effective ministers need to develop a 'liturgy of the heart'.

When I think back on the times I felt the urge to give thanks to no one in particular, these were when I felt truly myself, free of asking, free of striving, free of worry, free of anger. This could be dismissed as some sort of spiritual etiquette but it has brought me from the threshold into a sense, at times, of being enveloped by the mystery of the Eucharist given to us through the ancient and sustaining staples of bread and wine. Do we try to pin down, to limit the transforming power of the sacraments?

The phrase 'cultural Catholics' has been used disparagingly to describe those of 'vestigial faith' who take a more relaxed view of church attendance and rules. Culture, however, is a very powerful force and, in an atmosphere of love and generosity of spirit, may encompass what endures when doctrines fail to convince. Two thousand years of Christianity is as much a culture embodying a religion as the religion itself, and not to be dismissed. What is perceived as the vestiges of someone's faith today may be its green shoots tomorrow.

In my opinion, there were two seminal events within the Church that changed the face of Irish Catholicism in the last fifty years. The first one was Vatican II, whose spirit has yet to flower fully but nevertheless brought the people into the liturgy and the liturgy to the people. The second was the catastrophic cover up of child abuse. How much did the culture of passive acceptance and failure to think critically contribute to this situation and in the words of the Children's Penitential Rite, to the failure 'to show love', let alone justice?

As an institution, the Church seems to value conformity and orthodoxy at the expense of flexibility and creative thinking. Often, there's an overemphasis on rubrics, which of course have their place, but are not so important that, in the aftermath of the introduction of the revised Mass responses, one well-intentioned, but perhaps over-zealous celebrant kept interrupting the liturgy to remind the congregation to give the correct response! In these times, the pressing need, as I see it, is to care for the tree rather than polish a few of its leaves. In the seaside parish where I now live, in a wise and imaginative move, over ten years ago, it was decided to celebrate a Sunday Mass for the months of July and August in a space, close to the shore and open to the elements and to all passers-by. It brought people together in a way that was impossible in the cavernous parish church. The weather was almost always benign and in the sun and shade of the early morning, with the sound of the waves rising and falling, it was not hard to imagine the resurrected Christ on the shore behind us inviting us to breakfast. Maybe instead of lamenting the fall-off in numbers coming to Mass and struggling to maintain a certain number of parish Masses, more creative ways of setting the Eucharist free among the people might be explored. If the numbers turning up to, for example, graveyard Masses around the country are anything to go by, considerable interest is still there. Notwithstanding the shortage of priests, there may be something of a bunker mentality at work, where

> our temptation may be to try to 'protect' our faith by avoiding the questions which life today poses for faith. If we do this, we are like the man in the parable who buried the talent in the ground and earned for himself one of Christ's sternest rebukes. Our faith is given not to be locked away from prying eyes but to be put into circulation for the good of all God's people. We are not free to contract out of the struggle for relevance, precisely because we are ambassadors for Christ who makes his appeal through us. It is not permissible for us to hoard our own faith while glumly reflecting on the decline of faith in the world at large and moralising about the permissive society. Our commission is, after all, to go to that world and preach Christ crucified with joy and enthusiasm. Faith is the joyful denial of atheism.[4]

Forty or so years on, Ireland has gone from a largely homogeneous to a more multicultural society. Information technology has helped learning to become more democratic, with the internet and social media exerting huge influence, for better or for worse, over people's behaviour and lives. The commitment to church-going has waned. Interest in atheism seems to be growing although the default disposition of the human being since the dawn of time would seem to be a religious one. Confusion reigns between pluralism and secularism. The move by a society, educated and politicised by Christianity, towards one that attempts to airbrush references to its Christian heritage out of the picture, is worrying because of its shallow trendiness or fundamentalist simplemindedness, or both, masquerading as inclusiveness. 'A people without history is not redeemed from time' wrote T.S. Eliot (*The Four Quartets:* 'Little Gidding'). Without embracing the past that has shaped us, we remain confined by the present and perhaps, lost to the future. It is both ironic and reassuring to find that some of the staunchest defenders of Christianity's contribution to western civilisation, and to the world, are themselves atheists[5] but as Enda McDonagh has written (*The Furrow*, May 2011) 'the reign and reach of the Spirit of Christ and of God goes further than any religion, to the very ends of creation, at whose origins and in whose maintenance that same Spirit was and is active!'

I have been struck by the pertinence of Gabriel Daly's article on 'Prayer and Asceticism', forty-three years on. For his thirty-seven of those years as editor of *The Furrow*, Ronan Drury has facilitated our access to a plethora of inspiring writers, a tiny sample of which I refer to in this piece. In addition, he has kept a strong warp-thread on the theme of prayer running through its fabric. I think it is fitting that I should conclude with an apt reminder from Billy Swan in his article, 'Prayer Our Salvation' (*The Furrow*, June 2014):

> It takes broken soil to produce a crop, broken clouds to give rain, broken grain to give bread, broken bread to give strength.

Have we any prayer but 'Thanks'?

Ageing Titans: Church and State in Twenty-First Century Ireland[1]

TONY MCNAMARA

Consider the following two *vignettes*. One: As late as 1956, Richard Mulcahy, Fine Gael Minister for Education, saw himself as 'a kind of dungaree man' or 'plumber' who would 'take the knock out of the pipes', but would refrain from 'pontificating' on the deeper philosophical issues of education. He was careful to point out that teachers, syllabuses and textbooks in every branch of education should be informed by the 'spirit' underlying the Catholic conception of education. Second: In 2014, Ruairí Quinn, Labour Minister for Education, suggested that time devoted to religious education in our schools might be better used giving additional tuition in mathematics. On the face of it we are looking here at a shift in the balance of power between two important pillars of Irish society. I will contend in this essay that the changes are more complex than a mere shift in power between two institutions. I will contend that the nation state is morphing into a market state, while the church looks as if it is on the cusp of inevitable fundamental change. I will conclude that the relationship between these two institutions is changing radically and suggest that the challenge for both institutions is to embrace the reality of pluralism.

A Changed State

I suggest that the nature of the state in 'western' democracies has changed significantly in the past twenty years and that this is reflected in Ireland. Effectively the day of the 'nation state' in a democracy where political parties represented citizens' views, and governed accordingly when elected, has passed. What we have evolved to is a 'market state' where constitutional democracy – government *for* the people – has replaced popular democracy – government *by* the people. I will use two authors to underpin this suggestion, Peter Mair the renowned Irish political scientist and the American constitutional lawyer Philip Bobbit.

Mair (2013)[2] argues that, in the last decades of the twentieth century, political parties withdrew from the realm of civil society and moved to the realm of government. Party-voter distances increased and party-party differences shrunk (loc. 1255). Differences in policy goals seemed to matter less than shared cross-party ambition for office (loc. 931). Witness in Ireland the various combinations that have made up our coalitions in recent years, when sixty years ago 'coalition' was synonymous with Fine Gael–Labour. Opposition, structurally constituted, increasingly comes from outside party politics, whereas within politics parties it is either governing or waiting to govern. 'The articulation of popular interests and demands now occurs more and more outside the party world, with the preferred role of parties being that of the receiver of signals that emanate from the media or the wider society (loc. 1387).' In effect, citizens are becoming spectators rather than participants in government. One effect of this is that indifference to party politics presents us with either populist or ostensibly non-political experts (loc. 392). Decision-making authority is passed over to non-partisan bodies in which binding rules are adopted which deny discretion to the government of the day. In Ireland, An Bord Pleanála, the various Ombudsman offices, The Irish Human Rights and Equality Commission and the array of regulators that we have, come to mind, to name but a few. Mair concludes, in agreement with the American political scientist Russel Hardin, that governments are no longer in the business of redistributing resources or meeting collective needs. The issue of planning versus the markets has been settled – in favour of the markets (Hardin, 2000, p.32). Witness the central place of opinion polling and focus groups in the formation of the stances taken by Irish political parties.

Coming from an altogether different discipline, Bobbit (2002) arrives at similar conclusions about the state and the markets. For him the nation state in our time is in decline. It is withering and being replaced by the market state. The nation state is threatened on a number of fronts: (1) It can no longer guarantee the security of its citizens. Weapons of mass destruction mean that borders are no longer secure. Security threats do not even necessarily come now from other states. (2) Trans-national threats – disease, displacement of populations, climate changes – also ignore borders. Consider the horrendous weather events in Ireland in the early months of 2014 – seen by many as the result of climate change over which, on our own, we have no control. (3) In welfare matters the nation state is also vulnerable. Bad monetary policies anywhere in the world are reflected within minutes on Reuters screens in the trading rooms of the world. The control of the private movement of capital has given way to the virtually uninhibited flow of capital internationally. A consequence is a threat to the ability of nation states to provide continuous improvement to the welfare of their peoples. The recession in Ireland, from which we are still suffering, is an all-too sore reminder of this. Indeed the prime role played by the so-called Troika in Ireland comes to mind here as well. Indeed the pervasive influence of bodies such as the International Monetary Fund, the World Trade Organisation and the European Union are ready examples of nation states being at the mercy of trans-national organisations, not to mention trans-national commercial organisations. (4) Again, at the level of communications, there is erosion, erosion of national cultures. Equality between ethnic groups is a threat to the traditional nation-state. Immigration to Ireland, sometimes accompanied by xenophobia, comes to mind.

Bobbit is suggesting that no nation can assure its citizens of protection from weapons of mass destruction. No nation state can effectively control its own currency. No nation state can protect its own culture and its own way of life. No nation state can protect its citizens from trans-national threats such as disease or climate-related threats. Hence, the market state depends on international capital markets and multinational business to create stability. Its governance institutions are less representative than those of the nation state. It assesses its economic success in terms of the extent that it can secure more goods and services for its citizens, but it minimises its distributive function. It exists to maximise the opportunities of its people, and its yardstick for evaluation will be the quantifiable. It will be largely indifferent to norms of justice; as a corollary it will be difficult to get people to make sacrifices for a state that does not promote their cultural values. In summary it will exist to reflect, implement and diversify individual choice.

A recent opinion piece in *The Economist* (2014) echoes some of the thoughts above; it suggests that the way in which democracy is evolving today 'can result in a toxic and unstable mixture: dependency on government on the one hand, and disdain for it on the other. The dependency forces government to over-expand and over-burden itself, while the disdain robs it of its legitimacy'.

I am suggesting that we in Ireland fit the picture painted here of a hollowed out democracy acting as a market state. And it is to this 'state', or perhaps state of affairs, that we must look when we come to examine church/state relations.

A Changed Church[3]

Before turning to look at the church as it is evolving, I want to allude briefly to a vital aspect of the context in which it is evolving – the secular and secularism, borrowing from the work of the Canadian philosopher Charles Taylor in my comments.

Taylor (2007) asks: 'why was it virtually impossible not to believe in God in, say, 1500 in our Western society, while in 2000 many of us find this not only easy, but even inescapable?' (p.25). His response (in a major work[4] to which I can only do passing justice in this short piece) is to explain the crossover from an enchanted world to a disenchanted one. In the enchanted world of our ancestors, the natural world testified to divine purpose; God was implicated in the very existence of society; and the enchanted world was one of spirits, demons and moral forces. In the enchanted world there were outside forces impinging on the world. In the disenchanted world only those things that are in our minds, that we know, have reality. And crucially we have come to accept certain social imaginaries.

A social imaginary is a way in which people conceive of their social existence and it describes how they see themselves fitting together with others. It is a way everyday people think of their social surroundings, based on theories often only in the possession of a small minority, and which make possible common practices and a widely shared sense of legitimacy. Social imaginaries are both descriptive and prescriptive. They describe the way people believe things to be, but also how people think they should be. Taylor outlines three crucial social imaginaries.

The Economy

The 'economy', one of the imaginaries through which people see their society, is an interlocking set of activities of production, exchange and consumption, which form a system with its own laws and its own dynamic. The 'invisible hand' operates, securing mutual benefit, while individuals pursue their own ends. The crucial factor here is that this enmeshing of individuals in mutual benefit is not an order of collective action. Indeed the 'market' is the negation of collective action (Taylor 2007, p.183).

The Public Sphere

There are numerous public spaces where debate takes place, but there is an over-arching common space where members of society meet through a variety of media – print, electronic and face-to-face[5] – to discuss matters of common interest leading to a common mind. This is a locus which potentially can engage everybody and lead to a common mind. Thus constituted, it has acquired a normative status; government ought to listen to it.

Crucially, this has come to be seen as an essential feature of a free society – and this public sphere is outside power. It is not itself an exercise of power. It is an 'outside' thing that checks power, and it is constituted solely by the common actions of discussion and debate themselves. There is no need for some action-transcendent or higher order power to instantiate it. It is instantiated by itself, by the discussion in the public sphere.

The Sovereign People

The third imaginary which Taylor suggests underpins the modern self-perception of society is the concept of the 'sovereign people'. Hierarchy, kings, lords and masters have given way to this concept of the sovereign people. An idealised Natural Law has been appealed to; for instance in the USA, 'truths held self-evident' are evinced by 'we the people'. The shift has been to see elections as the only source of legitimate power.

The Direct Access Society

The three social imaginaries described above – the economy, the public sphere and the sovereign people – now underpin how we see our society operating. They have led us to a direct access society. No longer is access to opportunity mediated by some higher power as was the case in previous vertical societies. The principle of modern horizontal society is radically different. Each of us is equally distant from the centre. The three imaginaries are radically secular, in the sense of being of this age, and needing no action-transcendent origin.

And herein lies the crucial claim. Our secular age, as opposed to the pre-modern society of our ancestors, is one where no action-transcendent involvement is seen to be needed. It is this that makes it a radically secular age. And it is in this age that the church operates.

I suggest that the pervasiveness of the secular age mentality is far more important in coming to an understanding of the reduced state of the church in Ireland today than is the sexual violence against children scandal or any other shock. True, church insiders have experienced a catalogue of scene-changing events. To quote Mayo priest Brendan Hoban (2013), they have experienced ... 'the accumulated wreckage of the last few decades: paedophile scandals, failures of church leadership, vocations in free fall, haemorrhaging of our congregations: rising age-levels of priests ...' (p.605). But I think that, in line of what I have presented in the last few paragraphs above, Hoban's insight is correct, and more telling, when he observes:

'There's an immense gap between the Catholic Church and the "lived" lives of our people and we need a new approach, a new language to traverse it' (p.616).

Two further developments seem to me to be central when attempting to foresee how the church in Ireland will develop over the coming years. The first of these is the problem of a community dependent on a cultic priesthood which is fast disappearing. The strength of the church indeed is often measured by attendance figures at the weekly Eucharist. In the likely coming scenario when there will not be a weekly Eucharist, and where attendances continue to fall as the church population ages, there will be a crying need to redefine church. Thomas Whelan, Associate Professor of Theology at the Milltown Institute, suggests in this context that the current panic at the falling numbers of priests and the threat to the weekly Eucharist '… is somewhat shaped by our desire to retain and serve current structures rather than engage with an ecclesiology of communion and of pilgrimage, for example, which might suggest alternate ways of addressing the issue' (2014, p.234). It is hard to avoid the conclusion that the church will, if only of necessity, address its presence in Irish society by adopting alternate theologies of church. And this I suggest will present a different church to that of the twentieth century. And here I move to the second development to which I alluded above. I suggest that the newly 'discovered' Irish church will be nearer to what Pope Francis calls an 'evangelising' church. I turn now to Francis to see if his thoughts may give us a glimpse of what this might be, specifically in his much-heralded exhortation *Evangelii gaudium* (2013).

I have chosen two strands in Francis' *Evangelii gaudium* that are apposite I think to the discussion I am involved in here.[6] First, he is thoroughly convinced of the need for a decentralised liberating structure in the church as the three following quotes exemplify:

> Nor do I believe that the papal magisterium should be expected to offer a definitive or complete word on every question which affects the Church and the world (16).
> Excessive centralisation, rather than proving helpful, complicates the Church's life and her missionary outreach (32).
> More than by fear of going astray, my hope is that we will be moved by the fear of remaining shut up within structures which give us a false sense of security, within rules which make us harsh judges, within habits

which make us feel safe, while at our door people are starving and Jesus does not tire of saying to us: 'Give them something to eat' (Mk 6:37) (49).

Second, Francis also has a vision of a church which, though often misunderstood, will nonetheless continue to defend its core messages, even if this means at times going against the modern world.

> The process of secularisation tends to reduce the faith and the Church to the sphere of the private and personal. Furthermore, by completely rejecting the transcendent, it has produced a growing deterioration of ethics, a weakening of the sense of personal and collective sin, and a steady increase in relativism (64).
>
> As the bishops of the United States of America have rightly pointed out, while the Church insists on the existence of objective moral norms which are valid for everyone, 'there are those in our culture who portray this teaching as unjust, that is, as opposed to basic human rights. Such claims usually follow from a form of moral relativism that is joined, not without inconsistency, to a belief in the absolute rights of individuals. In this view, the Church is perceived as promoting a particular prejudice and as interfering with individual freedom'. We are living in an information-driven society which bombards us indiscriminately with data – all treated as being of equal importance – and which leads to remarkable superficiality in the area of moral discernment. In response, we need to provide an education which teaches critical thinking and encourages the development of mature moral values (64).
>
> The individualism of our postmodern and globalised era favours a lifestyle which weakens the development and stability of personal relationships and distorts family bonds (67).

Conclusions

I have painted pictures of the state and of the church which are remarkably different from the institutional actors of the twentieth century. The state, I am suggesting, is one which is less ideologically driven than heretofore, more particularly because, in common with other Western democracies, interests are less driven by political parties; a market mentality prevails. In summary it tends to exist to reflect, implement, and diversify individual choice.

The church early in this new century seems to be adrift in a structure and ecclesiology that has not taken account of the over-dependence on a cultic priesthood. Nonetheless in a new era of leadership it looks as if it will embrace decentralisation, while remaining true to those teachings that the church has traditionally defended against what it sees as libertarian individualism.

We have only passing examples of where tension reached a crisis stage between these two changing institutions in this century. In 2009, in the wake of the publication of the Murphy Report on sexual abuse in the Archdiocese of Dublin, the then Minister for Justice said, 'The bottom line is this: a collar will protect no criminal.' Again in 2011, in the wake of the report on sexual abuse in the Diocese of Cloyne, church and state involved themselves in diplomatic 'handbagging', famously exemplified in the following comment to the Dáil by the Taoiseach: 'The Cloyne Report excavates [sic] the dysfunction, disconnection, elitism ... the narcissism ... that dominate the culture of the Vatican to this day ...' Suffice it to say that in those encounters, institutionalism on the Rome side lead to papalism, legalism and dogmatism; and on the Irish state side we were treated to unimaginative secularism. But, those confrontations perhaps indicate the kinds of challenges which the changed circumstances of church and state will present to us in the coming years. We have never had heretofore to confront in this jurisdiction, or in this church, the problems of pluralism to any significant extent. I draw here on the work of Jeffrey Stout, Princeton Professor of Religion, to suggest some of the challenges that are before us. There will be a need to at least entertain the possibility that secularised political discourse in modern democratic societies can to some large extent be disentangled from the antireligious animus of some of its ideological defenders' (Stout, pp.102–3). We will have to learn to accept that 'the ideal of respect for one's fellow citizens does not in every respect require us to argue from a common justificatory basis of principles ...' (85). And we will need to 'articulate a form of pluralism, one that citizens with strong religious commitments can accept and that welcomes their full partici- pation in public life without fudging on its own premises' (296–7). Effectively the challenge will be to move beyond confrontation between secular liberalism and theological traditionalism (294).

Awakening: The Friendship between
D T Suzuki and Thomas Merton

EDWARD SELLNER

> ... to me it is clearly evident that you and I have in common and share
> most intimately precisely that which, in the eyes of conventional
> westerners, would seem to separate us. The fact that you are a Zen
> Buddhist and I am a Christian monk far from separating us makes us
> most like one another. How many centuries is it going to take for people
> to discover this fact?
>
> Merton's letter to D. T. Suzuki, 11 April 1959

In Zen Buddhism the word for 'awakening' is satori. It refers to an experience of personal transformation, of enlightenment, of the acquisition, as D. T. Suzuki says, of 'a new point of view as regards life and the universe'.[1] Thomas Merton defined it in his own terms as 'the explosive rediscovery of the hidden and lost reality within us'.[2]

For both men 'awakening' was one of the most significant experiences they held in common. Satori was a theme Suzuki constantly returned to in his writings on Zen, and Merton, years after his own transformative experience in Louisville, writes, 'I am just beginning to awaken and to realise how much more awakening is to come.'[3] The story of the friendship that developed between these two men in the mid-twentieth century – the Japanese scholar of Zen and the Trappist spiritual writer – has much to teach Christians today about important dynamics related to inter-religious dialogue, as well as perhaps inspire a new generation of seekers who are less aligned with specific religious traditions but yet deeply interested in a spirituality that incorporates the best from both East and West.

Satori in the Life of Daisetz Teitaro Suzuki

Daisetz Teitaro Suzuki (or D. T. Suzuki as most people knew him) was one of the most significant writers of the twentieth century. Not only did he introduce, almost single-handedly, Zen to the West, he also influenced positively the lives of many of his contemporaries, including Paul Tillich, Carl Jung, Erich Fromm, Alan Watts, Jack Kerouac, Allen Ginsberg, and Thomas Merton himself. As more people, disillusioned by World War II, began to search for other spiritual resources, Zen thought came to dominate broad segments of American and European society because of Suzuki's extensive writings. A so-called 'Zen Boom' unfolded across the spectrum of the intellectual world, especially in the 1950s, the time, as we will see, that the Trappist monk Thomas Merton began to read Suzuki too.

D. T. Suzuki was born 18 October 1870 in what is now the city of Kanazawa, Japan, the youngest of five children. His father, Ryojun Suzuki, died shortly after Suzuki's sixth birthday, and an older brother the following year. Such losses contributed to his later interest in the study of Zen, for, since his family followed that tradition, as he says in an autobiographical essay, 'Early Memories', 'it was natural that I should look to Zen for some of the answers to my problems.'[4] In 1891, following the death of his mother, Suzuki went to Tokyo to study with Imagita Kosen, who was abbot of Engakuji, an important Zen temple. When this beloved teacher died suddenly, Suzuki was thrown into what he describes as 'four years of struggle, a struggle mental, physical, moral, and intellectual'.

Not only was he facing grief once more, but his new Zen Master, Shaku Soen, changed his koan, the paradoxical word or phrase upon which a Zen neophyte would meditate, a meditation that hopefully might lead to enlightenment, satori. This Master, Suzuki says, gave him the word mu (untranslatable) as his new koan, and then proceeded to give 'me no help at all with the koan'; thus his struggle to discover its hidden meaning on his own.

Reading all the books on Zen he could find, he found a statement in one of them that proved helpful: 'All the knowledge and experience and wonderful phrases and feelings of pride which you accumulated before your study of Zen – all these things you must throw out. Pour all your mental force on to solving the koan ... When you reach that state something starts up within yourself and suddenly it is as though your skull were broken in pieces. The experience that you gain then has not come from outside, but from within yourself.'

Daily meditating on his koan, Suzuki kept busy during those four years translating various Japanese and Chinese writings into English. But the koan, he says, was 'my chief preoccupation', and what he put all his strength into solving – without success. A friend of his reported that at this time Suzuki even contemplated suicide. But, Suzuki writes, 'it often happens that just as one reaches the depths of despair and decides to take one's life then and there that satori comes ... To solve a koan one must be standing at an extremity ...'[5]

Suzuki's extremity came when it was decided that he should go to America to help Dr Paul Carus with the translation of the *Tao Te Ching*, the fundamental text of Taoism. As the time approached for his departure, he realised that it was now or never for him to solve the koan, and that he must put all his spiritual strength into this endeavour. It seems at this point he then surrendered, let go of his determination to understand the koan – a paradoxical stance that many others have discovered can lead to a spiritual breakthrough.

The breakthrough happened when 'I ceased to be conscious of *mu*' and 'became one with it so that there was no longer the separateness implied by being conscious of *mu*.' This happened while in a state of meditation, what he calls *samadhi*, and the moment of coming out of that state and 'seeing it for what it is – that is satori'. Suzuki writes that he has no idea how long he was in that state, but 'I was awakened from it by the sound of the [monastery's] bell.' He immediately went to his Master to discuss his experience of enlightenment. 'I remember that night as I walked back from the monastery to my quarters in the Kigen'in temple, seeing the trees in the moonlight. They looked transparent and I was transparent too.'[6]

As a result of his enlightenment experience, Suzuki spent the rest of his life exploring the meaning of satori in the numerous writings he did on Zen. For him, satori is 'the essence of Zen Buddhism'; it consists in the acquisition of 'a new viewpoint of looking at life and things generally'. It is, fundamentally, a *spiritual* experience, an experience affecting profoundly one's own spirituality. Though a trained, gifted master or mentor can help one prepare to receive this experience, no one – especially the seeker himself or herself – can make it happen. One can only, through prayer, meditation, and fasting, open oneself up to its occurrence. When it happens, it leads to an experience of union with all of creation rather than, as in the West, a dualistic perspective that divides reality into various parts or components, some seemingly more worthwhile. 'Satori,' Suzuki writes, 'may be defined as an intuitive looking into the nature of things in contradistinction to the analytical or logical understanding of it. Practically, it means the unfolding of a new world hitherto unperceived in the confusion of a dualistically-trained mind ... This is a mystery and a miracle.'[7]

Thomas Merton's Awakening: At the Corner of Fourth and Walnut
Thomas Merton, arguably the most influential American Catholic author of the twentieth century, wrote over seventy books and hundreds of poems and articles on topics ranging from monastic spirituality to social issues regarding racism, civil rights, nonviolence, the Vietnam War, and the nuclear arms race.

Merton was born in Prades, France, 31 January 1915. His father, Owen, was from New Zealand, and his mother, Ruth, from America. Both were artists, and both died young, leaving Thomas and his younger brother, John Paul, orphans at an early age. Merton's youth was characterised by what he later described in his autobiography as a life of dissolution and self-indulgence. Like Suzuki, however, who had lost his father, brother, mother and mentor when he was young, this profound sense of loss probably also contributed to Merton's search for meaning as well as a deep desire to belong.

He eventually was baptised a Roman Catholic and joined a community of Trappist monks at the Abbey of Gethsemani in Kentucky. Encouraged by his abbot to write, he composed *The Seven Storey Mountain*, the autobiography that made him a celebrity monk overnight. According to Michael Higgins, Merton expressed 'the deepest feelings of his contemporaries. He instinctively, viscerally grasped the spiritual longing of a generation, and gave it voice.'[8] He continued writing books, but as a recent convert and now a young monk, his books, though well-received, reflected a theology that was heavily dualistic in its emphasis, seeming to define 'the world' as a place of temptation, associated with his early life, and monasticism or Christian life as the only true escape from evil.

By the mid-1950s, at the time when his works were inspiring millions of his readers, Merton himself was experiencing, as his journals and letters reveal, something of a vocational crisis. He was unhappy in the monastery at Gethsemani, finding it too busy and in some ways too crowded for the solitary life to which he increasingly felt drawn. Underlying this restlessness was his intensified search for his 'true self'. Linked with that search was a conviction, as he expressed in a June 1958 journal entry, that 'I have not yet even begun to write, to think, to pray, and to live and that only now I am getting down to waking up.'[9] What would eventually contribute to his awakening would be his increasing knowledge of Zen Buddhism through his reading D. T. Suzuki's writings and eventually his friendship with the man.

Merton's interest in Asia went back to his adolescence. He was only fifteen when he had studied – and defended in a student debate – the ideas of Gandhi. As an undergraduate at Columbia University in New York, he also studied Eastern religions. There, he had even put the name Suzuki on a reading list of authors he hoped to become more acquainted with[10] – but evidently had not done so. In mid-winter of 1955, however, Merton wrote to his publisher, Jay Laughlin: 'Have you ever run across any books by

D. T. Suzuki … on Zen Buddhism? I am anxious to track some of them down and have them.' In May, 1956, he wrote once again to Laughlin that he had finally found the Zen books he was looking for in the Library of Congress, and was absorbing their wisdom. What he liked about Zen, he said, was how 'terrifically practical'[11] it was. By the summer of that year, he was reading everything he could find written by Suzuki, telling a friend, 'The very name of Suzuki produces in me electric currents from head to foot.'[12]

Reading Suzuki's work, he was increasingly becoming aware at this time of what he perceived as the similarities between his own translations of the sayings of the desert Christians with the stories of the Zen monks' pursuit of satori, the movement from dualistic thinking to a new, more intuitive sense of inner unity. And Merton was definitely searching for inner unity in a number of ways. In a journal entry, dated 28 April 1957, he wrote: 'If I can unite *in myself*, in my own spiritual life, the thought of the East and West, of the Greek and Latin Fathers, I will create in myself a reunion of the divided church and from that unity in myself can come the exterior and visible unity of the Church.'[13]

All of his reading and reflection on inner unity precipitated in Merton a highly dramatic turning point in his life, a satori experience that would change him irrevocably. Preceding it were journal entries related to his immersion in Zen. 15 November 1957, he wrote how 'there is no solution in withdrawal. No solution in conforming. A Koan! What sound is made by one hand clapping against itself? That is where I think Zen smart: in its absolutely fundamental psychological honesty.' On 27 February 1958, he returns once more to Zen, reflecting a growing sense of urgency: 'I suppose I have heard it before: that the moment in a bullfight is when the matador is to kill the bull is called "the Moment of Truth". Today [I] was suddenly struck and powerfully moved by the religious implications of this … Zen resonances in this expression, the "Moment of Truth" when the bull, the Koan, is killed.' Finally, on 19 March 1958, he writes of an experience the day before that took him, at last, beyond the dualism with which he had been struggling: 'Yesterday, in Louisville, at the corner of 4th and Walnut, [I] suddenly realised that I loved all the people and that none of them were, or, could be totally alien to me.'[14]

In selections from his journal, later published as *Conjectures of A Guilty Bystander*, he refines the original entry: 'It was like waking from a dream of separateness, of spurious self-isolation in a special world, the world of renunciation and supposed holiness. The whole illusion of a separate holy existence is a dream. Not that I question the reality of my vocation, or of my monastic life: but the conception of "separation from the world" that we have in the monastery too easily presents itself as a complete illusion; that by making vows we become a different species of being, pseudo-angels, "spiritual men, men of interior life ..."' He goes on to name what Suzuki equated with his own satori experience years before: 'This sense of liberation from an illusory difference was such a relief and such a joy to me that I almost laughed out loud. And I suppose my happiness could have taken form in these words: "Thank God, thank God, that *I am* like other men, that I am only a man among others ..."'[15]

This was a significant turning-point in Thomas Merton's life, this dramatic realisation of being one with all his fellow-creatures, one with himself and his own search for interior unity. It was a far cry from earlier writings in which Merton had stressed a disconnect between himself and the world. It marked a major transition – and speeded it along – of his becoming one of the most respected voices of the 1960s, a social critic while still being a member of a monastic community. From here on his writings express a new energy, a new inclusivity that is dramatically different from his earlier works which reflected a dualistic way of thinking and of being in the world. As a result of his satori experience, David Cooper says that he, Merton, came to realise that 'he was a man very much of his own century ... ; that he did not live in an intellectual climate of medieval saints.' A new voice began to take shape, what Cooper refers to as 'the voice of a more compassionate and flexible social critic'.[16]

An Exchange of Letters and Their Meeting
On 12 March 1959, within a year of his satori experience in Louisville, Merton wrote Suzuki directly, apologising for perhaps 'disturbing' him 'with a bad-mannered intrusion'.[17] It was the beginning of a long discussion between the two men on the similarities and differences between Zen Buddhism and Christianity. It was also the beginning of a friendship that lasted until Suzuki's death. At this point Merton had been reading Zen literature and Suzuki's works for years. He had decided to write Suzuki with a specific request, but seems to have intended much more. He wanted to ask the Zen scholar to write an introduction to what would later be published as *The Wisdom of the Desert* that would discuss the apparent similarities between the desert Christians and Zen Masters.

He also, by this time, was convinced that the contemporary Church had to take seriously the reality of the diverse religions in the world, and that religious dialogue was a spiritual necessity in the nuclear age. The West, he believed, needed 'the spiritual heritage of the East' or else the West would 'hasten the tragedy that threatens man and his civilisations'.[18]

Merton began his letter with humility: 'I will not be so foolish as to pretend to you that I understand Zen. To be frank, I hardly understand Christianity ... All I know is that when I read your books – and I have read many of them – and above all when I read English versions of the little verses in which the Zen Masters point their finger to something which flashed out at the time, I feel a profound and intimate agreement. Time after time, as I read your pages, something in me says That's it!' He tells Suzuki not to ask him to explain this, because he cannot, but, he says, 'I have my own way to walk and for some reason or other Zen is right in the middle of it wherever I go ... I'll say simply that it seems to me that Zen is the very atmosphere of the Gospels, and the Gospels are bursting with it ... But I still don't know what it is. No matter. I don't know what the air is either.'[19]

Evidently Suzuki was impressed with Merton's acknowledgment of ignorance, as well as his desire to learn. He wrote back almost immediately (31 March) and thanked Merton for his letter, saying that he agreed with the comparison of similar stories told 'in the annals of Zen' with those of the Desert monks. He also spoke of his desire to learn more about Christianity. For the next year they exchanged at least eight letters between them, after these first two, which covered a wide variety of topics: Merton telling Suzuki how the Zen Masters and desert Christians shared so many qualities, especially 'their quiet humour, blended with spiritual joy that transcends difficulties and sufferings', and how they both share similar views about Christianity and about Zen; Suzuki telling Merton how they were 'destined to differ' in some of their views, but being 'tolerant toward each other' was what counted. In one of his letters, Merton addresses directly the mystery of the Zen koan for satori to happen, comparing it to a Christian sacrament and his understanding of grace: 'The breakthrough that comes with the realisation of what the finger of a koan is pointing to, is like the breakthrough of the realisation that a sacrament, for instance, is a finger pointing to the completely spontaneous Gift of Himself to us on the part of God ... This is grace, this is salvation, this is Christianity. And, so far as I can see, it is also very much like Zen.'[20]

One of the most moving passages in Merton's letters is his apologising to his friend (and through him, to all Asian people) for the transgressions of the West against the East: 'I feel obliged to say this because of the huge burden of the sins of the western world, the burden of our sins toward the east: sins committed in the name of the Good and even in the name of Christ. I want to speak for this western world which has been and is so utterly wrong. This world which has in past centuries broken in upon you and brought you our own confusion, our own alienation ... And worst of all, that we have shared the Truth of Christ by imposing upon you our own confusion as if it came from Christ ... If only we had thought of coming to you to *learn* something ... If only we had thought of coming to you and loving you for what you are in yourselves, instead of trying to make you over into our own image and likeness.'[21]

In retrospect, what can be discerned in these letters are intimations of an approach to inter-religious dialogue from which anyone can learn basic dynamics necessary for it to be fruitful: first, the need to start with humility, acknowledging that one does not know fully either the other's traditions or beliefs NOR is one necessarily fully comprehending the mystery of one's own faith; second, the genuine desire to learn from each other rather than proselytise; third, while there certainly will be differences of opinion and of religious beliefs, both partners in dialogue should express the hope of discovering some common points of agreement, some common ground; fourth, the need at some point to acknowledge any harm that has been caused against one another's faith by the other's; fifth, bringing some degree of humour and joy to the discussions; and sixth, above all, recognising the importance of TRULY LISTENING. The last important dynamic, number seven, was revealed when the two men actually met.

Early in June, 1964, Merton received a letter from Suzuki's secretary inviting him to meet the Zen scholar in New York later that month. Although Merton had initially invited Suzuki to come to Gethsemani, his advanced age prohibited that journey, and he hoped that Merton would come to him. Although Merton had never received permission to travel by his abbot, this time an exception was made. Merton flew to New York on 15 June. On the 16th and the 17th, he met with Suzuki and his secretary, Mihoko Okamura, recording in his journal how much he enjoyed meeting both of them, and the special tea ceremony that they shared. They covered a wide variety of topics, from Paul Tillich to Heidegger to the German mystic Meister Eckhart. They also, of course, discussed Zen and their mutual interest in the mystics, both East and West. Then Merton recorded how the two friends parted, the Zen scholar and the Christian monk: 'The thing he insisted upon most – in Christianity and Buddhism – love more than enlightenment.'[22]

In a journal entry three days later, on 20 June, Merton acknowledges how pleasant their talks were, and how 'profoundly important to me – to see and experience the fact that there really is a deep understanding between myself and this extraordinary and simple man whom I have been reading for about ten years with great attention'. And, then, probably remembering his satori experience in Louisville, Merton names the gift Suzuki's writings had led him to: 'A sense of being 'situated' in this world.' Reflecting back upon those meetings, and the warmth he felt not only from Suzuki but Mihoko Okamura, he refers to an experience of homecoming for which he had so often searched: 'for once in a long time I felt as if I had spent a moment in my own family.'[23]

Conclusion

The two friends did not meet again. Suzuki died two years later, on 12 July 1966; Thomas Merton, on a pilgrimage to Asia, died suddenly at a conference outside of Bangkok, Thailand, 10 December 1968. Both men were aware, through their correspondence and friendship, of the necessary final element in any successful inter-religious dialogue: that, as Suzuki told Merton when they were parting, *love* is more important than anything else one brings to the discussions – even more important than satori, the experience of enlightenment. If, what Donald Allchin says is correct, that 'of all the aspects of Merton's work, his gift of crossing the frontiers between great world religions is perhaps the most significant for the future of humankind',[24] Merton himself would surely credit Suzuki as the Zen Master who helped him the most to do so. As he told a friend before he left for Asia, 'I do not believe that I could understand our Christian faith the way I understand it if it were not for the light of Buddhism.'[25]

The God who does not Exist

ENDA LYONS

The students I have been working with over the years are adults, almost all with a strong Catholic background. For the most part they are interested in theology for personal rather than professional reasons. They want to understand their faith better, to try to make sense of it, and, so, to deepen it. When we come to the question of 'God', by way of introducing the topic, I try to connect with their Catholic education. I ask them to write down privately, just for themselves and their own eyes, the answers to the following questions as they remember them from the Catechism: When did God begin? Who created God? Where is God? What kind of body has God? Not surprisingly their answers are invariably orthodox: God, they learned, has no beginning, is everywhere, has never been created but is Creator; has no body, but is 'pure spirit', has no limits, but is infinite. Then I ask them to reflect quietly for a few minutes on their answers. When they have done that I ask them to try to imagine what that God is like, even to draw for themselves an imaginary picture of that God. They are of course at a complete loss: they recognise that they simply cannot imagine the God of their faith.

I am always amazed, then, at their surprised reaction to a well-known passage of Karl Rahner – well known, that is, to theologians at least. Not that there is anything startlingly new in the passage: the biblical tradition, Paul in Athens, Augustine, Thomas Aquinas and other theologians throughout the centuries have emphasised the same truth. What seems to strike them about the passage is more the straightforward and direct way in which Rahner expresses that truth.

In the passage Rahner is talking about a God who does not exist. The background image he has in his mind is that of all the beings that ever existed or will exist thus making up together the entire family of beings. The God who does not exist is a God who would be yet another individual member of this family and who, together with them, would make up 'the larger household' of beings. In other words, Rahner is saying, God is not 'another being': we cannot tot up all the beings there are, and then add another Super Being, 'God'. Surprising as it may seem, anyone looking for such a God – and many of our contemporaries are – would be looking for a false God. Surprising as it may also seem, belief in such a God would be belief in a God who does not exist at all! A self-confessed 'atheist' who would reject such a God, would be right in doing so – right in refusing to believe in something which does not exist! So, Rahner points out:

> Both atheism and a more naïve form of theism (i.e. belief in God) labour under the same false notion of God, only the former denies it while the latter believes that it can make sense out of it. Both are basically false.
> (*Foundations of Christian Faith*, p.63)

I often find myself listening to people being interviewed on radio or television saying that they do not believe in God, but that they do believe in a Spirit of some kind and I find myself saying, 'Yes – rather like my own belief!'

It should appear obvious to anyone familiar with the traditional teaching about God, as the students mentioned above clearly were, that what Rahner says is traditional and orthodox. The God of traditional Christian theology, having no beginning and no end, to whose infinity there cannot be any limit, whose presence is not confined to any one place, but is everywhere, and, above all, who is Creator of everyone and everything, surely cannot be thought of '… as an individual being alongside of other beings, and who would thus as it were be a member of the larger household of reality' (*Foundations of Christian Faith*).

When we really think about it, even talking about God as 'an infinite being', is rather strange. If God were seen as a being, even an infinite being, God would really be seen as one being among others: why else would the article 'a' be used?

The naiveté of this understanding of God can be helpfully brought out, I think, by a very simple story – admittedly a highly unlikely one. Try to imagine this. The elderly lady was telling the little city girl about her garden. She talked about all the trees and shrubs and plants and flowers and birds and insects that were there. 'Of course', she added, 'there is a lot of light in my garden.' The little girl was fascinated by all of this, especially by the lovely sounds of the names the lady mentioned. 'I'd love to see your garden', she said. 'Will you bring me there?' The lady brought her to the garden and showed her around, and pointed out by name each shrub and plant and flower and even some wildlife. Again the little girl was fascinated. She was silent for a moment, but then said: 'But you said there was light in your garden. You did not show me the light!' Needless to say, the lady was amazed – and amused. She explained, as gently as she could, that light is not another shrub or plant in the garden or anything at all like these.

In saying that God is not 'an individual being alongside of other beings', Rahner is not, of course, at all denying the existence of God – no more than the lady in the story is denying the existence of light. Light is not 'another being' in the garden. But light is quietly and unobtrusively everywhere in the garden. In fact it is very powerfully in the garden. It is that which enables the garden to grow and glow. It is that without which there would be no garden at all. Though it is not something that in itself can be seen in the garden, it is that which makes all seeing possible. Nor in saying that God is not another being in 'the larger household' of beings is Rahner saying that God is an impersonal 'thing'. While God is not a 'person', or even three 'persons' in the same sense that we are persons, God is personal in the sense that God can 'think' and 'love' and, so, is more like a person than a thing. Far from denying the existence of God, Rahner is, on the contrary, leading us to a truer and more helpful concept of God. He is upholding the most basic and essential of all truths about God, that is, the utter and absolute 'transcendence' of God: he is emphasising, as all theology must do, that the God of faith is DIFFERENT, that God is above and beyond every created thing – beyond, not in terms of space, but in terms of BEING. The fact is the God of faith is not a being, but rather BEING ITSELF, the root and origin and source of all beings. God is BEING in which all the beings participate and have their being. That, of course, is not to say that all the beings are themselves God: that 'pantheisitic' view (literally 'everything is God') is obviously untrue. It is to say rather that all the beings have their being in God which is the true Christian position: it is called 'panentheism', meaning, that everything is in God.

This eternal truth about God which Rahner expresses so clearly opens up endless questions and can lead to, literally, eternal reflection: it touches on the very essence of God's contemplation on which eternal life consists. Here, however, I only want to emphasise one point. It should help us to know that we do not have to think of God as yet another being, even an almighty one, 'out there' or 'up there'. In fact that is how we often seem to think of God. We discuss, for example, whether God should be referred to as 'he' or 'she' when in fact God is altogether beyond such terms and is equally the source of male and female. We need to think of God more in terms of Light here in the garden of our universe: Light whose kindly presence pervades and warms the universe and all of us in it; Light which is the source of all life and colour and beauty in this garden. Or, to change from the garden image to that of the ocean: God is to us somewhat as the ocean is to the fish: '… it is in God that we live, and move, and exist' (Acts 17:28).

When we try to imagine what God is like in the Divine Self, we are indeed at a loss. How are we to imagine that which is not a being, but BEING ITSELF, that in which all beings participate? More importantly, perhaps, how can we possibly relate to such an apparently abstract Reality? How, for example, can we pray to God? Regarding how we are to imagine God, the plain fact is, that left to our own devices, we cannot. However, we are not left to our own devices. God who impinges on human life also guides us towards some way of thinking about God. Over the millennia, people have been aware of Mystery within which we live, and have tried to describe, or to image God. With the help of the Mystery itself they have succeeded. In particular each religion has its own image or images. In the Christian experiences, the image is Jesus of Nazareth. In the gospel according to John, perhaps in a moment of sheer frustration, the apostle Philip says to Jesus, seeming to stop him in his tracks, 'Show us the Father and it is enough for us!' The image that Jesus offered him was himself, Jesus himself: 'Philip, he who sees me sees the Father.' Jesus was not saying that he himself is simply identical with God, the Christian understanding of Jesus is that he is the Word of God Incarnate, God's self-expression in a human life. In the Christian experience, if we want to see what God is like in our terms, in our language, in our human situation, we look above all to Jesus of Nazareth, to his message and ministry, to his life of love, his sufferings, his dying, and his Resurrection. And the message and ministry of Jesus is about forgiveness and love. The literal meaning of the word 'theology' is 'a word about God'. We can say then with Karl Rahner that Jesus is 'the theology which God himself has taught us' (*Theological Investigations*, vol. 4, 117). And what that theology has taught us is that, in the words of Scripture, 'God is love' (1 Jn).

IV. Ethics of the Word

The Style of Virtue Ethics

James F. Keenan SJ

In thinking of a topic appropriate to recognise the leadership Ronan Drury provided for *The Furrow* and its readers, I began to think of a word that John O'Malley taught me thirty years ago, 'Style!' Style is not something over and against substance; rather, it's a lot more like a 'way of proceeding'. The way one proceeds captures one's style.

A Common Style: Vatican II, Pope Francis and Ronan Drury

In his brilliant work, *What Happened at Vatican II*, John O'Malley helped us to see that the Council changed us in our way of thinking of Church.[1] Earlier in an essay called, 'The Style of Vatican II', O'Malley explained why he thought the word was so important. 'Style – no other aspect of Vatican II sets it off so impressively from all previous councils and thereby suggests its break with "business as usual". No other aspect so impressively indicates that a new mode of interpretation is required if we are to understand it and get at its "spirit".'[2]

Anyone who reads O'Malley realises that the Vatican II style was radically different from the style that preceded it: 'It was a change in this closed, ghetto-like, secretive, condemnatory, authoritarian style that the council wanted to effect … In dramatic fashion, the council abandoned, for the most part, the terse, technical, juridical and other punitive language of previous councils. Believe this, or else!'

Unlike the legalistic, God-fearing style of the church that gave us the moral manuals, O'Malley sees that 'the style of the council was invitational. It was new for a council in that it replicated to a remarkable degree the style the Fathers of the Church used in their sermons, treatises and commentaries down to the advent of Scholasticism in the thirteenth century.'

Finally he turns to the language of the Council to write 'nothing is perhaps more striking in the vocabulary of the council, nothing perhaps so much sets it off from previous councils as words like "development", "progress" and even "evolution".' This is a sign of a break with the static framework of understanding doctrine, discipline and style characteristic of all previous councils. Vatican II never uses the word 'change,' but that is precisely what it is talking about regarding the church. What this implies, of course, is further change in the future. It suggests that its own provisions are somewhat open-ended. Whatever the interpretation and implementation of the council means, they cannot mean taking the council's decisions as if they said, 'thus far and not a step further'. The council's style is thus oriented to the future and open to it.[3]

I think here we see that the style of Vatican II is not unlike the style of Pope Francis or the leadership of Ronan Drury: it's a deeply theological style, resting in the tradition, open to the challenges of the present, shaping the future, and inviting all along the journey.

The Common Style of Virtue Ethics
The style of virtue ethics can be very much like the style of Vatican II, one that is responsive to the people of God and, I think, very much like the essays in moral theology that one finds in *The Furrow*.

It responds to believers who ask themselves how do I morally live out my faith, to activists who seek to answer the challenges of the world before them, and to theologians who ask themselves whether their research makes any difference to people of faith and of good will.[4] Let me run by some elements of its style.

1. Virtue ethics uses familiar, ordinary and fairly specific language
Virtue ethics' basic concerns deal with dispositions, practices and actions that are integral to the good life of any culture: justice, fidelity, wisdom, kindness, respect, temperance, courage, fortitude, honesty, righteousness, generosity, athleticism, piety, etc. It deals with direct, plain talk. It is used in the home, school, houses of worship, civic centers, sport arenas, in the media, in cross-cultural discourse and in inter-religious dialogue. It is taught to children from the earliest stages of their moral formation, whether they are at home, in school, in the playground, or at worship.[5]

Unlike other ethical systems, virtue ethics does not use language that is foreign or estranged from ordinary life. It does not invoke one to realise their categorical imperative. When a judgement is made, there is not an appeal to prove grounds of commensurability, nor an offer to establish proportionate reasoning. It does not compel anyone to obey a deontological rule.

Too much of modern and contemporary ethics looks like one needs a professor or at least a philosophical handbook in order to justify what one claims to be the right way of being or of acting. This infers that people do not know how to be ethical without a philosophical education. But this is not so.

Those who genuinely help us, as a society to move forward, are the very persons who as children understood and were responsive to commands like 'Be kind'. They learned as we learned through ordinary language and understood that through ordinary language they would grasp what was ethically expected of them.

Like great social reformers, great philosophers and theologians realise that moral language derives from ordinary language. Not surprisingly then Israel's Ten Commandments, the Confucian's Tao, and Jesus' Beatitudes are clear and familiar utterances. Their longevity arises in part from their easy-to-hear, remember and repeat claims. Parents, children, family, ministers, prison wardens, academic deans, teachers, soldiers and leaders invoke them as mainstays of moral insight.

Parents know this. They easily turn to virtue language as a well-spring of resourcefulness. Parents know that they need to be clear, instructive and supportive of their children's moral formation. They can say to their children, be friendly, be honest, and be respectful.

Let us not think that virtuous instructions are no more than admonitions to be good or do the right thing. These are fairly economical instructions, packed with very specific meaning. They are never without content and information. Be courageous, be respectful, be assertive are very specific summons.

The language of ethics needs to be familiar; it needs to be part of the fabric of ordinary human life. Moreover, it needs to be specific, urgent and immediately applicable. And it is.

2. Virtue ethics deals with ordinary life

Much of contemporary ethics looks like the exotically unsolvable. The more problematic, the more remote, and the more peculiar a case looks, the more it is appreciated and the more its exponent is considered brilliant. Ethics courses based on these type of rare cases can look like spectator sports: it's wild, unanticipated, chic, entertaining, and plays well in the media. Edmund Pincoffs saw this as a major challenge to any number of professional fields of ethics, when he coined the phrase quandary ethics.[6] Admittedly, on occasion, but not with enduring frequency, we need to entertain some quandaries, but ethics ought normally to deal with ordinary life.

In his *Summa Theologiae*, Thomas Aquinas makes a helpful distinction between a human act (any deliberate action) and an act of a human (which does not require any deliberate reason, such as stroking one's beard, an example he uses).[7] Later Thomas asks the question whether any human action can be morally indifferent. In an important claim he answers that 'every human action that proceeds from deliberate reason, if it be considered in the individual, must be good or bad'.[8] Effectively he claims that every human action is inevitably a moral action. He uses, as an example, the simple human act of going to bed.[9]

This gives us a much broader agenda for ethics than we normally imagine. Ethics is not primarily about the rare quandary issue; ethics is about ordinary daily life. Every human action that we perform is either a virtuous or vicious act: as we deliberate and act, we are realising ourselves as moral persons day by day.

3. Virtue ethics is a very active ethics
In order to fully appreciate how active this moral life is, Thomas again provides us with a distinction. He argues that virtuous and vicious activities are in themselves immanent activities. That is, the virtuous or vicious practices that one performs redound into the agent and further transforms the person accordingly. He uses the verb 'to do' to highlight his claim: practices that we do, shape us. We become, what we do. If I dance, story-tell, paint, write, I become the dancer, storyteller, painter or writer. Likewise if I do works of generosity, friendship, or kindness, I become shaped by the particular practices that I perform. All moral actions are then immanent actions and virtues are immanent habits formed by immanent practices and actions.[10]

Thomas distinguishes these activities from what he calls 'transient' ones, productive actions by which we 'make' some things. Here the object that we are making is shaped by our own intentionality and activities: I make dinner, a table, a glass of lemonade. My activity is not self-transformative per se; rather, it transforms something else: it is what Thomas calls 'transient' activity.

As in doing athletics (a very good metaphor for virtue!), our bodies, muscles, health, and spirit are shaped by immanent exercises. Borrowing from Avicenna, Thomas saw the life of virtue as one of reflection and exercise.

Like athletics then, a certain measure is needed for virtue. Unless we adequately exercise, we do not adequately become strengthened. For instance, weightlifting requires an athlete to know the tipping point between too little weight and too much. If we do not have adequate weights, we cannot adequately exercise. Such exercise is hardly worth it. Conversely, too many weights are dangerous; we can harm ourselves and our future. There is a need then to know what the mean between these two extremes are. Like weight-lifting, the mean for one person is very different than another, whence the need for real self-knowledge.

Virtue is much the same kind of immanent exercise. I need to know myself and my limits. I also need to push myself, to increase challenges to see where I am at a level of equi-poise. I need to anticipate the lifting I should do, as well as the breaks and timeouts. I certainly need to be spotted, as well.

4. Virtue ethics is fairly easy to teach

Every culture has its own heroes and heroines, significant figures bearing characteristic virtue traits that the culture recommends to be emulated. Stories or narratives of exemplars are the teaching materials of virtue ethics. In the United States, we have any number of narratives that easily couple with a particular virtue. Some of these belong to a long list of ways that we recommend the particular conduct of particular presidents. We can think, for instance, of the stories of Washington's honesty, FDR's courage, JFK's wit, or Lincoln's relentless fidelity to the nation. These virtues come alive not just for an individual but for a people and they are learned through stories and taught at very young ages.

Of course, these narratives pale in comparison to the stories of Jesus. Inasmuch as Christianity is the baptismal response to the call to discipleship, we seek to know the Lord. The Gospels are not simply a story then, but revelation itself. As such, the stories are themselves effective. By them we understand Jesus better and grow in the possibility of becoming like him. The stories not only give us a goal, they show us that Jesus makes the goal possible.

Nowhere is it more emphatic than in Jesus' answer to the question, 'And who is my neighbour?' Here Jesus responds with the parable of the Good Samaritan (Lk 10:25–37). The parable is a surprising one because its end is, unless we are not attentive, a reversal of the beginning. As the story begins, the neighbour seems to be the wounded man on the road. But by the end, the scribe tells us that the neighbour is the Good Samaritan, the one who shows mercy. In a way, Jesus is telling us not to look for a neighbour to love, but rather to be a neighbour who loves.

Throughout the tradition, many preachers and theologians have told the parable first as an allegorical narrative of Jesus' redemptive work and, in light of that work, then a call to imitation. The parable reveals the mercy of Jesus and in turn summons us to be merciful.

The parable has been preached in this way: the beaten man is Adam, wounded by sin and now exiled outside of the gates of the city, which was Paradise. Neither the Law nor the Prophets (the scribe nor the priest) help Adam. Then one not from the land of Adam, Jesus, the Good Samaritan, found Adam, tended to him, and carried him on his mule to the inn which is the church. There Jesus paid an initial price, our redemption, which will be paid in full when Jesus returns again at the end of time to take Adam to where the Samaritan lives, which is the kingdom.

Jesus is the neighbour who has entered our chaos to rescue and save us. The incarnation, passion, death, and resurrection of Jesus – that is, the saving mission of Jesus – was understood as a life of mercy. That life of mercy is what the disciples of Jesus are to live as they follow the one who goes before them. We are able to be merciful like Jesus because of what he has first done for us.

5. Virtues never stand alone

The virtues are related to one another. The thesis of the cardinal virtues, for instance, is the premise that human beings are complex and that if we do not understand and respond to that complexity, we will never grow virtuously. The virtues are called 'cardinal' from the Latin word *cardo*, which means 'hinge'. They are cardinal in that they are fundamental hinges upon which hangs the image of the moral person. Thomas wrote that these four virtues rightly order all our powers that enable us to act: prudence orders our practical reason; justice orders our will; temperance orders our desires; and, fortitude orders our fears. The four virtues are cardinal because they order all the dimensions of ourselves as we are engaged in moral acting.

Likewise there are three theological virtues: faith, hope, and charity. Though charity is the only virtue that exists in that next life, charity cannot live in this life without faith as its foundation and hope as its sustainability.

Like the cardinal virtues, even these gifts from God do not come into our lives as singular or solo. The function of the virtues is to connect.

6. Virtues are fundamentally social

We have just seen the intrinsic relationality of virtues: there can be no prudence without justice; there is no charity without faith. This inter-dependence means that virtues are disposed to animate not only the powers within a person, but more importantly to incorporate the person within the human community. Any virtue is never solely concerned with a personal good, but always also with the common good.

The more we look at the virtues and appreciate that no virtue can stand alone, the more we realise the social function and goal of virtues and their practices. For this reason we see the extraordinary usefulness of virtue ethics in articulating the mission of schools, parishes, corporations, hospitals and prisons. When institutions look to express their goals and the attendant practices and policies to realise those goals, they inevitably turn to the language of virtue for a comprehensive expression of their presence and work. Identity needs a story. In Christianity, Scripture is the story of a people called and led by God to be a distinctive community and a particular 'sort of person'.[11]

7. The Vatican II style of virtue ethics requires mercy

Any people can have a set of virtues, but it all depends on what set one has. Be obedient is a very different exhortation from be creative or be courageous. For us Christians, in the time of Vatican II and in the time of Pope Francis, we realise from Jesus in the Gospels that we need mercy as the key trademark of our identity. Otherwise, we might as well not bother with anything else.

Style Matters
PATRICK HANNON

When your words have been regularly vetted by someone for close on sixty years, you'd wonder about the wisdom of putting them before him again. That's the way with this scribe, one of the class that met Maynooth and Ronan Drury for the first time in 1958, as he embarked on the task of getting us to marry the demotic with some generally received pronunciation – not quite the RP of the southern counties of England perhaps, but decidedly not the pronunciation received in the southern counties of our own island. He combined with J. G. McGarry, to introduce us later to Sacred Eloquence, as Homiletics was then grandly called. And he was always helpful and often kind, though you wouldn't get carried away by the notion of rivalling Bossuet or Fenelon. Nor were you likely to think yourself an Arnold or Eliot of theology when you encountered his skills as Review Editor and Editor of *The Furrow*. Skilful and helpful he still is, as scores of Furrow contributors can testify, and he has never quite managed to disguise his kindness. So it's with thanks and pleasure that I offer a few reflections in honour of a gifted colleague and a good friend.

> I say this also thinking about the preaching and content of our preaching. A beautiful homily, a genuine sermon must begin with the first proclamation, with the proclamation of salvation. There is nothing more solid, deep and sure than this proclamation. Then you have to do catechesis. Then you can draw even a moral consequence. But the proclamation of the saving love of God comes before moral and religious imperatives. Today sometimes it seems that the opposite order is prevailing. The homily is the touchstone to measure the pastor's proximity and ability to meet his people, because those who preach must recognise the heart of their community and must be able to see where the desire for God is lively and ardent. The message of the Gospel, therefore, is not to be reduced to some aspects that, although relevant, on their own do not show the heart of the message of Jesus Christ.
>
> Pope Francis

Those words of Francis are from the interview he gave to the editor of *Civiltà Cattolica* six months into his papacy, and they came to mind as a starting point for these reflections, first because they give a glimpse of the style of Francis, and the style of Francis is going to be my main theme. But they're apposite also in a piece to honour Ronan Drury, for what they say happens to capture the theology that has informed his teaching of homiletics and his own homiletic practice. *A genuine sermon must begin with the first proclamation, with the proclamation of salvation*: the words might have been spoken in Loftus Hall or Long Corridor.

'The time is fulfilled, and the kingdom of God is at hand' is how Mark has Jesus begin. Of course there are other ways of conveying the priority of gospel, including the witness of the preacher's life and the whole tenor of a ministry. Kerygma must be first, though not necessarily literally so, in every homily, and a little catechesis in a homily on occasion mightn't come amiss; but catechesis needs time and a homily is meant to be short. *Then you can draw even a moral consequence*: but don't moralise, as many an earnest trainee-preacher heard from the back of the chapel in Maynooth. Francis too is adamant and clear: *The proclamation of the saving love of God comes before moral and religious imperatives.*

Today sometimes it seems that the opposite order is prevailing. It would be a great relief if commentators gave up parsing Francis for evidence of criticism of his predecessor. It must be clear by now that that isn't his line, that he's not that kind of person, as someone sensibly said the other day. It would be a relief too if we could all admit that it does sometimes seem that Christ's gospel consists in a handful of do nots, and it's not all the fault of the media. A grave misapprehension of course, putting law before gospel, negative and narrow in its picture of discipleship, uncorrected by any awareness of the concern for social justice that's now over a century old; described over forty years ago by a synod of the world's bishops as a constituent part of the gospel's message. The misapprehension is an obstacle to the spread of the gospel that sometimes seems intractable; and it's not reassuring to find highly-placed bishops among critics of the pope's attempts to set the balance right.

The short passage above is not just a summary of the pope's understanding of the preacher's role, it also conveys a sense of his ministry's style. The note it strikes was sustained even in the title *The Joy of the Gospel*, and Francis's deeds as well as his words have continued to resonate and harmonise with it. *Evangelii gaudium* is a programmatic statement of his vision for the church and its mission, touching on manifold practical and urgent concerns, but its underlying and persistent theme is that 'Christians have a duty to proclaim the Gospel without excluding anyone. Instead of seeming to impose new obligations, they should share their joy, point to a horizon of beauty and invite others to a delicious banquet.'[1]

It says something about the accuracy of the pope's reading of what church and world need now – about the magnitude of the task he himself faces – that church people have been discomfited by the emphases he has chosen to give his ministry. It's as if the Second Vatican Council had never taken place, with its commitment to renewal of the church, and its mission to share the gospel with all men and women, with whom Christ's followers share the joys and hopes and griefs and anxieties of the age.[2] Some reactions within the church seem strange when you think of the ministry of Jesus: a fear that the pope is diluting 'the demands of the gospel', that his outreach to people on the margins of the church will result in a cheapening of discipleship, and – verging on the ridiculous – something like a small child's jealousy of the attention he gives to people outside the household of the faith, and of the way he has engaged their interest.

So how are we to interpret Pope Francis's way, what to make of his style? A familiar answer contrasts it with Pope Benedict's: Benedict's is the academic, it's said, this pope's is more pastoral. And there is something to that, even if it's a simplification; nor should it suggest a weakness in either style. A parallel of sorts is the contrast that is made between *Lumen gentium* and *Gaudium et spes*, the first entitled a 'Dogmatic' Constitution, the second a 'Pastoral', though there's much that's pastoral in the one, doctrinal in the other. However, a better way to approach the question, perhaps, is with the aid of an insight of John W. O'Malley SJ, historiographer of the councils, and author of recent books on Vatican II and Trent.

The key to interpreting the documents of Vatican II, according to O'Malley, is to recognise that the genre of its enactments differs from that employed by any preceding council. He advances his contention through an analysis of the Council's vocabulary; for in his view 'the most concrete manifestation of the character of this genre … is the vocabulary it adopts and fosters. Nowhere is that vocabulary more significant than in Vatican II, and nowhere is the contrast greater between it and all preceding councils.'[3] And he suggests that the genre is best understood in terms borrowed from classical rhetoric, identifying it as *epideictic*, a mode of discourse found in patristic writing, studied by Cicero and Quintilian, and distinguished explicitly by them from the discourse proper to the legislator or the judge.

The epideictic genre, O'Malley explains, is a form of the art of persuasion. 'While it raises appreciation, it creates or fosters among those it addresses a realisation that they all share (or should share) the same ideals and need to work together to achieve them. This genre reminds people of what they have in common rather than what might divide them, and the reminder motivates them to cooperate in enterprises for the common good, to work for a common cause.'[4] Those are the traits that characterise the discourse of Vatican II: 'The Council was about persuading and inviting. To that end it used principally the epideictic genre. I am, of course, not saying that the bishops and theologians self-consciously adopted a specific genre of classical rhetoric as such. I am saying that the documents of the Council, for whatever reason, fit that pattern and therefore need to be interpreted accordingly.'[5]

Nor of course am I saying here that the pope has consciously adopted the epideictic mode, but it's surely a useful interpretative key to his preaching and teaching. His discourse is rarely that of a lawmaker, never that of the judge, and it does aim to persuade and invite. And he does seem to prefer to call upon what people have in common rather than to dwell on what divides, and to speak of common ideals, and summon to make common cause.

Of the Council's use of the genre, O'Malley says: 'Nowhere is the vocabulary more indicative of what the genre stands for, and therefore of the style of church the council promoted by means of it';[6] and one can add that the same may be said of the pope. There isn't space here to analyse the vocabulary that Francis favours when he speaks of the church's mission and of the style of church that he wants to promote. But it will serve our purposes to notice that what he thinks and seeks is caught in metaphor and striking image, in phrases as various as 'horizon of beauty', 'delicious banquet', 'fragrance of the gospel'; no less vividly in 'the cry of the poor', 'the church as field hospital', and of course 'the smell of the sheep'.

John O'Malley's observations appeared first in an article in *America* in which he is commenting on norms for interpreting the documents of Vatican II contained in the Final Report of the Extraordinary Synod of 1985, called to mark the twentieth anniversary of the ending of the Council. The specific context of his concern with genre is a norm which, as paraphrased by Avery Dulles reads: 'No opposition may be made between the spirit and the letter of the Council.' Whilst acknowledging the vagueness of the term 'spirit', O'Malley believes that it can be given content if attention is paid to the genre of the Council's documents. Not just to *what* the Council said but also to the *how*, as he puts it. 'Vatican II engaged in a new language-game for a council … [it] was in that regard as much a language event as an ecclesiastical or historical event. Perhaps another way of saying we must not separate the letter of Vatican II from the spirit is to say we must not separate the content from the language – from the *style*.'[7]

The church today has inherited the legacy of the Council, a legacy that is often controverted, sometimes acrimoniously; claim and counter-claim made about what may or may not change. Those charged with oversight have a special responsibility in the legacy's transmission, maintaining continuity with tradition but responsive to the need for change; and the bishop of Rome has a role that's uniquely significant in that process. Francis has given some explicit indications of his conception of the task, has indeed already instituted concrete change. But, as with the Council, perhaps it is to his style that we should look, to get a true sense of the shape of the church to come.

Writing of the shape of the church to come, Karl Rahner noted that difference of viewpoint, tension and even conflict is inevitable when Christians debate the nature of their task in the world. For Rahner, the answer is not to avoid the fray but 'to learn … to maintain the Church's unity and mutual love', something that 'must be constantly learned and practiced'.[8] It has been a great merit of Ronan Drury's stewardship of *The Furrow* that it has not avoided the fray though without becoming partisan, and that it remains a space where Christian community may be practised and learned. *Ad multos annos.*

A Voice for Justice

HUGH CONNOLLY

Surrounding mountains, high altitude, an active volcano, and a steep drop at the end of a short runway make flying into La Aurora International Airport in Guatemala City an interesting experience at any time of the year. Densely constructed barrios on impossibly sheer hillsides interspersed with deep ravines make one seriously ponder whether and where enough level space might realistically be found to land a plane. The familiar thud of rubber on concrete and the roar of engine-assisted brakes effectively answers that query albeit while giving rise to several not unrelated concerns.

Guatemala's geography has frequently influenced its history. Close to two-thirds of the country's total land area is mountainous. The rugged terrain provided refuge that allowed the indigenous peoples to survive the Spanish conquest in the sixteenth century, while the fertile valleys eventually produced fine coffees and other crops that have dominated the nation's economy ever since. Frequent volcanic eruptions, earthquakes, and torrential rains have often brought disaster and made building and maintaining roads and railways there very difficult.[1] The dozen or so of us who were guests of CIDSE – an international alliance of Catholic development agencies working together for global justice – got to experience these infrastructural deficits vividly during our weeklong observer mission to this beautiful yet tragic country in June 2014. The delegation representing Catholic development agencies from Ireland, Belgium, Switzerland, Spain and CELAM, the South American Union of Bishops' Conference, visited projects and contexts deep within the Guatemalan interior. I was privileged to be there as guest of *Trócaire*, the official overseas development agency of the Catholic Church in Ireland.

Two mountain chains traverse Guatemala from west to east, dividing the country into three major regions: the western highlands, where the mountains are located; the Pacific coast, south of the mountains; and the Petén region, north of the mountains. These areas vary in climate, elevation, and landscape, providing dramatic contrasts between dense tropical lowlands and highland peaks and valleys.[2] Guatemala's highlands lie along the Motagua Fault, part of the boundary between the Caribbean and North American tectonic plates. This fault has been responsible for several major earthquakes in historic times, including a 7.5 magnitude tremor on 4 February 1976 which killed more than 25,000 people. Nevertheless it is perhaps fair to say that the greater tragedies and more significant faults of Guatemala's recent history are arguably those which were entirely preventable, those which were wrought regrettably by human injustice and corruption.

As well as its challenging topography, Guatemala has one of the most significant indigenous populations in Latin America. While a very significant forty-three per cent of the people of Guatemala still self-identify as indigenous, in fact the vast majority of Guatemalans are in one way or another descended from indigenous people. During a very packed and thoroughly memorable week in the interior, we experienced at first hand the rich culture of these warm and welcoming people in La Puya, Alta Verapaz, El Quiché and many of the other places we visited. We were privileged to witness their linguistic, cultural and religious traditions and beliefs as well as their extraordinary dignity and attachment to their homelands. Among the indigenous 'Mayan family' are the Ixil people who live in three municipalities in the mountains of the El Quiché department and who were the primary hosts of our delegation.

Over the course of the last several decades, the homelands of the Ixil, as well as vast areas of this strikingly beautiful country, have seen much violence and strife culminating in political repression and civil war. In the early eighties, the Ixil community was one of the principal targets of a genocidal operation, involving systematic killings, forced displacements and orchestrated hunger. At the 2013 trial of erstwhile president, Efraín Ríos Montt, eventually found guilty of having ordered the deaths of 1,771 Ixil people, the presiding judge, Jazmin Barrios, declared that 'The Ixils had been considered public enemies of the state and had been victims of virulent racism, as well as being branded an inferior race.' According to a 1999 United Nations truth commission, between seventy and ninety per cent of Ixil villages were razed and sixty per cent of the population in the altiplano region forced to flee to the mountains between 1982 and 1983. By 1996, it was estimated that some 7,000 Maya Ixil had been killed. The violence was particularly heightened during the period 1979–85 as successive Guatemalan administrations and the military pursued an indiscriminate *tierra arrasada* or scorched-earth policy.

Our own immediate host in the village of Xix, an hour's drive along a dirt road from Nebaj, was Don Tiburcio, a catechist of Ixil origin who has a very familiar face and for good reason – he was one of the chief protagonists of *Trócaire*'s 2003 lenten campaign, aimed at raising awareness of land rights issues in Guatemala and advocating justice for those that had lost their lives, their loved ones and their land in Guatemala's thirty-six year internal armed conflict. The first massacres in Tiburcio's neighbourhood began in 1981. In February 1982, while on watch with other community leaders, he raised the alarm that the army was coming and the whole village fled to the mountains. There he lost his first wife and children who died from malnutrition. Tiburcio was captured by the army in 1983, accused of being a guerrilla and was kept prisoner for three years. During this time he was subjected to repeated torture, interrogation, starvation and incomprehensible levels of cruelty at the hands of the Guatemalan military.[3]

Don Tiburcio was gratified by the opportunity to share his testimony and his reflections on the trial with us when we visited his home. Over the course of nearly three hours he recounted with incredible detail the story of the persecution of his community, how he came so close to death three times, that he thought he had actually died: 'I prayed to God to take me if it was my time – I thought I would die, but by the grace of God I managed to survive.' An estimated 200,000 of his fellow Guatemalans were murdered or 'disappeared' during the conflict, eighty-three per cent of whom were of indigenous ethnicity.[4] The genocide of the Ixil community was the most extreme expression of an ideology of racism that festered at the very core of a state; such that they were deemed an 'internal enemy' which had to be 'annihilated'.

After the bloodshed in December 1996, a peace agreement finally settled Guatemala's thirty-six year civil conflict and hopes were high that the country had reached a new beginning. But moving from a culture of war to peace is never an easy thing. Some of the combatants wasted little time in pursuing the only course of action they knew and turned to crime. Many indigenous leaders told us they are disappointed with the scarce improvements in opportunities for their people, who make up roughly half of Guatemala's population and who most keenly suffered the war's wrath.[5] Another dark cloud over Guatemala, even today, is the criminalisation of human rights workers as well as the subtle and at times, not so subtle, 'blackening' of their work and good name. 'Terrorists' and 'Marxists' are some of the labels used in what they describe as '*la campaña negra*'. There is also frequent recourse to dubious arrest warrants and indefinite detentions as well as continued discrimination against these people. As a consequence, one of the extraordinary tasks that development agencies are called to do, is simply to be 'companions' to these defenders. The very fact of being in the presence of a westerner while walking on the street or driving in one's car greatly reduces the likelihood of their being targeted in a hit and run shooting or bombing.

Nowadays, all over Guatemala, there remains a strong sense among the indigenous peoples of their still not being considered equal human beings with fellow *'guatemaltecos'*. This is fuelled by what they refer to as *'la impunidad'*, the immunity from justice still enjoyed by those who were key architects of the genocide. The recent high profile genocide trial of Ríos Montt, guilty verdict and subsequent setting aside, overruling and annulling of that verdict, confirmed the fears of many. As a consequence there is now a profound lack of confidence that guilty parties will ever be brought to justice. There is also a deep foreboding that some mechanism may be found for 'brushing things under the carpet of history'.

In Guatemala today, among those who suffered most, there remains a lack of any sense of closure. There is a shared feeling of not being able to grieve, of not being able to arrive at a common understanding of what truly happened. More concretely there is the frustration and pain of still not being able to discover what became of 'disappeared' family members and loved ones. As one of the community leaders put it 'we need to heal the past in order to live the present and to have any hope of approaching the future as one people.'

Our short observer mission concluded with a briefing of national ambassadors and government officials on the Friday morning back in Guatemala City. We emphasised our strong impression of a wonderful indigenous culture still not being fully accepted or recognised; a sense that it was continuing to be pushed to the margins and suppressed by a monolithic mono-culture that was largely unrepresentative of this beautiful country and its people. We also recounted our first-hand witness to a worrying lack of basic human rights and services such as sanitation, water, roads and infrastructure, healthcare, energy and even sufficient food and nutrition, not to mention basic access to justice and security and other fundamental state services. We related too how we had the privilege of revisiting with survivors the extraordinarily tragic and traumatic recent history of Guatemala; and having spoken with and listened to them at some length, had been dismayed to find that there was still no real acknowledgement by the State of the suffering and the slaughter during this bleak episode. Neither was there any bringing to justice or accountability for those who were the protagonists, actors and key agents in this most brutal chapter of Guatemalan history.

Our formal work of reporting over, we concluded our week with a visit to the newly opened Casa de la Memoria de Guatemala. Under the motif *'para no olvidar'* [so as not to forget] this centre does its best, with quite scant resources, to present Guatemalan history in an inclusive and truthful way so that the horrors of the immediate past will never be forgotten, or worse still, revisited. There are, in a glass case on permanent display, tens of thousands of items of correspondence. These include the 22,000 letters, written by Irish people to the Guatemalan government in 2003, demanding justice for Tiburcio and fellow victims and survivors of the conflict on foot of the Lenten Campaign. They were channelled through the *Trócaire* offices in Maynooth, Cork and Belfast. Seeing those handwritten notes, some carefully handwritten, others hastily scribbled, but all pleading for Tiburcio's release and many bearing a *Maigh Nuad, Cill Dara* postmark, brought home to me in a striking way how social justice and global solidarity can never be allowed to become mere abstractions and how, as members of one Christian family within this global village, we have real and tangible responsibilities toward each other – especially toward those who are our most vulnerable.

Earlier in the same week, I had another echo of those responsibilities and global ties when I chanced to meet with a religious sister from my own native heath who has spent a life time in Central and South America in the service of the Gospel among indigenous communities. 'I don't think we ever met before' I ventured as I grasped her hand. 'No but I've read you a couple of times in *The Furrow*' she retorted. Both episodes were a vivid reminder of how the written word can reach beyond boundaries of distance and difference to harness the energies of all of those who simply wish to stand in solidarity with their neighbour no matter which corner of the globe they should inhabit.

Reflecting on the invitation to share some of the flavour of my Guatemalan visit in these pages, while in turn celebrating the extraordinary contribution of a remarkable theological journal, it struck me that over the last half century, each of these Maynooth-based institutions have in their distinctive and quite separate ways shown us different dimensions of one and the same mission, as each has sought to build up Christ's kingdom at home and abroad. Concrete expressions of our call to discipleship, to shed the light of the gospel on our human condition and to allow *the living word* challenge our comfort and complacency, have been brought into our very living rooms and breakfast tables via the pages of *The Furrow* and the annual re-appearance of the *Trócaire* Lenten Box. Both have been instrumental too in reminding us that faith is never separable from our understanding of human life and dignity and each has brought to the fore our tradition of social justice with its roots in the Hebrew prophets.[6] They are each in their distinct ways a 'voice for justice' and a contemporary echo of those ancient voices that once announced God's special love for the poor and called God's people to a covenant of lasting love and justice. That well known motto *Novate vobis novale* famously echoes the prophet Jeremiah's words and has inspired generations of *Furrow* contributors to take up their pens and 'till the untilled ground'. That very same inspiration and summons to justice has also fired up many of those who strove and still strive to 'do the work of justice' through *Trócaire* Lenten Campaigns, 24-hour fasts and the many other concrete acts of solidarity and support for our sisters and brothers who suffer throughout the world. Like the prophetic wisdom from which they draw their inspiration, each institution has played its part 'in comforting the afflicted and afflicting the comfortable'.

Ultimately, 'doing the work of justice' takes courage, whether it be writing in the pages of a journal or working on the streets of a *favela*. Whether it be facing up to the injustices of our world or shining a light on those more near at hand, within our society, our homes, our church and our hearts. In the end it all comes back to the life and words of Jesus himself, who came 'to bring glad tidings to the poor … liberty to captives … recovery of sight to the blind' (Lk 4:18–19), and to following in the footsteps of the One who identified himself with 'the least of these', the hungry and the stranger (cf. Mt 25:45).[7]

A decade after the *Trócaire* letter campaign, Don Tiburcio finally had the opportunity to give his powerful testimony to the Guatemalan Supreme Court as a survivor of and witness to genocide. Those 22,000 carefully composed letters and petitions reminded him, and more importantly the Guatemalan government, that he was not alone. They remind all of us too I think that we each, on occasion, have to 'plough up the hard ground'[8] in order to allow the seeds of 'justice peace and joy in the Holy Spirit' take root afresh in our hearts and to let ours too become another 'voice for justice'.

Ecology as a Moral Issue:
An Ongoing Journey
PÁDRAIG CORKERY

In his many years as editor of *The Furrow*, Ronan Drury always succeeded in attracting contributors who engaged with issues that were of concern to Irish society, the Irish Church and the global community. Furthermore many of his contributors actively participated in a 'reading of the signs of the times' by reflecting on issues that were at the cutting edge of societal and church discourse. Many editions of *The Furrow*, indeed, dealt with issues in ways that introduced new perspectives that helped to open up discussion and move the debate forward. This is particularly true of the many articles that engaged with a) questions concerning the role of men and women in the life of the church; b) the challenges facing the Christian family in a radically changed culture and; c) issues relating to human relationships, both heterosexual and homosexual.

In from the margins
Concern for the environment as a moral issue is a relatively new phenomenon in the life of Church, state and society. Over the past fifty years, the Church's reflections on this crucial issue have become more frequent, more urgent in their tone and content and more theologically rooted. This is seen both in the documents of the universal Church and those of the local Church.[1] It is also to been seen in the many works of theologians over the past number of decades.[2] Equally the political community has begun to seriously engage with the issue, resulting in numerous conferences worldwide and the enacting of significant pieces of legislation aimed at halting environmental destruction. Within society many interest groups and individuals continue to raise awareness of this vital global issue through debate, lobbying and the embracing of alternative 'greener' lifestyles.

The pages of *The Furrow*, under the stewardship of Ronan Drury, reflected this growing interest in ecology as a moral issue. Irish theologian Seán McDonagh was a consistent and creative contributor over the decades. One of his early contributions placed ecology as a vital concern for theology and theological ethics.[3] A few years later, in the pages of *The Furrow*, he reported on the Justice, Peace and Integrity of Creation Convention, held in Korea in March 1990.[4] The developing corpus of

Church teaching on the topic was analysed and critiqued by McDonagh over the years.[5] Seán McDonagh's status as the leading Irish 'green' theologian is reflected in the fact that many of his publications were the subject of review articles in *The Furrow*.[6]

The theological roots of our concern for creation were the subject of the popular and successful, Furrow Guided Reading Programme (1987–8), when Denis Carroll's book, *Towards a Story of the Earth*, was the textbook chosen by Gabriel Daly OSA. The hierarchy's interest in the issue was reflected in an early publication by Cahal B. Daly, then Bishop of Down and Connor.[7] Concern for the environment in political, scientific and theological circles intensified worldwide with the dawn of the new millennium. This heightened sense of urgency was reflected in *The Furrow* articles by, amongst others, John O'Donoghue,[8] Donal O'Mahony,[9] Dermot A. Lane[10] and Donal Dorr.[11]

The response of the Church to concerns about the environment has developed and matured over the decades. Early references to the ecological issue in Church documents were often fleeting and superficial and not in any way integral to the documents.[12] Moreover many references to the environment were often presented in the language of self interest; if humans continue to cause environmental pollution and destruction, they will reap the consequences. Gradually this approach was replaced by a more adequate approach that viewed the destruction of the environment as a *theological* and *moral* issue rather than a merely pragmatic or aesthetic issue. Pope John Paul II, in January 1990, published the first document dedicated exclusively to the issues surrounding the environment. The document's title *Peace with God the Creator, Peace with all Creation* succinctly sums up the approach of the Christian tradition; our relationship with creation, in all its diversity and complexity, is rooted in our understanding of God as a loving Creator who has gifted us all we have and are.

In the remainder of this short essay, I will look at the central elements of the analysis found in Church documents and the remedies proposed therein for the reversal of the degradation of the environment.

Ecological Destruction: Contributing factors
The primary contributory factor to environmental destruction is identified as an attitude which sees the earth as an infinite resource to be used and manipulated by humanity for the exclusive benefit of humanity. In this

mindframe humankind sets itself 'up in place of God and thus ends up provoking a rebellion on the part of nature, which is more tyrannised than governed by humanity.'[13] Such an attitude fails to appreciate the integrity of creation, its finite nature and the inter-related nature of all created reality. It leads inevitably to an ethic of domination, rather than an ethic of responsible stewardship, which pays scant attention to consequences or to the integrity of creation.

Grinding poverty is a reality in many communities across the globe. It is a reality that forces people to eke out a living in ways that are ecologically unsound and in the long term unsustainable.[14] This reality of poverty in the midst of a world of abundance highlights the lack of solidarity within nations and, especially, between developed and developing nations. The ongoing reality of war and armed conflict continues to wreak havoc on the environment and to use up resources that could be directed towards the alleviation of poverty and human suffering. War contributes to the ecological crisis and the ecological crisis can lead to war. This link between peace building and environmental protection has been highlighted in a recent World Day of Peace Message.[15]

The predominance of a culture of consumerism has played a significant and ongoing role in environmental destruction. Such a culture, with its emphasis on 'what we have' rather than 'who we are', leads to lives of irresponsible consumerism. In their reflections on consumerism and its consequences, the Irish Bishops, in a pastoral letter written during the Celtic Tiger years of rapid economic growth, argued that 'an ethic of consumption is probably the least developed area of Church social teaching today'.[16] An adequate response to environmental destruction must include, particularly for developed nations, a credible 'ethic of consumption'.

Finally, the Compendium proposes that one possible consequence of a growing lack of belief in God is that 'nature is stripped of its profound meaning and impoverished'.[17] This severing of a link to a loving Creator God does have the potential to devalue creation in the eyes of some. To view creation, including humanity, as the consequence of chance, rather than a loving gift, could contribute to a culture of indifference or hostility to creation.

Response: A change of attitude and lifestyle needed
The response of Church teaching to the ecological crisis can succinctly be summed up in the call for a change of attitude and a change of lifestyles. The former challenges us to change how we view creation and our relationship to it. The latter impresses upon us the need to conscientiously examine our lifestyles.

At the core of the Church's developing approach to ecology is an acceptance of creation as a gift from a loving Creator. In nature 'the believer recognises the wonderful result of God's creative activity, which we may use responsibly to satisfy our legitimate needs, material or otherwise, while respecting the intrinsic balance of creation'.[18] All of creation is linked to a common source in a creator God and reflects the wonder and majesty of God. Indeed as the psalms and prayer tradition of the Church testify, contemplation of the wonders and beauty of creation can lead us to a greater and deeper appreciation of the sacred.[19] Each element of creation has its own 'grammar'[20] or 'prior God-given purpose'[21] which we are called to honour and protect. This implies that human stewardship of creation excludes attitudes and actions that violate the integrity of creation. Rather, responsible stewardship involves attitudes that are respectful and actions that promote flourishing. The 'gift' nature of all we are and have should shape the attitudes and actions of the believer. This attitude towards creation should be 'essentially one of gratitude and appreciation'.

In recent publications the intrinsic bond between all of creation has received more explicit attention. *Caritas in veritate* emphasised that 'the book of nature is one and indivisible'[22] and involves not only the environment but also all that contributes to integral human development. Human stewardship involves attention to environmental ecology and human ecology. We cannot be for all that is 'green' and remain indifferent to all that crushes or endangers the dignity of persons. And vice versa. We are called to respect the integrity of both ecologies and work towards creating societies where they flourish. That can only be accomplished if our world view incorporates an attitude of respect, reverence, and thankfulness that leads to lifestyles that are just, temperate and inclusive. Lifestyles that are life-giving in every sense of the word. The document further argued that 'the way humanity treats the environment influences the way it treats itself and vice versa'.[23] This is, I think, a very profound point because it emphasises that attitudes of disrespect towards any part of God's majestic creation can corrode and desensitise us and lead to a hardening of hearts that impacts on all relationships.

The ecological crisis has highlighted the need for solidarity between nations, especially between developed and developing nations. In particular the countries that are highly industrialised must lower their domestic energy consumption and work towards a 'worldwide redistribution of energy resources' so that poorer nations can have access to them.[24] Given that the ecological crisis has global consequences and is a global responsibility, wealthier nations have a duty to assist poorer nations towards developing practices that are ecologically sound.

The ecological crisis has obvious implications for how we conduct business and construct economic programmes. This is an urgent issue both for governments but also for the leaders of industry and commerce. Programmes of economic development must carefully 'consider the need to respect the integrity and the cycles of nature ... because environmental protection cannot be assured solely on the basis of financial calculations of costs and benefits'.[25] The maximisation of profit cannot be the sole goal of economic programmes. Rather, the goal must be the promotion of the global common good which includes the protection of the environment. A central insight of Catholic Social Doctrine is that economic activity is not an end in itself. Rather its *raison d'etre* is to serve the 'whole person and every person'.

Church documents have consistently highlighted the reality that the ecological crisis must be viewed from the perspective of inter-generational justice.[26] We have a responsibility – rooted in our shared humanity and a sense of solidarity – to hand on the environment to the next generation so that they too can be blessed by its beauty, diversity and bounty. Our responsibility for the environment – the common heritage of humankind – extends not only to this present generation but to future generations.

The contribution that poverty and conflict makes to environmental degradation is readily accepted by all. If we are serious about responding to the ecological crisis, the global community, and especially believers, have an obligation to confront the economic structures and policies that keep so many in dehumanising poverty. People in the first world must accept that attention to the rights of the poor will have consequences for first world lifestyles. Just trade between developing and developed nations will have inevitable consequences for richer nations. This point has been consistently made in the social teaching documents of the Church and was sharply articulated as far back as *Populorum progressio*; 'Is (s)he prepared to pay higher taxes so that public authorities may expand their efforts in the work of development? Is (s)he prepared to pay more for imported goods, so that the foreign producer may make a fairer profit.'[27]

Challenges going forward

Though concern for creation has come in from the margins in the teaching of the Churches, and in the priorities of many governments and societies, it has still some distance to go, I think, before it is recognised by many Christian believers as a core Christian concern. Though Church teaching on this issue is now theologically rooted and delivered with a great sense of urgency, it has not penetrated the minds and hearts of many believers. Maybe this can be explained by a dearth of preaching on this subject at parish liturgies. Or maybe some people are just not convinced that concern for the environment, or, indeed, concern for social justice are really Gospel imperatives. A particular challenge in the years ahead then is to try and convince more believers of the oneness of the Christian life; the call and challenge to live in right relationship with God, self, others and God's creation. The Christian life is an integrated life where the values of the Gospel shape these four relationships. The language of the two ecologies, found in *Caritas in veritate* and elsewhere, could, I think, be very fruitful in inspiring believers because it emphasises the link between humankind and the rest of creation in God's loving design.

A second challenge, particularly for people of the developed world, is that of lifestyle change. The developed world has contributed more to environmental degradation than any other section of humanity. We have done this primarily through over consumption of energy and created goods. The necessary reduction in consumption will have (minor) negative implications for the quality of our lives but (significant) positive implications for the environment and future generations. This is a daunting but worthwhile challenge for a people rooted in the Gospel, and called to solidarity and service.

A third challenge is to face up to the direct link between poverty and environmental destruction. Any serious effort at addressing the ecological crisis must confront the reality of poverty and the sinful structures that perpetuate that inter-generational reality. In this regard the analysis and principles of Catholic social doctrine can make a valuable contribution. The principle of the Universal Destination of Goods boldly asserts that the world and its goods were made for everyone rather than a select few. The right to private property is subordinated to this principle and to that of the common good. The virtue and principle of solidarity, rooted in our shared humanity and destiny, challenges us to work for the good of all because 'we are *all* really responsible for *all*'.[28] The language of 'social sin' and 'structures of sin' enable us to accurately describe social, political and economic realities that imprison, impoverish and demean individuals and communities and should motivate us towards dismantling these sinful structures. In this regard Pope John Paul II wrote about the danger of believers failing in their duty to confront what is contrary to Gospel values because of 'laziness, fear or the conspiracy of silence, through secret complicity or indifference ...'[29]

Finally, in that same Apostolic Exhortation, Pope John Paul II proposed that some neglect the call to create a better world by taking refuge 'in the supposed impossibility of changing the world ...'[30] This is a real danger for the Christian community as it faces the attitudinal and lifestyle challenges generated by the ecological crisis and, indeed, by the reality of poverty and exclusion. Change seems so difficult and slow. Yet, believers must trust that change is possible. Human structures – political, social and economic – are constructed and maintained by human choices and priorities. These can be challenged and reversed by people of good will working together to build a more inclusive, 'greener' world. This is a special challenge, privilege and responsibility for a believing people called to be 'the salt of the earth and the light of the world'.

From Hippocrates to Bioethics
GINA MENZIES

Bioethics in the News

Issues in bioethics continue to attract a great deal of attention and play a growing role in public debate. We have all become more concerned with who lives, who dies and who decides.[1] In the summer of 2014, the case of Baby Gammy, a Down Syndrome twin born to a surrogate Thai woman, commissioned by an Australian couple, and subsequently reportedly abandoned by them, featured in news coverage around the world. In the same month, the World Health Organisation[2] declared the Ebola crisis in West Africa to be an international emergency. Early in the crisis, the World Health Organisation said that, in the special circumstances, it was ethical to allow drugs untested on human subjects to be given to patients with the condition, even though there was no certainty of effectiveness or safety.

In 2013, a case in Belgium grabbed international attention. Belgian doctors euthanised forty-five-year-old identical deaf twins who were going blind and requested assisted suicide. Marc and Eddy Verbessem were born deaf, never married and lived together, working as cobblers. When they discovered they had a form of glaucoma they asked for euthanasia as they believed their lives would be unbearable if they could no longer see. The euthanasia debate usually centres on cases of the terminally ill or those suffering intolerable pain, but neither featured in this instance. A few days later, the Belgian government announced that it would amend the law to allow minors and people with dementia be euthanised. This became law in 2014,[3] despite the opposition of 160 paediatricians and the Catholic Archbishop of Michelen-Brussels.

In Ireland, Marie Fleming, suffering from multiple sclerosis, took a landmark case to the Irish High Court for the right to die with the assistance of her partner. In April 2013, the High Court[4] ruled against her and this judgement was upheld by the Supreme Court.[5] In delivering the ruling, the Supreme Court noted that there was nothing to stop the Oireachtas from legislating to allow for assisted suicide in such cases, once it was satisfied that appropriate safeguards were put in place. In 2010 the DPP for England and Wales published a Policy for Prosecutors in Respect of Cases of Encouraging or Assisting Suicide.[6] These legal and medical cases raise significant ethical issues, which are nowadays addressed by what is known as Bioethics.

Bioethics

Bioethics can be defined as a branch of ethics that studies the philosophical, social, and legal issues arising in medicine and the life sciences. It is chiefly concerned with human life and well-being. Within academia it is a relatively new discipline derived from biology and moral philosophy; one a life science, the other an ethics of human behaviour in the field of medical practice and scientific research.

Methodologically it is similar to evidence based medicine. It is necessary to line up as many facts and as much information as possible, medical, social, legal and relational with a view to doing justice to the dignity and human rights of all patients. It has become a formal element in medical education since the 1990s in Ireland and since the 1970s in the United States. By the 1970s, bioethics had become the discipline for discourse on the problematic side of the new medicine and science.

Today, bioethics relies on diverse resources to analyse, assess and judge the morality of interactions between physicians and patients and the wider society. It is interdisciplinary in its methodology. Edmund Pellegrino, philosopher and doctor describes medicine as encounters involving a dialectic between clinical medicine and philosophy.[7] Philosophically, bioethics uses theories of Deontology and Utilitarianism. The former emphasises the need for rules, norms, duties, and respect for persons. The latter, the need to maximise benefits for the majority of people but bioethics never holds to them in an absolutist fashion. Casuistry, the study of cases is consistently used to illustrate the demands of doing the good in a variety of instances. National codes such as those of Medical Councils in various countries and international codes such as that of the World Medical Association reflect the insights of contemporary bioethics.

Earlier Days

Medical practice up to the middle of the twentieth century was more concerned with comfort than cure.[8] The patient was the passive recipient of the professional expertise of the doctor. Frequently, a poor diagnosis was withheld from the patient in order to prevent further anxiety. Paternalism was the prevailing attitude. Consent for medical treatment was rarely sought. There was an assumption that what the doctor ordered was also what the patient would want. Today, the model of patient doctor collaboration is the ideal taught in most medical schools in the western world. Informing the patient of options and outcomes and seeking consent are the cornerstones of this model.

Earlier efforts to articulate an ethical code go back to the fourth century BCE when the school of Hippocrates produced an oath for doctors. This oath, which physicians were required to take, was to act always for the good of their patients and to keep confidences. It also required them never to cut – that would forbid surgery today! An English doctor, Thomas Percival wrote the first book to bear the title medical ethics in 1803.[9] He was asked to provide some guidance for a dispute in the Manchester Royal Infirmary which broke out between surgeons, physicians and apothecaries. In 1847, the American Medical Association published a code which borrowed many of Percival's precepts.[10]

Two developments converged in the middle of the last century which increased the urgency for a renewal of ethics in medicine. These were the scientific advances to improve healthcare and the scandals of unethical research.

Scientific and Medical Advances

At the dawn of the twentieth century, the greatest threat to human health came from infectious diseases, which frequently claimed the lives of the very young. Babies born in 1900 often did not reach fifty years of age.[11] Immunisation has eliminated smallpox and has almost eliminated polio and measles. Currently, non-communicable diseases, such as heart disease, cancer, obesity and diabetes reflect life style changes and mainly affect adult populations. Dementia, especially Alzheimer's disease, has become one of the conditions whose incidence frequently increases dramatically with age.

Medical developments such as cardiac resuscitation, assisted reproduction, organ transplantation, genetic engineering, embryonic stem cell research and enhanced diagnostics as well as the creation of new therapies and drugs have contributed significantly to improvements in the quality and length of life for those who live in the developed world, alongside ongoing debates concerning the allocation of healthcare resources. The quality and quantity of our days is ever growing. The global number of centenarians is projected to increase tenfold between 2010 and 2050.[12]

The advances in medicine after World War II heightened the need to reconsider the ethical aspects of medical practice. Penicillin, discovered in

1928, became the treatment for pneumonia and other infections during the 1960s. Polio vaccines were introduced in the 1950s. Chlorpromazine became available to treat schizophrenia. Full cardiac resuscitation was introduced in 1958. The first heart transplant was carried out by Dr Christiaan Barnard in 1967 and now thousands of heart transplants are carried out every year throughout the world. Since 2005, fifty face transplants have been performed for patients with serious burns and disfigurements.

Earlier ethical frameworks were not enough to deal with the 'big item' issues in the area of genetics, reproduction technology, research and even the definition of death itself as well as the myriad of dilemmas which occur frequently in a medical setting, such as:

- Who receives the donated kidney?
- Should an unconscious Jehovah's Witness be transfused?
- Should an anorexic teenager be force fed against expressed wishes?
- Should all who suffer cardiac arrest be resuscitated?
- Should a terminally ill patient be assisted to die?
- Should we legislate to allow or ban surrogacy?
- How do we respond to a colleague who is behaving unethically?
- How do we distribute the health budget?

Exposure of Medical and Scientific Scandals in the Twentieth Century
Nazi doctors were put on trial at Nuremberg following World War II. They had been involved in what they claimed were legitimate research and experiments, more accurately described as cruel and inhumane treatment resulting in many deaths and extreme suffering. They were accused of murder, torture and other atrocities committed in the concentration camps. Seven of the doctors were sentenced to death and nine were imprisoned. In their defence they claimed they were conducting medical research. In the execution of these experiments they broke every canon of medical practice. The ten principles of the Nuremberg Code drawn up after the trials focused on consent, voluntariness and the need to avoid unnecessary injury to the participants.[13] Despite the existence of the code, there was little change in medical ethics during the 1950s.

One of the worst scandals was revealed in the United States in Alabama by a whistleblower and reported in *The Washington Post* in 1972. This sandal was the Tuskegee syphilis experiment, which continued for forty years (1932–72). Black, illiterate poor men with syphilis were led to believe they were receiving treatment when those caring for them were merely tracking the pathology of the condition. This was carried out under the auspices of the United States Public Health Service. Even when penicillin became available these men did not receive treatment. The defence offered by the doctors involved was as spurious as that offered in the trials of the Nazi doctors – that the work was for the greater good of science! 'It was the longest non-therapeutic experiment on humans in medical history.'[14] In 1997 President Clinton apologised on behalf of the United States and compensation was paid to those still alive.

Other scandals in research exposed by whistleblowers had a profound impact on the medical profession and scientists. Two doctors, one a Professor of Research in Anaesthesia in Harvard Medical School, Henry Beecher and Maurice Pappworth, a medical ethicist and medical educator in England, exposed many examples of unethical research in the 1960s. Beecher wrote a famous article 'Ethics & Clinical Research' published in the prestigious *New England Journal of Medicine* in 1965. Beecher cited twenty-two medical experiments where patients were exposed to risks and which were conducted without the consent of the participants, who were often poor or mentally incapacitated. Around the same time, Pappworth who was in correspondence with Beecher wrote *Human Guinea Pigs: Experimentation on Man* in 1968, exposing similar practices.[15] Pappworth went a step further then Beecher by naming those involved in conducting over two hundred unethical experiments. Both men suffered severe criticism from their colleagues but are today recognised as pioneers who initiated necessary changes in medical ethics.

The Belmont Report
The US Government established a commission to examine the American scandals especially the Tuskegee case. The result was the Belmont Report. Its findings suggested a number of core principles to govern ethical research involving human subjects: respect for persons, beneficence and justice.

By 1979, these appeared in a framework theory, called Principlism, devised by ethicists, Tom Beauchamp and James Childress.[17] They proposed four principles which incorporated the principles of the Belmont report. Respect for persons was encapsulated in the principle of autonomy, non-maleficence, the principle not to inflict harm on others was added to the three recommended in the report.[18]

The shadow of Nuremberg, scientific and medical progress and the exposure of a number of scandals led to the search for a new moral code in medicine.

Theologians Enter the Search for a New Medical Ethic

Life, death and justice are issues long pondered by theologians and philosophers. A natural partnership developed between theologians teaching moral theology in American Universities and those in search of a new medical ethic. Albert Jonsen, a former Jesuit, and teacher of philosophy at Loyola University, recognised the necessity for a new model of medical ethics. The old ethics were too frail to meet the challenges posed by the new science and medicine.[19]

As bioethics was coming into being, Catholic moral theology was also entering a new phase. The second Vatican Council called for a renewal in Catholic moral theology which up to then had had a strong emphasis on an interpretation of natural law in terms of the purpose and structure of human functions. Richard McCormick describes the pre-Vatican II morality as a system based on legalism and absolute obedience to a rule-based morality that provided little space for growth in moral maturity. He describes this in an extreme example of removing ham pieces from split pea soup on Fridays![20]

The call for renewal emphasised a more biblical, nuanced pastorally-based theology: one that was less absolutist with recognition of context when deliberating on the morality of an action. Taking culture seriously was given expression and meaning in the phrase 'historical consciousness', acknowledging that culture affects our moral awareness and development.

This created space to reconstruct a more meaningful connection between gospel and life and to recognise the messiness of reality. Reading the 'Signs of the Times' provided a paradigm shift from a morality based on rules and paternalism to one of personal responsibility.[21] John Mahoney SJ emphasised the need to recognise that there is not always a ready answer to individual questions and that reality is essentially relational and conscience is primary.[22]

The paternalistic challenge to moral theology and medical ethics converged. A collaborative relationship between doctor and patient became the new norm. It is not therefore surprising that theologians who were grappling with new insights from Vatican II and the need for a more authentic moral theology were invited into conferences and discussions, which led to the birth of bioethics.

The Hastings Center[23] and The Kennedy Institute for Ethics[24] sought theologians as natural dialogue partners to explore the new questions. Paul Ramsey, a Methodist lecturer in Christian ethics at Princeton, and James Gustafson, a divinity lecturer at Yale, were invited onto the board of The Hastings Center. The Kennedy Institute was directed by a Mennonite theologian, Le Roy Walters, and its first scholars were Charles E. Curran and Richard McCormick. McCormick became Professor of Christian Ethics at The Kennedy Institute of Georgetown University and he is credited with the notion of proportionalism in moral deliberations.

Moral theologian Charles Curran critiqued the stance on contraception taken in *Humanae vitae* (1968). He invoked fresh thinking in many areas of sexual morality and focused on the primacy of conscience. He was rewarded for his efforts by dismissal from his teaching post at Catholic universities by the then Cardinal Joseph Ratzinger, Head of the Congregation for the Doctrine of the Faith. Curran continues to teach in the Methodist University in Dallas.

Joseph Fletcher, an Episcopalian Minister, was the first to challenge the common practice of withholding truth from a patient even if the motivation was paternalistic and done to protect the patient from further anxiety. He is also credited with the theory of situational ethics: a moral stance which insists that context is a pertinent element of any ethical dilemma. It is clear how many of these theological insights immediately lent themselves to the new study of bioethics. Many of these theologians, initially partners in the birth of medical ethics, became the first generation of bioethicists.[25]

Bioethics Today
Moral theology serves a very practical purpose: it focuses on how we live in the light of Gospel values. The early bioethicists in the field of medicine and science had a similar task – to bring a new moral ethic to the practice of medicine and science for the twenty-first century. Bioethics, like moral theology, is a pragmatic exercise in resolving dilemmas. While moral the-

ologians deal with how we live our lives, bioethicists deal with the practice of medicine on a day-to-day basis. Bioethics is also an academic discipline which does not make extravagant claims for recognition but is as pertinent to patient well-being as the skills and competencies of its practitioners.

Auricular Confession:
Some Inadequacies
CHARLES E. CURRAN

It is a privilege to contribute to this Festschrift in honour of Ronan Drury, Emeritus Professor of Homiletics at Maynooth and longtime Editor of *The Furrow*. *The Furrow* has made an outstanding contribution to pastoral theology – relating theology to the life of the Church and the world. In keeping with this focus, the present article will discuss some inadequacies in the sacramental rite of auricular confession, especially in the light of contemporary theological understanding.

Sin, forgiveness, and penance have been central realities in the Christian life. So important are these realities that in the Catholic tradition, penance is one of the seven sacraments. The reality of penance involves more than just the sacrament, but the sacrament gives a special importance and significance to the reality of penance.

Historical Development
History reminds us of the developing practice of sacramental penance in the Church.[1] The New Testament testifies to the forgiveness of sin and the reconciliation of the sinner with the Christian community, but various forms of such reconciliation have taken place over time. One of the most significant developments in the early history concerns the possibility of receiving reconciliation or penance more than once – a controversy that continued until the seventh century. From the fourth to the sixth centuries there emerged what is most properly called 'canonical penance' since it was governed by the canons or church laws. Sometimes this has been called public penance and on the basis of that a few thought it involved the public confession of sins, but such was not the case. The canonical penance took place in three stages – entry into the order of penitents through the hands of the bishop, a long stage of severe expiation, and finally reconciliation with the Christian community through the hands of the bishop. Since this very severe process could not be repeated, it gave way in the seventh and later centuries to what was called tariff penance. The minister was the priest or monk, not the bishop; confession played a larger role; the minister assigned a penance to be done according to what was found in the penitential books; then what was now beginning to be called absolution

was given. In all these variations of sacramental reconciliation there were questions and even abuses that had to be addressed.

The Fourth Lateran Council in 1215 and especially the Council of Trent in its fourteenth session in 1551 inaugurated what became the format of the sacrament of penance until the present time. Trent called for the confession of all mortal sins to the priest at least once a year according to their number and species. The emphasis was now on confession; satisfaction was reduced to a prayer; and the priest gave absolution after the confession of sins and the assignment of the penance.

As a result of this format the sacrament became known as confession. The Catholic Reformation stressed the role of confession in the life of the faithful. So important was the sacrament of confession that it shaped the course of moral theology in seminaries that existed from the Council of Trent until Vatican II. The courses in moral theology had the purpose of training future confessors in determining what acts were sinful and the degree of sinfulness. By the twentieth century, the confession of devotion involving just venial sins, became very common. On Saturday afternoons and evenings lines of penitents waiting to go to confession were commonplace in Catholic churches. Religious women and men and priests were expected to go to confession on a weekly basis.[2] Confession played a very important role in the life of all Catholics. Today confession plays a much smaller role. The sharp decline in confession in the period after Vatican II is acknowledged by all.

The Pre-Vatican II Experience

How does one evaluate the practice of confession that played such a significant role in the pre-Vatican II Church? There can be no doubt that for some people the role of penance was truly an experience of the forgiveness and mercy of God, and helped the penitent to transform her life. This was especially true of penitents who had experienced special crises or problems in their lives. Also for some the devotional confession was a source of spiritual growth.

On the other hand, the Catholic practice of confession in the pre-Vatican II Church is associated with some negative aspects. The practice of penance contributed to the phenomenon known as 'Catholic guilt'. So commonplace is this concept and reality that even Wikipedia has an article on 'Catholic Guilt'. At the very minimum some of the context surrounding confession, especially the parish mission, contributed to the existence of

Catholic guilt. Parish missions were an important part of Catholic devotional life. A number of studies have documented the role of the parish mission in Ireland and the United States in the latter part of the nineteenth and early part of the twentieth century. These missions were usually held once a year in every parish. The preaching aimed to bring people to confession and the fear of hell was the primary motivating factor. The emphasis on fire and brimstone brought about guilt which then brought the person to confession. Parish missions still exist today but they are no longer that prominent in Catholic life. In addition the newer approach to missions stresses God's love, mercy, and forgiveness.[3]

Closely associated with guilt is fear. Many Catholics approached confession with trepidation and even fear. The surroundings of the stark and dark confessional box greatly contributed to the trepidation of the penitent. Many penitents never experienced the joy of celebrating the mercy of the loving God whom we call Mother and Father. The theological context for confession conceived of the Christian life as a life of duty in obeying the commandments of God and not the loving response to the gift of God's love. The motivation of the fear of hell played a major role in motivating Catholics to do their God-given duties.

Connected with the emphasis on sin and the fear of hell was the phenomenon of scrupulosity. The scrupulous person experiences the fear of sinning in all that one does. Scrupulosity paralyses the person who always lives in fear of committing sin and going to hell no matter what one does. Scrupulosity affected many Catholics in the area of sexuality, especially because every sexual sin involves a mortal sin that would send one to hell. Another manifestation of scrupulosity, which some older readers might still remember, was the difficulty many priests had in praying or saying the words of consecration. Some priests repeated the words a number of times because they were fearful that if the words were not said correctly there would be no consecration of the bread and wine, and the priest himself would commit a grave sin. No priests were ever scrupulous in making sure they said exactly the opening prayer of the Mass (*Introibo ad altare Dei*) because the validity of the sacrament did not depend on saying these exact words.

Post-Vatican II Practice and Theory
Since Vatican II the role of confession (the name of the sacrament has properly been changed to reconciliation, but the basic ritual remains the same)

in the Church has changed dramatically. The people of God for the most part no longer see confession as an important part of their lives. This article will now show that there are good theological reasons why the vast majority of Catholics today do not go to confession. The Christian moral life is no longer understood as the duty of doing God's law under the fear of eternal damnation. The Christian life involves, rather, a loving response to the gift of God's love. The primary motivating factor of the Christian life is not fear, but the good news that we have been justified by God through Jesus and the Holy Spirit with the gift of God's love and the call to friendship with God.

The centrality of confession in the present ritual does not recognise in practice the broader dimensions of the reality of penance. From the time of Thomas Aquinas in the thirteenth century, Catholic theology has recognised three fundamental acts of the penitent – contrition, confession, and satisfaction. Even the manuals of moral theology with their narrow focus on training confessors for determining what acts were sinful and the degree of sinfulness continued to recognise the three fundamental acts of the penitent.[4] The present ritual, however, so stresses confession that contrition as the basic change of heart and satisfaction are for all practical purposes neglected.

There is also a more basic problem with the present ritual – the understanding of sin itself. Sin is seen as an act against the law of God. For many in the pre-Vatican II Church, confession involved reciting a laundry list of particular actions. The contemporary understanding of sin has changed. Sin is now seen in relational terms. Contemporary Catholic moral theology in general sees the moral life in relational terms – our multiple relationships with God, neighbour, world, and self. The basic scriptural summary of the Christian life – to love God above all things and to love our neighbour as ourselves – sees the life of the disciple of Jesus in relational terms. Our relationship to God by definition includes all the relationships to others, the world, and self. How can you love the God you do not see if you do not love the neighbour you do see? Christian moral life involves growth in these basic relations. Acts have a meaning and importance only insofar as they manifest and develop these relationships.

Such a relational approach also affects our understanding of sin. Sin is not primarily an act but involves our multiple relationships with God, neighbour, world, and self. Elsewhere I have pointed out in some detail how the first chapter of Genesis well-illustrates the relational understanding of sin.[5] The sin of Adam and Eve was not primarily their disobedience of God's command but rather their deeper refusal to accept the relationship of loving dependence on God. This broken relationship is illustrated by the fact that after their sin, when God came down in the cool of the evening to walk with them in the garden, they hid themselves. Also in the end they had to leave God's garden because they had broken their relationship with God. But sin also affects our relationship with others. Adam and Eve were to become two in one flesh, totally committed to one another, but when confronted by God about what they had done, Adam put the blame on Eve – she did it, not me. The mythical story of Genesis tells how their son killed his brother as a consequence of sin. Sin affected also their relationships to the world. In accord with the cultural understanding of the time, as a result of sin Adam experienced toil and weariness in his work and Eve brought forth her children in labour and pain. With regard to their relationship to one's self, it was only after sin that they experienced division within themselves as illustrated by the fact that they felt the need to cover their nakedness.

The Catholic understanding today recognises both mortal sin and venial sin in relational terms. In a relational approach, mortal sin involves the breaking of our multiple relationships while venial sin weakens the multiple relationships. The relationship to God is known and manifested in these other relationships to neighbour, world, and self.

In the light of the relational model of sin, the inadequacy of seeing sin as an act against the law of God becomes evident. One cannot determine the state of a relationship based only on observing one act. My being angry with my friend may very well be a sign that the relationship is broken, but it might also indicate only that I had a bad night. Most people would consider it a rash judgement if one judges another person on the basis of one act alone. The inner heart of the person can only be understood in the light of a variety of different individual acts. If mortal sin is understood as a particular act then obviously there can be many mortal sins. In a relational understanding there is no doubt that mortal sin is a much less frequent occurrence in the Christian life than it was thought to be in the pre-Vatican II Church.

A relational understanding of sin goes hand-in-hand with the relational understanding of growth in the spiritual and moral life. Catholic spirituality has consistently emphasised the need for growth in the spiritual life. The New Testament insists on the importance of growth. Some decades ago George T. Montague published his book, *Maturing in Christ: Saint Paul's Program for Christian Growth*. The Christian through the Spirit is a new creature called to be transformed into the fullness of life.[6]

Throughout the centuries spiritual writers have emphasised this growth in various stages. For some spiritual growth involves moving from one virtue to another. In the first stage the Christian serves God through fear; in the second stage one serves God through hope and expectation of recompense; in the third stage, the Christian serves God through charity and love. Others such as St Bernard describe the stages of growth in terms of progress in one virtue, such as progress in love or charity. Many are familiar with the three ways proposed by Ignatius of Loyola in the *Spiritual Exercises*. The purgative stage involves struggle against sin and temptation, insisting on mortification and the reception of the sacraments. The second stage – the illuminative way – concerns growth and progress in the virtues through the imitation of Christ, who is light and life. The third stage, the unitive way, is identified with the mystical life involving a deeper level of union with God in prayer and emphasising the role of the gifts of the Holy Spirit.[7]

The Constitution on the Church of Vatican II in its fifth chapter emphasised the call of the whole Church to holiness. All the faithful of whatever status are called to the fullness of the Christian life and to the perfection of charity.[8] The pre-Vatican II Church insisted on the distinction between the laity as those who live in the world and obey the Ten Commandments and the religious who leave the world to follow the evangelical counsels. The gospel after Vatican II was not a counsel for a few, but a call for all the baptised. Moral theology today must recognise and develop the call to holiness of all the baptised.

The relational understanding of the Christian life furnishes a good way of describing the Christian call to holiness and perfection. Just as sin is seen in terms of multiple relationships, so too conversion involves multiple relationships. Even before Vatican II, Bernard Häring insisted on the basic reality of conversion as the fundamental reality of the Christian moral life. The very basic conversion is the change from sin to grace, which is the very opposite of mortal sin as the move from grace to sin. Häring, however, stressed the need for continual conversion in the Christian life after this basic conversion. Continual conversion puts flesh on the bones of the call to holiness.[9] Continual conversion is likewise to be understood today in relational terms – the growth in our relationships with God, neighbour, world, and self. The insistence on the multiple relationships and the inter-relatedness of the relationships overcomes the danger in some forms of spirituality mentioned above which restrict holiness only to our relationship with God. On this basis one can appreciate why the International Synod of Bishops in 1974 insisted that action on behalf of justice and the transformation of the world is a constitutive dimension of the preaching of the gospel.[10] Growth in spirituality must include more than just growth in our direct relationship to God.

The sacrament of penance seen in a relational anthropology of sin and conversion thus should contribute greatly to the realisation that all the faithful are called to growth in their moral and spiritual lives.

The Sacramental Aspect

As mentioned, the ritual of auricular confession flourished in a context which conceived the moral life primarily as a series of duties based on obedience to God's commands, and not the contemporary context of a loving response to the God who has first loved us. As a result, the contemporary understanding of sacramentality remains very much in the shadows in the celebration of the rite of confession. The sacraments are saving encounters in which the love of God comes to us through Jesus and the Holy Spirit and we change our hearts in response to this love. The sacraments in general are joyful celebrations of God's gift of love to us and our response. The sacrament of penance or reconciliation in particular celebrates the mercy and forgiveness of God who is willing to embrace us even after we have broken our relationships or fallen short in them. The sacrament of reconciliation therefore should be a joyful celebration of the mercy and forgiveness of God. Our first response is praise and thanksgiving for this totally undeserved gift.

The sacrament of penance, however, is not magic; it also calls for a response on the part of the penitent. To its credit, the Thomistic understanding of auricular confession avoided a one-sided magical understanding of the sacrament. Thomas Aquinas as an anthropological realist recognised that the sinner must always have the change of heart, whether forgiveness occurs inside or outside the sacrament. In fact,

Aquinas held that forgiveness often occurs before the sacramental celebration itself. The person's heart is already changed before the sacrament is celebrated. The grace of the sacrament does not supply for any lack or deficiency on the part of the penitent.[11] However, the format of auricular confession fails to recognise the primacy of God's merciful gift and the sinner's first response of praise and thanksgiving.

Sacramental rituals reveal much about our understanding of God. The theological context and the ritual of auricular confession portray God as the sovereign Lord who is to be obeyed. The contemporary sacramental approach stresses the primacy of God's love and mercy, recognises God as the gracious Mother and Father who without any merit on our part shares love and life with us and is always willing to show mercy and forgiveness in our sinfulness and shortcomings. In Catholic practice today there is still too much emphasis on God as the one who is to be obeyed rather than the loving parent who makes us adopted children and sisters and brothers of Jesus.

Another aspect of sacramentality that is missing in auricular confession is the reconciliation with the Church. The confessor acts as a minister of the Church, but the role of the Church is really not visible. Sacraments by their very nature are called to make visible and present the realities they celebrate. The older canonical penance gave a very significant role to the ecclesial aspect. The sinner was installed into the order of penitents, and after a long, harsh penance, the sinner was reconciled to the Church community through the laying on of hands by the bishop. The role of reconciliation with the Church is a difficult one for many people to appreciate today. To make this aspect more present in the sacramental celebration will not be easy, but at least a more community celebration of the sacrament is a good start.

This essay has emphasised the inadequacy of the present rite of auricular confession in light of contemporary understandings of sin, conversion, growth in the Christian life, and sacramentology. The theological positions developed here give some direction toward a renewed ritual for the sacrament of penance but this essay does not attempt to develop such a rite.

Society, the Institutional Church and Homosexuality

BEN KIMMERLING

Next year the Irish government will be asking the citizens of this state to decide whether or not same-sex couples should be allowed to marry. Such a proposal would have been unthinkable a generation ago. However secular society has been changing rapidly. Homosexuality has been decriminalised. Civil Partnership has been introduced. People who are gay are no longer invisible. They now talk honestly to heterosexual people about their own often painful experiences as gay people, who had to live in an oppressive society. Their honesty has challenged our assumptions, changed our attitudes and invited us into an encounter with them as normal vulnerable human beings.

Although this change of attitude towards people who are gay is noticeable, it is not however uniform. Consequently the discourse on the legalisation of gay marriage has been at times fractious. Is there perhaps a better way to conduct the conversation in the months ahead – one based on mutuality? Instead of attacking one another, each side could reflect on its own attitudes and assumptions in order to understand how their experiences have shaped them. This kind of dialogue, which has already been started by the gay community, could, if it is continued, promote greater understanding and would be less bruising on all sides. The success of such a conversation would require great honesty, but it would encourage the growth of empathy on all sides. Obviously it is not so easy for heterosexual and homosexual people to imaginatively inhabit one another's physical world. But surely, given our common humanity, it must be possible if we listen with openness, to develop some understanding of the emotional and intellectual world of the other and to bring that understanding to the public conversation.

The Gay Journey into Awareness

Many people who are gay have spoken about the growth of their awareness of their sexual orientation. This appears to have occurred in stages over a period of time. It manifested itself at first as an inchoate unarticulated physical awareness – below the level of conscious thought. Then, as this knowledge emerged into consciousness, it became a more explicit emotional and intellectual awareness. This often didn't chime with the understanding of sexuality which the person received from the surrounding culture. This dissonance gave rise to negative feelings – such as confusion, unease, resistance, fear, anger, turmoil and even temporarily, outright denial. Eventually, and sometimes after much anguish, the internal conflict between the physical, emotional and intellectual levels of the person's personality were reconciled and an acceptance of the individual's sexual orientation took place. It was usually at this point of integration that the gay person felt ready to 'come out'. This journey towards integration was painful because it was conducted in a society which was often intolerant of homosexuality. It is not surprising then that some people who are gay may feel anger, rage, or bitterness towards that society.

However what is rarely adverted to is the fact that, until relatively recently, many heterosexual people were simply ignorant of the existence of homosexuality. So they too have been making a journey into awareness and acceptance of the homosexual orientation. This parallel journey is certainly not as painful as the gay journey. But the person making it does go through certain stages before a mature acceptance of the gay orientation is achieved. If a civilised conversation is to be conducted in the period between now and the referendum, then everyone, including the gay community, needs to understand this. If gay people take a long time to accept their own orientation, then they should understand that heterosexual people too may take time to move from ignorance to full acceptance. Human acceptance and understanding rarely arrive ready made.

We need to remember too that intolerance and repression didn't only come from the heterosexual side. Intolerance sometimes came from gay people who repressed their own homosexuality and who therefore were very hard on their own kind. And ignorance was not all on one side either. Gay people were often ignorant too. That is why they sometimes thought that there was something wrong with themselves.

A Heterosexual Journey into Awareness
The wide-spread acknowledgment of the gay orientation is a relatively new phenomenon. Acceptance of it has been gathering pace in the past thirty years. I see this reflected in my own family. Twenty-five years ago, when my mother was in her nineties she asked me 'what is homosexuality?' She had no idea such an orientation existed until she began to

see references to it in the papers. The concept was not part of her known world. So her ignorance of it was total. Could she be accused of being homophobic? I think not, because culpability requires awareness. Twenty years later, my grandchildren have routinely met gay couples who have been guests in their home. So awareness of homosexuality is part of their everyday reality.

But what of the generations in between – my own and my daughters' generation? Our life experience encompasses both poles. I was totally unaware of homosexuality when I was growing up. By my late twenties, the word was probably in my vocabulary, but I had no occasion to use it, or think about it and only vaguely understood it. Then in my mid-thirties I attended a talk given by a married couple. The husband spoke first. He said that having married, he then discovered that he was gay. He talked of his struggle at first to suppress it, and then having failed, of his efforts to express it in casual, furtive encounters. His wife spoke of her devastation when she discovered the truth and of her suffering as she watched her husband's infidelity with other men.

So I was confronted by the human face of homosexuality for the first time. It was like discovering an unknown continent. I found it extra-ordinary. I had a variety of responses. Emotionally I was deeply moved. I was filled with compassion for the suffering which both endured. I found it profoundly thought-provoking. Homosexuality seemed strange, mysterious, foreign, like hearing about life on another planet but without having any desire to go there. And lastly, if I am to be really honest, I felt an initial spontaneous reaction of distaste. Fortunately however, that reaction was overshadowed by the deep compassion which I felt as I listened to those two vulnerable human beings.

As I write it now, I recall hearing that word 'distaste' in another context. I was in my forties. An elderly priest friend – now long dead – confided in me that he was homosexual – a brave confession at that time. He had a breakdown in his fifties and spent a number of years attending a psychoanalyst. During his analysis he acknowledged his homosexuality and found a way of integrating that aspect of his personality into his priestly life. That he did this successfully was evident: when I knew him, he was loved by both men and women for his humanity and holiness. As he talked to me about being homosexual, he explained that he felt a physical 'distaste' towards women's bodies. I heard his use of this word 'distaste' as a relevant fact, but not as a slight on me as a woman, because it co-existed comfortably with his regard for me as a human person. A fact he demonstrated by confiding in me.

I believe now that this spontaneous use of the word 'distaste' by two people of different sexual orientations, was no coincidence. This may be a quite normal reaction of many gay and heterosexual people towards one another's physical sexuality. The problem is that in the absence of a personal encounter, both heterosexual and gay people can get stuck in that place of distaste. Consequently they may fear, judge or condemn the other orientation.

I was fortunate to have the opportunity to listen to that couple, and especially to listen to that man, who happened to be gay, talking honestly about who he really was. When he spoke he was vulnerable, he was human. And my humanity responded to his. If I had met him on a superficial level I might perhaps have judged him. But because he revealed himself with honesty, all my judgements were erased and respect moved in to fill the space. That encounter challenged me, it changed me, it moved me on. I understand now that authentic human encounter has the potential to change minds and hearts. It carries within it a call to conversion.

So I am suggesting:

- that it may be quite normal for gay and heterosexual people to feel an initial distaste towards each other's physical sexuality; that this is a neutral fact. It does not mean that one is passing judgement on the other's orientation. It is about one's sexual 'taste'. It is I suppose an indicator of one's own sexual orientation.
- that this reaction need not prevent the growth of respect and love between heterosexual and homosexual people.
- that in a transitional society such as ours, both gay people and heterosexual people go through a journey, which may involve emotions such as ignorance, confusion, disbelief, anger, etc. before understanding is achieved. So patience is needed all around, particularly in regard to the older half of the population whose youth was spent in a different world.

If there is any truth in what I am suggesting, then perhaps our conversation in the months before the referendum could be conducted in a different tone.

Secular Society – A Challenge to the Institutional Church?
What is the Institutional Church's attitude towards gay marriage? Unsurprisingly it is against it. And what is its attitude towards people who are gay? It is not against them, it insists, but it is against their homosexual acts. A fine theological distinction which may be clear to the Institutional Church's leaders, but is too fine a point for most homosexual people to accept. The Church declares that God created all human beings including homosexual people. It accepts that homosexual people through no choice of their own have homosexual inclination. It insists the God loves them *but* only provided they do not act on those innate inclinations which God implanted in them. But I wonder whether perhaps the institutional Church has misread the mind of God on this matter?

Wouldn't it be a strange God who would create someone with certain innate characteristics, which are felt to be an intrinsic and inseparable part of her/his personality, yet who only loves them on condition that they completely ignore this part of themselves. Perhaps the institutional Church has been distorting the message of God's love in this respect, by making it conditional. Is Pope Francis perhaps hinting at that when he said 'Who am I to judge?'

The church's opposition to homosexual behaviour has its origins in its historical antipathy towards physical sexuality. It sprang from dualistic thinking and manifested itself in a morbid pre-occupation with sexual behaviour. A hair-splitting neurotic theology was built up around the morality of particular acts. This antipathy, until recently, encompassed marital sex, which was only tolerated because of its usefulness in procreation. And while there has been a welcome re-think on the meaning of heterosexual married love, the antipathy continues to encompass homosexual acts right up to the present time. The Institutional Church, in its obsessive preoccupation with physical/sexual details, sometimes seems to forget that it is dealing with sensate human beings. So I think that what is required now on the part of the Institutional Church is a lot more psychology and a lot less 'dogmatic' theology. Otherwise homosexual people will never be convinced that they are accepted and welcomed by the Church.

It is notable that on a pastoral level, where priests meet people who are gay, opposition often melts away. It is what Martin Buber calls an I – THOU encounter which changes the minds and hearts of good pastors. An I – THOU encounter is one where a person is not chopped up into segments;

where some bits are then accepted, while other bits are rejected. Instead it is an encounter where a human being is accepted in her/his totality. It is what I imagine an encounter with Jesus would have been like. It is what homosexual people should experience in their Church.

The Church's emergent theology of human sexuality speaks inspiringly about the unitive and the procreative aspects of married love. When the Church talks about the procreative aspect of that love, it is not merely speaking of the creation of children. It is also speaking about the pro-creativity of the sexual love of childless people. It recognises that the fecundity of their love can manifest itself in their loving outreach to others. This theology offers a vision of sexual love as Trinitarian – a love that of its very nature cannot be confined to two people. If it is genuine it must flow outwards towards others. This is obvious in the birth of a child – the entry of the 'other' into the relationship. But birth is also symbolic. It invites childless couples to think imaginatively beyond that physical event, to the possibility that their love could also bring 'New Life' – in a psychological/spiritual sense – to others who cross their path.

Gay and lesbian couples are often childless – in the sense that they cannot together produce a child of their own. There are convincing ethical arguments against using surrogacy or sperm donation to acquire a child – regardless of whether a childless couple is gay or straight – because of the possible adverse psychological effect it may have on the future child. Some childless gay couples share these ethical concerns. Yet childless love – including homosexual love – needs to bear fruit in some form. It must eventually spill outwards to others. Human love, because it participates in Divine love, has a universal as well as a personal dimension. The love of spouse and children in heterosexual marriage can be understood as witnessing to the personal dimension of God's love. Celibacy can be seen as witnessing to the universal dimension of God's love. Perhaps the time is now ripe for the Church to change its attitude towards homosexual acts, to re-think its position on homosexual love and to realise that the committed love of a gay or lesbian couple, could witness to both the personal and the universal dimensions of God's love.

And now let us allow our theological imaginations take flight. Let us imagine a future where this attitudinal conversion has taken place; where the Church has expanded its rich theology of Trinitarian heterosexual married love to include the sexual love of gay couples; a Church which accepts that their love too can be both unitive and procreative. And imagine the Church acknowledging that this love is sacramental – a place where God's love can erupt into the world and flow out towards others. Imagine the Church valuing it so highly that it wants to bless it in a special way – maybe even to create a special sacrament to dignify and foster it.

Wouldn't this vision of committed homosexual love, witnessing to both the personal and universal dimensions of God's love, be a beautiful alternative to the Institutional Church's present attitude of condemnation. Currently it offers no vision at all to homosexual people, other than a negative vision – the via dolorosa of abstinence. And people – including gay people – do need an uplifting inspiring vision, to give meaning and purpose to their human love. Is it any wonder that in the past, when society turned its back on homosexual people, they were forced underground into furtive, shortlived, dehumanising encounters. The Church in its teaching reinforced and legitimised that oppression. So it too must take its share of the blame. It too should make amends.

People who are gay are now holding their heads up with pride. They are seeking to replace those furtive short-term potentially dehumanising encounters, with long-term committed relationships based on love. Shouldn't our Church be the first to encourage and welcome that? Could such committed same-sex relationships not be recognised as a vocation and be integrated into Church life? Perhaps there could even be a recognised ministry in parishes where, with the Church's blessing, two committed gay people could live and work purposefully as a couple, to bring the 'Good News' of God's love to others. A little far-fetched you may think. Perhaps, but only for those who lack imagination!

V. Preaching the Word

Mary: Mother of God

STANLEY HAUERWAS

A Sermon for Christ Church Cathedral
22 December 2013

Isaiah 7:10–16
Psalm 80:1–7; 16–18
Romans 1:1–7
Matthew 1:16–18

'Do you believe in the virgin birth?' That *was* the question people asked one another when I was a boy growing up in that Southern Baptist dominated land called Texas. It was *the* question because how you answered would indicate who you were, what you believed, as well as where you stood in the world. If you expressed any doubts about the birth of Jesus by a virgin you were identified as one of those liberals that did not believe that the Bible was inspired. That is to put the matter in too general terms. It was not that you not only failed to believe the Bible was inspired but you refused to believe that every word of the Bible was inspired.

Refusal to believe in the virgin birth also entailed ethical and political implications. If you did not believe in the virgin birth you were probably a person of loose morals which meant you also wanted to destroy everything we hold dear as Americans. In particular if you did not believe in the virgin birth it was assumed you did not believe in the sacredness of the family and, if you did not believe in the sacredness of the family, it meant you were an enemy of the democratic way of life. In short, a failure to believe in the virgin birth was a sure indication that you were a person not to be trusted.

One of the anomalies, at least what I take to be an anomaly, of this use of the virgin birth to determine one's standing in the world is those that used the virgin birth as the test case for moral rectitude often seemed to forget who it was that was the virgin. What was crucial for those that used the virgin birth in the manner I am describing is what seemed to matter to them was some woman that was a virgin had given birth. It did not seem to matter if Mary was the one that had been impregnated by the Holy Spirit.

But Isaiah does not say that 'a' virgin or young woman will bear a child. Isaiah says 'the' young woman will bear a child. 'The' is a definite article indicating that not anyone would give birth and still be a virgin, but someone in particular would be a virgin mother. We did not know who the 'the' would be until Mary was singled out to be the mother of Jesus, but we knew it would be a 'the'. Not just any young Jewish girl would do. The one to carry Jesus would be named 'Mary'.

That 'the' made all the difference for how the church fathers read this text. For them what was significant was that Mary, the mother of Jesus, was the virgin. An indication of how important her singularity was regarded is that at the Council of Ephesus in 431 she was given the name 'Mary, the Mother of God'. That title meant that Mary is not a replaceable instrument in the economy of God's salvation. Rather she is constitutive of God's very life making it impossible to say God without also saying Mary.

Such a view of Mary, a view held throughout the Christian tradition, was not how those that used the virgin birth as a test understood matters. They had a high view of virginity, but a low view of Mary. They had a low view of Mary because the last thing they wanted was to be identified with the Roman Catholics. Roman Catholics even seemed to think you could pray to Mary. Those whose focus was primarily on the virgin birth assumed that such a prayer bordered on being idolatrous.

Those that used the virgin birth as a test to determine your character were and continue to be identified as people who are theologically and politically conservative. In general that assumption is probably true. I think, however, this way of thinking about Christianity can also be found among those who represent more liberal theological and political positions. Conservatives and liberals alike assume that any account of Christianity that can pass muster in our time will be one in which the Christian faith is understood to be a set of strongly held ideas. Conservatives have the virgin birth and satisfaction theories of the atonement. Liberals have love and justice. Conservatives and liberals understand the Christian faith as a set of ideas because so understood Christianity seems to be a set of beliefs assessable to anyone upon reflection.

But then there is Mary. She is not just another young Jewish woman. She is the betrothed to Joseph. She has known no man yet she carries a child having been impregnated by the Holy Spirit. In Luke we have her annunciation in which her 'let it be' indicates her willingness to be the mother of the Son of God. In Matthew we have the annunciation of Joseph who is told to take Mary for his wife and he faithfully does so. Accordingly Joseph is given the task of naming Mary's baby. He names him Jesus, Emmanuel, because this child is the long awaited sign that 'God is with us.' The son of David, the King of Israel, has been conceived and born.

Mary and Joseph are not ideas. They are real people who made decisions on which our faith depends. Christianity is not a timeless set of ideas. Christianity is not some ideal toward which we ought always to strive even though the ideal is out of reach. Christianity is not a series of slogans that sum up our beliefs. Slogans such as 'justification by grace through faith' can be useful if you do not forget it is a slogan. But Christianity cannot be so easily 'summed up' even by the best of slogans or ideas. It cannot be summed up because our faith depends on a young Jewish mother called Mary.

Mary and Joseph are real people who had to make decisions that determined the destiny of the world. Isaiah had foretold that a Mary would come, but we had no idea what Isaiah's prophecy meant until Mary became the Mother of God. This is no myth. These are people caught up in God's care of his people through the faithfulness of the most unlikely people. They are unlikely people with names as common as Mary and Joseph, but because of their faithfulness our salvation now depends on acknowledging those names.

This is the last Sunday of Advent. Advent is a time the church has given us in the hope we can learn to wait. To learn to wait is to learn how to recognise we are creatures of time. Time is a gift and a threat. Time is a gift and a threat because we are bodily creatures. We only come into existence through the bodies of others but that very body destines us to death. We must be born and we must die. Birth and death are the brass tacks of life that make possible and necessary the storied character of our lives. It is never a question whether our lives will be storied, but the only question is which stories will determine our living in and through time.

Stories come in all shape and sizes. Some are quite short such as the story of a young Texan trying to figure out what it means to believe or not believe in the virgin birth. Other stories are quite long beginning with 'in the beginning'. We are storied by many stories which is an indication that we cannot escape nor should we want to escape being captured in and by time.

Jesus, very God, became for us time. He was conceived by the Holy Spirit and born of a virgin named Mary. Jesus, so born, is very man. He is fully God and fully man making it possible for us to be fully human. To be fully human means that through his conception and birth we have become storied by Mary. We are Mary's people.

What could it possibly mean that we are Mary's people? In his monumental book, *A Secular Age*, Charles Taylor characterises the time that constitutes our time as 'empty'. By 'empty' Taylor means as modern people we think of time as if it were a container that can be filled up by our indifferent likes and dislikes. As a result our sense of time has a homogeneous character in which all events can be placed in unambiguous relations of simultaneity and succession. Taylor suggests our view of time has a corresponding account of our social world as one constituted by a horizontal space, that is, a space in which each of us has direct access to time without the assistance of a mediator.

If Taylor's characterisation of our time as empty (a characterisation I suspect many of us will find forces a self-recognition we would prefer to avoid), is accurate we can better understand why we have trouble knowing how to acknowledge we are Mary's people. We may be ready to acknowledge that the stories that constitute our lives are ones we may not have chosen but we nevertheless believe that when all is said and done we get to make our lives up. But Mary did not choose to be Mary, the one highly favoured by God. Rather she willingly accepted her role in God's salvation by becoming the mother of God – even while asking 'How can this be?'

How extraordinary it is that we know the name of our Lord's mother! The time we live in as Christians is not empty. It is a time constituted by Isaiah's prophecy that a particular young woman will bear a son whose name will be Emmanuel. It is a time constituted by a young woman named Mary who was chosen by God to carry and give birth to one fully human and fully God. It is a time that is made possible by Joseph, her husband, who trusted in what he was told by the Holy Spirit. It is that time in which we exist. It is a time that gives us time in a world that thinks it has no time to worship a Lord who has Mary as a mother.

'Do you believe in the virgin birth?' was a question generated by a world that had produced people who feared they no longer knew the time they were in. That is they had no other way to tell time but to think they must force time to conform to their fantasy that they could make time be anything they wanted it to be. 'Do you believe in the virgin birth?' was a desperate question asked by a desperate people. It was a question asked by good people lost in a world they feared threatened all they held dear. Yet it was a question that could only distort the Gospel by failing to see that the good news is Mary is the Mother of God. I fear, however, that question, 'Do you believe in the virgin birth?' remains in the hearts of many who count themselves Christians.

If you try to answer that question I fear you will only distort the gospel. Mary, the Mother of God is not an answer to that question. Mary, the Mother of God, is not an answer to a question. Mary, the Mother of God, is a declarative assertion that makes clear that it was from Mary that Jesus assumed our humanity by becoming a creature of time.

That Mary is the Mother of God means we do not begin with speculative accounts about God's existence or nature. Our God is to be found in Mary's womb. Because our God is to be found in Mary's body we believe that same God desires to be taken in by us in this miraculous gift of the holy Eucharist, the body and blood of Christ. By partaking of this gift, a gift that if pondered leads us to ask with Mary, 'How can this be?' But the gift makes the question possible because through this gift we become participants in a time that is filled with God's providential care of us. We are Christians. We live in Mary's time.

Such a time is anything but empty. Rather it is a time storied by people whose lives witness to the Lord of time, the Lord who encompasses all life and death. I suggested above that there was a politics often associated with the question 'Do you believe in the virgin birth?' There is also a politics that is entailed by our affirmation that Mary is the Mother of God. The politics of Mary is a politics of joy characteristic of a people who have no reason to be desperate. They have no reason to be desperate because they have faith in the Lord of time.

So on this Sunday, a Sunday when Christmas seems so near, let us remember because we are Mary's people we are in no hurry. Let us wait in patience for the Christ-child whose own life depended on the lives of Mary and Joseph. The Word of God was made flesh. He came so that we might experience the fullness of time. Let us wait with Mary and Joseph for the child who will redeem all of time. Let us wait with patience and hope so that the world may discover that time is not empty; rather time remains pregnant with God's promise found in Mary, the Mother of God.

Corporus Christi
MARY GORDON

Today is the feast of the Body and Blood of Christ. When I was growing up in the good-old, bad-old pre-Vatican II days, the feast was known as Corpus Christi – the Latinate version naming the body and not the blood. In 1969, the feast was changed to the body and blood of Christ because there had been a special feast just for the blood, and the Church in its wisdom, decided to consolidate. The feast actually came into being through the sustained efforts of a woman. A sister Juliana of Liege who lived in the thirteenth century, had a dream of the moon with one dark spot in it: the dark spot being the absence of a feast honouring the Eucharist. Traditionally, the day was marked by processions; it was an occasion for genuine festivals, some of them noteworthy for their originality. In Catalonia, Corpus Christi is also known as the feast of the dancing egg; an egg is hollowed out and placed at the top of a stream of water gushing from a fountain so that it appears to dance. In the small town of Murcia in Spain, the feast is marked by The Dance of the Babies also called Baby Jumping in which an old man dresses in yellow, carries oversize castanets and jumps in and out of an obstacle course made up of babies under one year's old. No babies apparently have ever been hurt; the only reported injury has been a jumper's pulled hamstring. Nevertheless, as a grandmother, I'm glad it's not my home town. In my childhood, there was a procession; the children who had made first communion that May appeared in their white outfits, piously walking up the streets into the church.

Because I have been for all of my living memory, a reader and a writer, I associated the feast of Corpus Christi with a scene in a novella by Flaubert. Many of you may know Flaubert as the author of *Madame Bovary* but this scene occurs in an uncharacteristically tender fiction of Flaubert's called *A Simple Heart*, a story about a devoted servant whose life, in the dignity of her doing her job well and the pure love of her heart, is seen as heroic. At the novella's very end Felicite, the hero of the novella, is dying. Flaubert's choice of the name Felicite, the French for happiness, is deeply ironic, because she has had a life much more composed of difficulty than happiness. But one of the sources of her happiness was her parrot Lulu. Now Lulu was a perfectly terrible bird, he bit people, he caused Felicite enormous anxieties by escaping for long periods, he was given to embarrassing utterances of a blasphemous or obscene nature, taught him by a former owner. When Lulu dies, Felicite grieves for him deeply, and a friend suggests that she have him stuffed. This idea gives her great consolation and she places her stuffed parrot on the table beside her bed. So in her final illness Lulu is the first thing she looks at in the morning and the last thing at night. As the feast of Corpus Christi approaches she knows she is dying, but she wants to participate in the feast which is an important event for the community. The custom is to decorate the altar with objects that are considered precious and valuable by the townspeople: fine lace, fine silver, precious glassware. Felicite asks that her stuffed parrot, now worm eaten and mouldy, be placed on the altar because it is her most precious possession. The priest agrees, and as the community processes past her window, Felicite dies, smelling incense and happy in the knowledge that her mouldering parrot is on the altar. Her last vision is of the Holy Ghost who comes to her not in the form of a dove, but a parrot.

Mouldy stuffed parrots, jumping over babies, and dancing eggs. What does this have to do with the body and blood of Christ? Well everything, representing, as it does, the best of what Christianity can be but too rarely is. The particular genius of Christianity is that we worship an incarnate God, a God not only of spirit but of flesh, who is worshipped in our attachment to the material of this world: who is loved in all our loves, however un-sublime and un-exalted, even a mouldy stuffed parrot or an obstacle course of babies. The ritual life of the church, its sacramental life, insists upon a connection to materiality. The water of baptism, the bread and wine of the Eucharist, the oil of the anointing of the sick: these are not abstractions, and not merely symbols; they are an insistence upon an understanding that makes holy the material of this world.

And so the feast of the Body and Blood of Christ is a feast that celebrates the Incarnate God. But let's think of the word Incarnate. Incarnation. When I thought of it, the word that shares a root with it came to my mind and that word is carnivore, which means of course, meat-eater. I remembered being in Italy and feeling a kind of shock when I heard the translation of the Word Made Flesh … *La parola e carne* … the word was *carne*, the word for meat, the same word I had used when I ordered a steak the night before at my local trattoria. When I heard these words, I made another literary association, and this was to the beautiful poem 'Love' by the great seventeenth-century poet George Herbert, himself an Anglican priest. It gives me great pleasure to share this with you now.

LOVE

Love bade me welcome; yet my soul drew back,
    Guilty of dust and sin.
But quick-eyed Love, observing me grow slack
    From my first entrance in,
Drew nearer to me, sweetly questioning   5
    If I lack'd anything.

'A guest,' I answer'd, 'worthy to be here':
    Love said, 'You shall be he.'
'I, the unkind, ungrateful? Ah, my dear,
    I cannot look on Thee.'   10
Love took my hand and smiling did reply,
    'Who made the eyes but I?'

'Truth, Lord; but I have marr'd them: let my shame
    Go where it doth deserve.'
'And know you not,' says Love, 'Who bore the blame?'   15
    'My dear, then I will serve.'
'You must sit down,' says Love, 'and taste my meat.'
    So I did sit and eat.

'You must sit down says love and taste my meat', the meal that does away with shame and guilt. A meal of meat. The shocking implication of the Incarnation, like the words of the Consecration of the Mass, have been blunted by constant use, like a coin whose image has been worn away by years of passing from hand to hand. We have heard the words thousands of times Take and Eat, This is my Body, Take and Drink, This is my Blood. But what are those words saying? Eat my body. Drink my blood. Who eats human flesh and drinks human blood? Cannibals. Vampires. Is this what Jesus is demanding of us?

You can relax. I don't mean that we are vampires and cannibals. And, to use a phrase that has made its way to costume jewellery and chip clips, that's not what Jesus meant. Because cannibals and vampires use violence to take the flesh and blood of unwilling victims, people who would much rather, thank you, hold on to their flesh and blood. What Jesus has done is to offer himself as gift most radically and completely, an offering of a total self made through love, an offering that insists upon our participation, our active consumption, an offering of the self as gift of food, to be taken in the most intimate way possible, for our nourishment and growth, for the very formation of ourself and our identities. Jesus does insist, in his words, upon being consumed. So if we can free ourselves of the charge of being cannibals or vampires, we must accept the role of consumers. In participating in the ritual of the Eucharist, we are a community of consumers. It's not about iPads or Lexus cars or Prada bags or Jimmy Choo shoes. We are consumers of the sacred. We take it into our bodies, where the sacred is already lodged, and we are transformed, or perhaps it is better to say, that the sacred which is necessarily always part of our bodily selves is nourished, revitalised, reawakened. Maybe even fattened up.

In our hyper civilised world, our tidy and decorous religious practice, we lose sight of one of the major reasons why human beings have seemed, against all odds, to have continued in an impulse to worship. We need, as a species, to connect the visible and the invisible, not to separate spirit and flesh but to celebrate their inevitable connection. Body AND Blood. Oh yes, it's bloody, it's not neat, it's not quite safe. Transformation is never safe. Or predictable. The fourteenth-century prayer *Anima Christi* asks that the blood of Christ should inebriate us. Make us drunk. Get us out of our sure, safe, predictable cells into the radical uncertainty of pure gift. A pure gift that celebrates our impurity, that we are as creatures, hybrids, flesh and spirit, body and mind, and that we worship a God who manifested himself, like us, in an impure form: the incomprehensible infinity of God made visible: a baby, a wounded criminal, a host offering everything to us as a community of flesh and blood, knowing ourselves and the transcendent in the ordinary stuff of bread and wine.

Biographies

Hugh Connolly is a priest for the Diocese of Dromore. He is currently President of St Patrick's College, Maynooth.

Eamonn Conway is a priest of the Tuam diocese, Professor and Head of Theology and Religious Studies at Mary Immaculate College, University of Limerick. His recent publications include *Priesthood Today: Ministry in a Changing Cultural Context* (2013), and *Blueprint for the Church: An Introduction to the Joy of the Gospel* (2014).

Michael A. Conway is Professor of Faith and Culture at the Pontifical University, St Patrick's College, Maynooth, and a priest of the Diocese of Galway. His publications include *The Science of Life: Maurice Blondel's Philosophy of Action and the Scientific Method* (2000). He is Director of the Irish Centre for Faith and Culture and has served as Editor of the *Irish Theological Quarterly*.

Pádraig Corkery is Dean of the Faculty of Theology, Maynooth and Head of the Department of Moral Theology.

Brian Cosgrove is Professor Emeritus of Maynooth University, and was Head of the English Department for some fourteen years before retiring in 2006. He is the author of *Wordsworth and the Poetry of Self-Sufficiency* (Salzburg: University of Salzburg, 1982). He has a particular interest in the interface between literature and philosophy / theology.

Charles E. Curran is the Elizabeth Scurlock University Professor of Human Values at Southern Methodist University. He has served as president of three national academic societies – the American Theological Society, the Catholic Theological Society of America, and the Society of Christian Ethics. He has published eight volumes in the Moral Tradition series from Georgetown University Press, the last of which was *The Development of Moral Theology: Five Strands* (2013).

Gabriel Daly OSA has retired from teaching theology in Trinity College Dublin and the Irish School of Ecumenics. He has written four books and hopes to publish another on reform in the Church shortly.

John F. Deane is a poet and fiction writer, founder of *Poetry Ireland* and *Poetry Ireland Review*. His latest poetry collection is *Snow Falling on Chestnut Hill* (Carcanet 2012). Forthcoming in 2015 is a new collection of poems, *Semibreve*, from Carcanet and a 'faith memoir', *Give Dust a Tongue*, from Columba.

Eugene Duffy is a priest of the diocese of Achonry. He is currently a lecturer in Theology and Religious Studies at Mary Immaculate College, University of Limerick and a former President of the Irish Theological Association. He has lectured and written extensively on issues of ecclesiology and pastoral renewal. He has edited *Catholic Primary Education: Facing New Challenges* (Columba Press, 2012) and *Parishes in Transition* (Columba Press, 2010). He previously taught Theology at All Hallows College, Dublin and was Director of the Western Theological Institute, Galway.

Mary Gordon is the author of seventeen books: novels, stories, essays, memoirs, a biography of Joan of Arc and a study of the Gospels, *Reading Jesus*. She lives in New York City and teaches at Barnard College.

Thomas Groome is Professor of Theology and Religious Education at Boston College and Chair of the Department of Religious Education and Pastoral Ministry within BC's School of Theology and Ministry. Born in Co. Kildare and a graduate of St Patrick's College, Carlow, Groome went on to do graduate and doctoral studies in Theology and Education at Fordham University and Columbia University, and has been teaching at Boston College since 1976. His most recent book is *Will There Be Faith* (HarperCollins, 2012).

Patrick Hannon is a priest of the diocese of Cloyne and Professor Emeritus of Moral Theology in Maynooth. His most recent book is *Right or Wrong?* (Veritas, 2009).

Stanley Hauerwas, an American theologian, ethicist, and public intellectual, was the Gilbert T. Rowe Professor of Theological Ethics at Duke Divinity School with a joint appointment at the Duke University School of Law. In the fall of 2014, he assumed a Chair in Theological Ethics at the University of Aberdeen. He is a well known and prolific author in Christian Ethics.

Mark Patrick Hederman is abbot of Glenstal Abbey, a Benedictine monastery in Limerick. Formerly headmaster of the school, he has lectured in philosophy and literature in many countries, as well as in Ireland. A founding editor of the cultural journal *The Crane Bag*, and author of several books, including *Kissing in the Dark*, *Underground Cathedrals*, and *Dancing with Dinosaurs*. His most recent book, *The Boy in the Bubble: Education as Personal Relationship*, was published in 2012.

Brendan Hoban, a priest of the diocese of Killala, was born in Ballycastle, Co. Mayo. A columnist with the *Western People* for more than thirty years, he has presented a weekly religious magazine programme on Mid West Radio for the last twenty-five years. He is at present researching the history of Killala diocese. His most recent book is *Who Will Break the Bread for us?* A founder member of the Association of Catholic Priests, he is at present PP, Moygownagh, Co. Mayo.

John Horgan is a well known journalist who worked for the now defunct *Evening Press*, the *Catholic Herald* and, from 1963–1973 for the *Irish Times*. From 1973 to 1976, he was Editor of *Education Times*. He was a Labour Party senator, TD and MEP before becoming Senior Lecturer and eventually Professor of Journalism at Dublin City University until retirement in 2006. He became Ireland's first Press Ombudsman, an office from which he retired on 1 September 2014. He is now Visiting Professor at Boston College.

James F. Keenan SJ is Canisius Professor at Boston College and Director of the Jesuit Institute and of the Presidential Scholars Programme. He is the Founder of Catholic Theological Ethics in the World Church, which he co-chairs with Linda Hogan. He is presently working on two books, *University Ethics* (Rowman and Littlefield) and *A Brief History of Catholic Theological Ethics* (Paulist Press).

Ben Kimmerling is a facilitator and occasional writer. She has worked with both religious and secular groups in Ireland and overseas.

Dermot A. Lane is Parish Priest of Balally in Dublin 16 and teaches in the Mater Dei Institute of Education, DCU. He is author of *Stepping Stones to Other Religions: A Christian Theology of Interreligious Dialogue* (2011) and *Religion and Education: Reimagining the Relationship* (2013).

Enda Lyons, a priest of the diocese of Tuam, was ordained in 1958 and received a DD at Maynooth in 1961. He is a founder member of the Institute of Religious Studies, Mount Oliver, Dundalk, where he taught Theology for ten years. In more recent years he has been working at theology with groups, mostly in the West of Ireland. He is author of *Partnership in Parish: A Vision for Parish Life and Ministry*, and *Jesus: Self-portrait by God*, both published by the Columba Press, Dublin.

Pádraig McCarthy was ordained in 1967 for the diocese of Dublin, and has served in nine parishes. He has contributed articles to *The Furrow* to promote discussion on a variety of topics over that time.

Enda McDonagh is former Professor of Moral Theology at Maynooth. He has lectured at universities around the world and published some twenty-five books.

Tony McNamara worked in the Institute of Public Administration for thirty years. On retirement he enrolled in the School of Religions and Theology in TCD where he was awarded a PhD in 2009.

Oliver McQuillan graduated in Ancient Classics from St Patrick's College, Maynooth. He subsequently worked in a range of industries both in Ireland and

abroad. Originally a member of the celebrated Lantern Theatre, he recently returned to the stage, and has also worked in film, television and radio. He has written several plays including *The Ghost Room*, an exploration of the fears and failures
of Catholic clerics; and *The Trial of Dr Luther* which he performed in Dublin's New
Theatre in 2011. His most recent play, *The Puffin's Nest*, is scheduled for performance in that theatre in January 2015. He is a regular contributor on ecumenical
themes to *The Furrow*.

Gina Menzies teaches bioethics in The Royal College of Surgeons from where she
graduated with a MSc in Medical Ethics and Law. She holds degrees in Modern
Languages from Trinity College and in Philosophy and Theology from the Milltown Institute where she carried out postgraduate research in Moral Theology. She
is a member of the College of General Practitioners Ethics Research Committee; a
former member of the Higher Education Authority, the board of Gonzaga College
SJ, and the Irish Sports Council and currently serves on the board of the National
Concert Hall. She is an active member of We Are Church.

Breandán Ó Doibhlin is former Professor of Modern Languages at Maynooth
University. He is known for his writing in Irish: novels, drama and literary
criticism. He has translated several major works of French literature into Irish and
has a particular interest in problems of cultural identity.

Gerry O'Hanlon SJ is a staff member of the Jesuit Centre for Faith and Justice and
Associate Professor of Systematic Theology at the Milltown Institute. Among his
recent publications are *Theology in the Irish Public Square* and *A New Vision for the
Catholic Church: A View from Ireland* (Columba Press, 2011). He is a frequent contributor to *The Furrow*.

Michael Olden is a priest of the diocese of Waterford and Lismore. In recent years
he has been parish priest successively of Kilsheelan and Kilcash, SS Peter and Paul's
Clonmel, Tramore and Carbally. Previously he was Dean, Professor of Church History and President of Maynooth College. He now lives in retirement in Waterford.

Mary Redmond is a CEDR qualified mediator (see one-resolve.ie) and a Consultant
Solicitor and author specialising in Employment Law. Her most recent publication
is *The Pink Ribbon Path*, authored in her married name, Ussher, a book of prayers,
reflections and meditations for those facing serious illness. In 2004 she was made
an Honorary Fellow of Christ's College, Cambridge and in 2014 was conferred with
an LL D Hon Causa by Trinity College Dublin. Redmond is founder of two national
charities, the Irish Hospice Foundation and The Wheel.

Aidan Ryan is a priest of the diocese of Ardagh and Clonmacnois, ordained in 1969. In the early years of his ministry he served successively as Diocesan Catechist (Primary), as a Fidei Donum missionary in Zambia and as Spiritual Director at the Irish College in Rome. Since 1990 he has been in full-time parish ministry, latterly (since 1999) in the parish of Ballinahown, between Athlone and Clonmacnois.

Dr Fáinche Ryan is Assistant Professor of Systematic Theology at the Loyola Institute, Trinity College Dublin. A native of Kerry, Dr Ryan has also worked with the Irish Redemptorists on their mission team, and is a regular contributor to periodicals such as *Doctrine and Life*, *Spirituality*, *The Furrow* and *Reality*. She is also author of *The Eucharist: What do we believe?* (Columba Press, 2012).

Edward Sellner is Professor of Theology at St Catherine University, St Paul, Minnesota, where he has taught for the past thirty-four years. He is the author of twelve books, most recently *Finding the Monk Within: Great Monastic Values for Today* (Paulist Press, 2008) and *The Double: Male Eros, Friendships, and Mentoring – From Gilgamesh to Kerouac* (Lethe Press, 2013).

Anne Thurston is a theologian and a writer. She has been a contributor to *The Furrow* for many years. She was recently awarded a PhD (Trinity College Dublin) for her work on discerning textures of faith through a practice of reading contemporary literary texts.

Catherine Twomey was born in Dublin in 1954 and has taught at first and second level in schools in Ireland, England and Japan. She is currently living and teaching in Co. Waterford. From 1999 to 2005, she co-edited *Harvest* – a magazine for the Diocese of Waterford and Lismore. She has had a small amount of poems published in various magazines and anthologies and is an occasional reviewer for *The Furrow*.

Eoin de Bháldraithe (Waldron) was born in 1938 near Ballyhaunis in Beakan Parish, Co. Mayo. He entered Mt St Joseph Abbey, Roscrea in 1956 and was ordained a presbyter in 1963. Two years later he received a Master's degree in Theology from the Benedictines in Rome and was sent to the new monastery near Moone, Co. Kildare where he worked on the farm for forty years. During this time he forayed forth into various church controversies. Now retired from farm work, he tries some more serious theology.

Des Wilson was born in 1925, and educated at St Malachy's College, Belfast, Queen's University, and St Patrick's College, Maynooth. He studied Community Education at the University of Ulster and co-founded the independent adult education project, Springhill Community House, Belfast 1972, working there ever since.

Endnotes

The Priest, the Editor, and the Man of Many Talents—Michael Olden

1. It is of interest that on the day when Gerry McGarry was buried in Ballyhaunis, Tomás Ó Fiaich and I were standing together at the graveside. During the prayers he whispered to me that he had to be in the Apostolic Nunciature that evening. I wished him well. A few hours later in the Nunciature he was given the disquieting news that he was appointed archbishop of Armagh. I feel sure that McGarry noted the coincidence with gentle humour!

Letters to Ronan—Anne Thurston

1. Section XII, 'Route 110' in Seamus Heaney, *Human Chain*, London: Faber & Faber, 2010.
2. Walter Brueggemann, *The Bible and Postmodern Imagination: Texts Under Negotiation*, London: SCM Press, 1993, p.30.
3. www.theguardian.com/books/2011/mar/20/a-hundred-doors-michael-longley-review
4. Section XII, 'Route 110' in Seamus Heaney, *Human Chain*.

Hopes for Religious Education: Was Danger Mulally onto Something?— Thomas Groome

1. Charles Taylor, *A Secular Age*, Cambridge, MA: Harvard University Press, 2007. See 25–28 for Taylor's summary of 'exclusive humanism'.
2. The centrality of the historical Jesus is a dominant theme in contemporary scholarship. See, for example: John Dominic Crossan, *The Historical Jesus: The Life of a Mediterranean Jewish Peasant*, San Francisco: HarperSanFrancisco, 1991; Gerhard Lohfink, *Jesus of Nazareth: What He Wanted, Who He Was*, Collegeville: Liturgical Press, 2012; Jose Pagola, *Jesus: An Historical Approximation*, Miami: Convivium Press, 2009.
3. 'The Church in the Modern World', #43, in Walter Abbott, ed., *Documents of Vatican II*, New York: America Press, 1966, p.243.
4. The most complete account of a shared Christian praxis approach can be found in Thomas Groome, *Sharing Faith: A Comprehensive Approach to Religious Education & Pastoral Ministry*, San Francisco: Harper SanFrancisco, 1991.
5. For the best, less technical explanation of the life to faith to life approach see Groome, *Will There Be Faith?*, San Francisco: HarperSanFrancisco, 2012.

Communication and the Church: A Memory and a Meditation—John Horgan

1.   Michael O'Neill (1958), 'The Priest and the Press', *The Furrow*, (9) 12, December 1958, p.775.
2.   John 3:8, King James version. Louise Fuller, *Irish Catholicism Since 1950: The Undoing of a Culture*, Dublin: Gill and Macmillan, 2002, p.85.
3.   In private life an official of the Customs and Excise Service.
4.   The elephant trap lying in wait for those who had imbibed not wisely but too well became evident only at the leave-taking, when each of us had, with varying degrees of steadiness, to bend the knee to, and kiss the ring of, Dr McQuaid himself, on the way out. His enjoyment of our embarrassment was palpable.
5.   I cannot remember its correct title, much less the year in which the survey was carried out, but it was probably in the late 1960s, when I remember I reported it for the *Irish Times*.

Encountering *The Furrow*—Eoin de Bháldraithe

1.   A. Flannery (ed.), *The Conciliar and Post Conciliar Documents*, Dublin: Dominican, 1975, pp.474–9.
2.   Ibid., pp.508–14.
3.   David Woodworth, 'Inter-Church Marriage: An Anglican View', *The Furrow* 22 (1971), 603–14; now in E. McDonagh, V. MacNamara (eds), *An Irish Reader in Moral Theology: The Legacy of the Last Fifty Years*, vol. 2, pp.254–62.
4.   Some of the effects of the cardinal's approach can be seen in 'Go for it and be happy', the story of Katherine and James', pp.22–3 in *Mixed Emotions: Real stories of mixed marriage*, Belfast: Northern Ireland Mixed Marriage Association, 2012.

The Tacit Reform of Vatican II—Gabriel Daly OSA

1.   Leo XIII, *Aeterni patris* (art. 31).
2.   M.D. Petre, *Autobiography and Life of George Tyrrell*, London, 1912, vol. 2, p.337.
3.   Pius X, *Motu Proprio: Doctoris angelici* (1914).
4.   Tromp was to be Cardinal Ottaviani's peritus at Vatican II and was one of the most extreme scholastic reactionaries at the council. Ottaviani dropped him when the defeat of their position had become inevitable.
5.   Pius XII, *Humani generis* (art. 34).
6.   John Paul II, *Fides et ratio* (art. 49).
7.   John W. O'Malley, *What Happened at Vatican II*, Cambridge, Massachusetts: Belknap Press, 2008, p.46.
8.   See Gabriel Daly, *Transcendence and Immanence: A Study in Catholic Modernism and Integralism*, Oxford: Clarendon Press, 1980, p.106.
9.   *Pensées*, fr. 278 (Krailsheimer edition and translation), Harmondsworth: Penguin Books, 1966, p.58.

Priesthood, Authority and Leadership—Michael A. Conway

1. See, for example, the first issue of the French magazine, *La Boussole*, which is entirely dedicated to 'L'Autorité Positive: comment elle peut changer notre vie' (La Boussole, Spring Issue, 2014).
2. 'In every well-ordered community each man has his appointed task which he must perform' (Plato, *The Republic*, 406 c3–4).
3. See, for example, Charles Taylor, 'Magisterial Authority', in *The Crisis of Authority in Catholic Modernity*, Michael J. Lacey and Francis Oakley (eds), Oxford: OUP, 2011, pp.259–69. This entire volume contains a number of important essays on authority in the Catholic tradition.

The Reform of the Church in her Missionary—Gerry O'Hanlon

1. See Richard P. McBrien, *The Church*, New York: HarperCollins, 2008, pp.254–6. Interestingly McBrien notes that there are only two places in the entire corpus of Catholic Social Teaching where the teachings on social justice and human rights are explicitly applied to the Church itself.
2. Gerard Mannion, 'An Acute Symptom of a Much Deeper Malaise: The Abuse Crisis in its Wider Ecclesiological Context', in Patrick Claffey, Joe Egan and Marie Keenan (eds), *Broken Faith*, Bern: Peter Lang, 2013, pp.239–41.
3. Michael J. Lacey, 'The Problem of Authority and its Limits', in Michael J. Lacey and Francis Oakley (eds), *The Crisis of Authority in Catholic Modernity*, Oxford: Oxford University Press, 2011, pp.1–25 at 6.
4. Ladislas Orsy, 'The Divine Dignity of Human Persons in Dignitatis humanae', *Theological Studies*, 75, 2014, pp.8–22 at 12.
5. For a critique of the 'power-over' approach associated with the 'institutionality' of the Church, see Michael A. Conway, 'Christianity in Europe – a Future?', *The Furrow*, 65, July–August, 2014, pp.331–8.
6. Antonio Spadaro SJ, 'Wake Up The World', conversation with Pope Francis about religious life, 12 November 2013 – original text in Italian (*La Civilta Cattolica* 2014, I, pp.3–17). See also *EG*, 226ff.
7. Spadaro, op. cit., 3 – 'I am convinced of one thing: the great changes in history were realised when reality was seen not from the centre but from the periphery.'
8. Our Mission and Justice, 10, 34th General Congregation of the Jesuits, 1994.

'From the Bishops down to the last of the lay faithful'—Fáinche Ryan

1. 'ab Episcopis usque ad extremos laicos fideles', St Augustine, De Praed. Sanct., 14, 27: PL 44, p.980.
2. Ronan Drury, 'Canon J. G. McGarry: Editor 1950–1977', *The Furrow*, vol. 28, no. 9 (Sep. 1977), p.535.

3. The Archbishop of Armagh, 'The Furrow and Its Programme' *The Furrow*, vol. 1, no. 1 (Feb. 1950), pp.6–9: 6.

4. The Archbishop of Armagh, 'The Furrow and Its Programme', *The Furrow*, vol. 1, no. 1 (Feb. 1950), pp.6–9: 6.

5. The Archbishop of Armagh, 'The Furrow and Its Programme', *The Furrow*, vol. 1, no. 1 (Feb. 1950), p.8.

6. Thomas Aquinas, in Heb 1:8, 9 [64] http://dhspriory.org/thomas/SSHebrews. htm (accessed 4 July 2014).

7. Ben Kimmerling, 'Theology for Lay People – Reflections on *"The Furrow"* Theology Course', *The Furrow*, vol. 36, no. 12, Dec. 1985, pp.736–41.

8. www.vatican.va/roman_curia/synod/documents/rc_synod_doc_20131105_ iii-assemblea-sinodo-vescovi_en.html (accessed 4/7/2014).

9. Dennis Coday, 'Irish bishops: Vatican synod questionnaire reveals challenges families face'in *The Tablet*, 18 Mar. 2014, http://ncronline.org/news/accountability /irish-bishops-vatican-synod-questionnaire-reveals-challenges-families-face (accessed 4 July 2014).

10. Dennis Coday, 'Irish bishops: Vatican synod questionnaire reveals challenges families face', *National Catholic Reporter*, 18 Mar. 2014. http://ncronline.org/news/ accountability/irish-bishops-vatican-synod-questionnaire-reveals-challenges (accessed 7 July 2014).

11. Christopher Lamb, 'Family life survey findings must be kept under wraps – Vatican' *The Tablet*, 16 April 2014 www.thetablet.co.uk/news/686/0/family-life- survey-findings-must-be-kept-under-wraps-vatican (accessed 7 July 2014).

12. Mary Luke Tobin, 'Women in the Church since Vatican II' in *America. The National Catholic Review*, 1 Nov. 1986. http://americamagazine.org/issue/100/ women-church-vatican-ii (accessed 7 July 2014).

13. The Archbishop of Armagh, '*The Furrow* and Its Programme', *The Furrow*, vol. 1, no. 1 (Feb. 1950), p.8.

14. The phrase *usque ad extremos* might better be translated as 'all the way, up (to), even (to)'.

A Pope from the Global South: Redirecting Evangelisation—Eamonn Conway

1. Comparable therefore with John Paul II's *Redemptor hominis* (1979), and Pope Benedict's homily at the mass with cardinals immediately following his election (20 April 2005).

2. Bryan Froehle, 'Changing Face of Global Catholicism: Implications for Theology and Theological Education', unpublished paper to the 2011 Network Council Meeting of the International Network of Societies for Catholic Theology, De Paul University, Chicago.

3. Allen, J., *The Global War on Christians: Dispatches from the front-lines of Anti-Christian Persecution*, New York: Image, 2013.

4.   Froehle, op. cit.

5.   Papal Address at the University of Regensburg. See: http://www.zenit.org/en/articles/papal-address-at-university-of-regensburg (accessed 4 August 2014).

6.   Rahner, K., 'Basic Theological Interpretation of the Second Vatican Council', in *Theological Investigations*, 20, London: Darton, Longman & Todd, 1981, p.78.

7.   Rahner, op. cit., p.83.

8.   The historically defining character of European culture for Christian faith merits more detailed study. In that regard, Charles Taylor's work on cultural and acultural readings of modernity is worth considering. See, inter alia, Taylor, C., 'Two Theorie of Modernity', in *The International Scope Review*, vol. 3, issue 5, 2001, pp.1–9.

9.   See Victor Manuel Fernández and Paolo Rodari, *La Iglesia del Papa Francisco – Los Desafíos desde Evangelii gaudium*, Madrid: San Pablo, 2014, p.11. Archbishop Fernandez is the only living theologian cited in *Evangelii gaudium*. Rector of the Catholic University of Argentina, and a close collaborator with then Cardinal Bergoglio in producing the document that resulted from the conference of Latin American Bishops, at Aparecida in 2007, Fernandez was made a titular archbishop by Pope Francis shortly into his pontificate and is one of his key theological advisers.

10. See 'Concluding Document', V General Conference of the Bishops of Latin America and the Caribbean, *Aparecida*, May 2007.

11. See http://insightscoop.typepad.com/2004/2013/12/evangelii-nuntiandi-the-greatest-pastoral-document-that-has-ever-been-written.html (accessed 29 August 2014). See *Instrumentum Laboris*, n. 33, and Message, n. 1, of the XIII World Synod of Bishops; also *Evangelii gaudium*, n. 73.

12. See 'A big heart open to God', exclusive interview by Antonio Spadaro SJ, with Pope Francis, *America*, 30 Sep. 2013.

Pope Francis and the Agenda for Pastoral Reform—Eugene Duffy

1.   http://en.radiovaticana.va/storico/2013/03/27/bergoglios_intervention_a_diagnosis_of_the_problems_in_the church/en1-677269 (accessed, 26 August 2014).

2.   'What I would have said at the Consistory: An interview with Cardinal Jorge Mario Bergoglio, Archbishop of Buenos Aires', http://www.30giorni.it/articoli_id_16457_l3.htm (accessed, 26 August 2014).

3.   V General Conference of the Bishops of Latin America and the Caribbean: Disciples and missionaries of Jesus Christ, so that our Peoples may have life in Him. Concluding Document, *Aparecida*, 13–31 May 2007.

4.   Ibid., no. 244.

5.   Ibid., no. 247.

6.   *Evangelii gaudium*, no. 264.

7.   Concluding Document, *Aparecida*, 13–31 May 2007, no. 391.

8.   Ibid., no. 393.

9.   *Evangelii gaudium*, no. 198.

10. 'Message of the fifth general conference to the peoples of Latin America and the Caribbean' in V General Conference of the Bishops of Latin America and the Caribbean: Disciples and missionaries of Jesus Christ, so that our Peoples may have life in Him. Concluding Document, *Aparecida*, 13–31 May 2007.

11. *Evangelii gaudium*, no. 23.

12. 'What I would have said at the Consistory: An interview with Cardinal Jorge Mario Bergoglio, Archbishop of Buenos Aires', http://www.30giorni.it/articoli_id_16457_l3.htm (accessed, 26 August 2014).

13. *Evangelii gaudium*, no. 16.

14. Ibid., no. 32.

15. 'What I would have said at the Consistory: An interview with Cardinal Jorge Mario Bergoglio, Archbishop of Buenos Aires', http://www.30giorni.it/articoli_id_16457_l3.htm (accessed, 26 August 2014).

16. *Evangelii gaudium*, no. 119.

17. Ibid., no. 30.

18. Ibid., no. 262.

Poets, Theologians and God—Dermot A. Lane

1. Dennis O'Driscoll, 'Missing God', *Exemplary Dangers*, London: Anvil Press Poetry, 2000, pp.29–31.

2. Dennis O'Driscoll, 'Intercession', *Reality Check*, London: Anvil Poetry Press, 2007, pp.18–20.

3. Susan Millar DuMars, *The God Thing*, Salmon Poetry, 2013.

4. *The Furrow*, February 2014, pp.122–8.

5. 'Undiscovered', p.19.

6. Charles Taylor, *A Secular Age*, Cambridge: The Belknap Press of Harvard University Press, 2007.

7. James Sweeney, 'Faith in Culture', *New Blackfriars*, 2013, pp.148–59 at 150.

8. See Christian Woman, *My Bright Abyss: Mediation of a modern believer*, New York: Farrar, Straus, and Giroux, 2013, p.124. The reception of the translation of the Roman Missal into English comes to mind as an illustration of both of these problems.

9. See Rowan Williams, *Faith in the Public Square*, London: Bloomsbury, 2012, Chs 1 and 2.

10. Gen 1–2:7 and Rom 5:5.

The Furrow on Film—Mark Patrick Hederman

1. *The Furrow*, April 1950, pp.164–6.

2. Kevin Rockett, *Irish Film Censorship, A Cultural Journey from Silent Cinema to Internet Pornography*, Dublin: Four Courts Press, 2004, p.20. Most of the information

about cinema censorship which I use in this article is gleaned from his definitive study.

3. J.J. Lee, *Ireland 1912–1985: Politics and Society*, Cambridge: Cambridge University Press, 1989, p.158.

4. Chairperson of An Chomhairle Ealaeon/The Arts Council of Ireland, by appointment of the Government of Ireland with responsibility for funding all the contemporary arts in Ireland from 1993–98, in 'Ideologies and Irish Arts Policies, 1921–91,' which he wrote the year before he was appointed.

5. Ciarán Benson, 'The place of the Arts in Irish Education, Report of the Arts Council's Working Party on the Arts in Education', 1979.

6. Encyclical Letter of Pope Pius XI on motion pictures [29 June 1936] 'Vigilant Care'.

7. *The Furrow*, August 1950, p.382.

8. Ibid. p.383.

9. *The Furrow*, July 1951, pp.472–4.

10. Cf. for example his review of Elia Kazan's East of Eden [1955] in *The Furrow*, December 1955, pp.754–5.

11. *The Catholic Herald*, 15 January 1965.

12. John C. Kelly, 'The Morality of Films,' *The Furrow*, January 1965, pp.20–3.

13. Kevin Rockett, op. cit., pp.314–16.

Fógairt an tSoiscéil i gCultúr Briste (Ar Chothrom Caoga Bliain *Gaudium et Spes*)—Breandán Ó Doibhlin

1. Deirtear 'détheangach' le pobal atá ar a mbealach ó theanga amháin go teanga eile, san áit gur riocht seasta an diglossia mar a bhfuil dhá theanga beo taobh le taobh ach a bhfuil úsaid difriúil acu faoi seach sa tsochaí, ar nós Spáinnis agus Guaraní i bParaguay.

2. J. Sesboué, *Le Dieu du Salut*, p.482.

3. Naomh Eoin Pól II, ag caint leis an Congresso del Movimento Ecclesiale di Impegno Culturale, 16 Eanáir 1982.

A Dualistic Theophany: Nature as Source of Fear and Love in Wordsworth—Brian Cosgrove

1. 'Instinct' is here an adjective: the sense of the line is, 'As if filled with voluntary power.'

The Contemplative Christian Lawyer—Mary Redmond

1. With distinctions between different branches of law, the subject of a different discussion.

2. See Leonard L. Riskin: 'The Contemplative Lawyer: On the Potential Contributions of Mindfulness Meditation to Law Students, Lawyers, and their Clients, vol. 7, 2002, Harvard Negotiation Law Review. His is a comprehensive article and a good starting point.

3. See 'Why do I teach Restorative Justice to Law Students?' by US Justice Janine Geske, *The Bar Review* February 2014, p.14.

4. See Dr Barry White, www.MeditatioNewsletter/March_2014.

5. www.wccm.org and http://www.wccmmeditatio.org and for Ireland see www.christianmeditation.ie.

6. John Main OSB came across meditation in the writings of John Cassian, such as his 'Cenobitic Institutions' and 'Conferences'. 'The Desert Spirituality', and especially the teaching of Evagrius, provided a contemplative way to pray for ordinary Christians which flowered for about two centuries in the deserts of Egypt, Palestine and Syria and went on to feed the spirituality of the Orthodox Church. John Cassian brought meditation to the West in the early fifth century.

7. Gift and Call, Dublin: Gill & Macmillan, 1975.

8. John Main, *The Way of Unknowing*, Norwich: Canterbury Press, 2011.

9. See for instance the Guidance and Ethics Committee of the Incorporated Law Society which has issued several practice notes on subjects such as Ethical Barriers within a Firm or, Ten Steps to Improve Productivity.

Living the Questions—Catherine Twomey

1. *The Furrow*, vol. 22, no. 11 (Nov. 1971), pp.671–85.
2. Gabriel Daly, op. cit.
3. Padraig J. Daly, *Afterlife*, Dublin: Dedalus Press, 2010.
4. Gabriel Daly, op. cit.
5. Kevin Myers, 'The gospel according to Trinity is truly a testament to stupidity', *The Sunday Times*, 6 April 2014. Available at www.thesundaytimes.co.uk.

Ageing Titans: Church and State in Twenty-First Century—Tony McNamara

1. This essay is not based on any empirical research. Rather I present reflections based on apposite literature.
2. P. Mair, *Ruling The Void: The Hollowing Of Western Democracy*, Verso Books, New York and London. The book was started in 2007. Mair died in 2011 and the book was published posthumously in 2013, brought together from his manuscripts by a colleague Francis Mulhern.
3. My focus is on the Roman Catholic Church.
4. *A Secular Age* is 874 pages long and analyses the evolution to the secular state. Here I do not visit the detailed arguments of the book, but rather call on some of Taylor's conclusions to underpin my analysis.

5. And presumably social media, which was not in the ascendance it is now when Taylor wrote.
6. There are of course other themes in the exhortation. Notably there is a very strong emphasis on the option for the poor and on social justice, a striking contrast to his predecessor's predilection for an emphasis on charity.

Awakening: The Friendship between D. T. Suzuki and Thomas Merton—Edward Sellner

1. See D. T. Suzuki, *Essays in Zen Buddhism*, New York: Grove Press, 1949, p.237.
2. Thomas Merton, *Mystics and Zen Masters*, New York: The Noonday Press, 1961, p.50.
3. Thomas Merton, 'January 25, 1965', in *Dancing in the Water of Life: The Journals of Thomas Merton*, vol. 5, San Francisco: HarperSanFrancisco, 1997, p.195.
4. See D. T. Suzuki, 'Early Memories', in *A Zen Life: D T Suzuki Remembered*, Masao Abe, ed., New York: Weatherhill, 1986, pp.3–4.
5. Ibid., pp.9–11.
6. Ibid., p.11.
7. See D. T. Suzuki, 'On Satori – The Revelation of a New Truth in Zen Buddhism,' in *Essays in Zen Buddhism*, pp.229–66.
8. Michael Higgins, *Heretic Blood: The Spiritual Geography of Thomas Merton* (Toronto, Canada: Stoddart Publishing, 1998), p.36.
9. Thomas Merton, 'June 22, 1958', in *A Search for Solitude: The Journals of Thomas Merton*, vol. 3, San Francisco: HarperSanFrancisco, 1996, p.207.
10. See Michael Mott, *The Seven Mountains of Thomas Merton*, Boston: Houghton Mifflin Co., 1984, p.307.
11. Thomas Merton and James Laughlin, *Selected Letters*, David Cooper, ed., London: W. W. Norton, 1997, pp.108, 114.
12. See Roger Lipsey, 'Do I want a small painting? The Correspondence of Thomas Merton and Ad Reinhardt', in *The Merton Annual*, 18, Victor Kramer, ed. Louisville, KY: Fons Vitae, 2006.
13. Thomas Merton, 'April 28, 1957', *A Search for Solitude*, p.87.
14. Ibid., pp.139, 174, 181–2.
15. See Thomas Merton, *Conjectures of a Guilty Bystander*, New York: Doubleday, 1965, pp.156–8.
16. David Cooper, *Thomas Merton's Art of Denial: The Evolution of a Radical Humanist*, Athens, GA: University of Georgia Press, 1989, pp.101, 106.
17. Robert Daggy, ed., *Encounter: Thomas Merton & D T Suzuki*, Larkspur Press, 1988, p.5.
18. Thomas Merton, *Mystics and Zen Masters*, p.46.
19. Robert Daggy, ed., *Encounter: Thomas Merton & D T Suzuki*, pp.5–6.
20. Ibid., pp.11–13, 17, 23, 47.

21. Ibid., 23–4.

22. Thomas Merton, *Dancing in the Water of Life: The Journals of Thomas Merton*, vol. 5, San Francisco: HarperSanFrancisco, 1997, pp.114–15.

23. Ibid., pp.116–17.

24. A. M. Allchin, 'Foreword', in William Shannon, *Silent Lamp: The Thomas Merton Story*, New York: Crossroad, 1992, p.xiii.

25. David Steindl-Rast, 'Epilogue,' in Donald Mitchell and James Wiseman, eds., *The Gethsemani Encounter*, New York: Continuum, 1998, p.274.

The Style of Virtue Ethics—James F. Keenan SJ

1. John O'Malley, *What Happened at Vatican II*, Cambridge, MA: Harvard University Press, 2010.

2. John O'Malley, 'The Style of Vatican II', *America*, February 24, 2003; http://americamagazine.org/node/146401.

3. Ibid.

4. On whether academicians can make any difference, see Keenan, 'Impasse and Solidarity in Theological Ethics', Catholic Theological Society of America Proceedings, 64 (2009), pp.47–60.

5. See William Werpehowski and Kathryn Getek Soltis, ed., *Virtue and the Moral Life: Theological and Philosophical Perspectives*, Lanham: Lexington Books, 2014.

6. Edmund Pincoffs, *Quandaries and Virtues: Against Reductivism in Ethics*, Lawrence: University of Kansas Press, 1986.

7. Thomas Aquinas, *Summa Theologiae* I. II. 6.

8. Ibid., 18. 9c.

9. Ibid., 18. 9. ad3.

10. Ibid., I. II. 74. 1c.

11. On Virtue and Scripture, see Yiu Sing Lúcás Chan, *The Ten Commandments and the Beatitudes*, New York: Rowman and Littlefield, 2012; N J Mahwah, *Biblical Ethics in the 21st Century: Developments, Emerging Consensus, and Future Directions*, Paulist Press, 2012; Daniel Harrington and James F. Keenan, *Jesus and Virtue Ethics: Building Bridges Between New Testament Studies and Moral Theology*, Lanham, Md.: Sheed and Ward, 2002; *Paul and Virtue Ethics*, New York: Rowman and Littlefield, 2010.

Style Matters—Patrick Hannon

1. par. 15

2. par. 1

3. J. W. O'Malley SJ, *Vatican II: Did Anything Happen?*, New York and London: Continuum, 2008, pp.76–83 at 76.

4. Ibid., p.76.

5. Ibid., p.77.

6. Ibid.
7. *America*, 31 March 2003.
8. E. Quinn, tr., *The Shape of the Church to Come*, London: SPCK, 1974, p.126.

A Voice for Justice—Hugh Connolly

1. http://www2.faulkner.edu/o/admin/websites/rtrull/mfc/Guatemalainfo.htm
2. Idem.
3. http://www.trocaire.org/blog/justice
4. Evers, Liz, http://www.trocaire.org/blogs/testimony-survival-and-dignity-face-genocide.
5. Habegger, Larry, and O'Reilly, James. http://articles.chicagotribune.com/1998-02 01//9802010097_1_guatemala-crime-victims February 01, 1998.
6. http://www.usccb.org/beliefs-and-teachings/what-we-believe/catholic-social-teaching/sharing-catholic-social-teaching-challenges-and-directions.cfm
7. http://ccdocle.org/social-action/education-and-training/catholic-social-teaching.
8. Hosea 10:12 and Jeremiah 4:3.

Ecology as a Moral Issue: An Ongoing Journey—Pádraig Corkery

1. See for example the contribution of the Irish Catholic Bishops' Conference, 'The Cry of the Earth: A Pastoral Reflection on Climate Change', 2009.
2. See, Tobias Winright (ed.), *Green Discipleship: Catholic Ethics and the Environment*, Anselm Academic, 2011.
3. Seán McDonagh, 'Good Earth – Reflections in Ecology and Theology', *The Furrow*, 35, pp.430–40 (1984).
4. Seán McDonagh, 'Chronicle: Justice, Peace and the Integrity of Creation', *The Furrow*, 41, pp.452–5 (1990).
5. See for example Seán McDonagh, 'The Earth is forgotten in Veritatis Splendor', *The Furrow*, 45, pp.454–6 (1994), 'To Protect Creation—a teaching in its infancy', *The Furrow*, 61, pp.363–74 (2010).
6. See for example Donal Dorr, 'To Care for the Earth', *The Furrow*, 38, pp.455–60 (1987), John Feehan, 'Towards a Greener Theology', *The Furrow*, 52, pp.54–6 (2001).
7. Cahal B. Daly, 'Caring for the Earth: A Work of Peace', *The Furrow*, 41, pp.81–91 (1990).
8. John O'Donohue, 'The Wisdom of the Earth', *The Furrow*, 54, pp.609–12 (2003).
9. Donal O'Mahony, 'The Voice of the Earth – towards an ecological spirituality', *The Furrow*, 56, pp.152–9 (2005).
10. Dermot A. Lane, 'The Cry of the Earth', *The Furrow*, 59, 153–7 (2008).
11. Donal Dorr, 'Ecology – The Theological Issues' (Featured Review), *The Furrow*, 61, pp.311–16 (2010).

12. See for example 'Justice in the World', (1971), #11: 'Furthermore, such is the demand for resources and energy by the richer nations … and such are the effects of dumping by them in the atmosphere and the sea that irreparable damage would be done to the essential elements of life on earth, such as air and water, if their high rates of consumption … were extended to the whole of humankind.'

13. Pope John Paul, II, *Centesimus annus*, 1991, #37.

14. 'The environmental crisis and poverty are connected by a complex and dramatic set of causes – in such cases hunger and poverty make it virtually impossible to avoid an intense and excessive exploitation of the environment.' Compendium of Catholic Social Doctrine, #482.

15. Pope Benedict XVI, If You Want to Cultivate Peace, Protect Creation, Message for World Day of Peace, 2010. Reprinted in Tobias Winright, op. cit., pp.60–72.

16. Irish Catholic Bishops' Conference, Prosperity with a Purpose, Veritas, 1999, p.73.

17. Compendium of Catholic Social Doctrine, #487, #464.

18. Pope Benedict XVI, *Caritas in veritate*, 2009, #48.

19. The Cry of the Earth, p.14.

20. *Caritas in veritate*, #48.

21. *Centesimus annus*, #37.

22. *Caritas in veritate*, #51.

23. Ibid.

24. Ibid., #49.

25. Compendium of Catholic Social Doctrine, #470.

26. *Caritas in veritate*, #48.

27. Pope Paul VI, *Populorum progressio*, 1967, #47.

28. *Sollicitudo rei socialis*, #38.

29. Pope John Paul II, *Reconciliatio et paenitentia*, 1984, #16.

30. Ibid.

From Hippocrates to Bioethics—Gina Menzies

1. Albert R. Jonsen, *Bioethics Beyond the Headlines: Who lives? Who Dies? Who Decides?* Lanham: Rowman & Littlefield, 2005.

2. World Health Organisation, 13 August 2014, http://www.who.int/csr/don/2014_08_13_ebola/en.

3. The Belgian law of 28 May 2002 permitting euthanasia for adults under certain conditions was amended on 28 February 2014 to permit euthanasia for minors.

4. Fleming v. Ireland, 2014 IEHC 2.

5. Fleming v. Ireland, Appeal No. 019/2013, Denham CJ, 29 April 2013.

6. Policy for Prosecutors in Respect of Cases of Encouraging or Assisting Suicide Issued by The Director of Public Prosecutions for England and Wales, February 2010.

7. Edmund D. Pellegrino, *The Philosophy of Medicine Reborn*, H. Tristram Engelhardt, Jr. and Fabrice Jotterand (eds), Notre Dame: University of Notre Dame, 2008.
8. Deirdre Madden, Medicine, Ethics & the Law, Dublin: Butterworth, 2002, p.17.
9. Thomas Percival, *Medical Ethics, or a Code of Institutes and Precepts, Adapted to the Professional Conduct of Physicians and Surgeons*, Manchester: S. Russell for J. Johnson, 1803.
10. Code of Ethics of the American Medical Association, adopted May 1847.
11. 'Global Health and Aging', World Health Organisation, US National Institute on Aging and National Institutes of Health, NIH Publication 11–7737, October 2011.
12. Ibid.
13. George J. Annas and Michael A. Grodin, *The Nazi Doctors and the Nuremberg Code: Human Rights in Human Experimentation*, New York, Oxford University Press, 1992.
14. James H. Jones, *Bad Blood*, New York: The Free Press, 1993.
15. Maurice Henry Pappworth, *Human Guinea Pigs: Experimentation on Man*, Routledge and Kegan Paul, 1967
16. Ethical Principles and Guidelines for the Protection of Human Subjects of Research, The National Commission for the Protection of Human Subjects of Biomedical and Behavioural Research, US Department of Health & Human Services, 18 April 1979.
17. Tom Beauchamp and James F. Childress, *Principles of Biomedical Ethics*, 1st edn, New York, Oxford University Press, 1979. The book is now in its 6th edition, 2009.
18. Ibid.
19. Albert R. Jonsen, *The Birth of Bioethics*, New York, Oxford University Press, 1998.
20. Richard A. McCormick SJ, *The Critical Calling, Reflections on Moral Dilemmas since Vatican II*, Washington D.C., Georgetown University Press, 1989, p.10.
21. Richard McCormick SJ, op. cit., p.21.
22. John Mahoney, SJ, *The Making of Moral Theology: A Study of the Roman Catholic Tradition*, Oxford, Clarendon Press, 1987.
23. Founded in 1969. See list of recipients of award, beginning with Beecher in 1976 and including Beauchamp and Childress 2010, Richard McCormick, Paul Ramsey and Joseph Fletcher. The Centre produces a bimonthly journal promoting ethics in health, medicine and the environment.
24. Founded in 1971.
25. Jonsen, op. cit., p.58.

Auricular Confession: Some Inadequacies—Charles E.Curran

1. James Dallen, *The Reconciling Community: The Rite of Penance*, New York: Pueblo, 1986.
2. Susso Mayer, 'Devotional Confession,' *Orate Fratres*, 18 (1944), pp.159–65; Mayer, 'Devotional Confession II: Reasons Recommending its Practice,' *Orate Fratres*, 18 (1944), pp.258–64.

3. Michael Baily, 'The Parish Mission Apostolate of the Redemptorists in Ireland', in *History and Conscience: Studies in Honour of Sean O'Riordan CSsR*, Raphael Gallagher and Brendan McConvery (eds), Dublin: Gill and Macmillan, 1989, pp.274–96; Brendan McConvery, 'Hell Fire and Poitín Redemptorist Missions in the Irish Free State,' at www.historyireland.com/twentieth-century-contemporary-history/hell-fire-poitin-redemptorist-missions-in-the-irish-free-state-1922-1936; James A. Wallace, 'Reconsidering the Parish Mission', *Worship*, 67 (1993), pp.340–51.

4. Bernard Poschmann, *Penance and the Anointing of the Sick*, New York: Herder and Herder, 1964, pp.168–79.

5. Charles E. Curran, *The Catholic Moral Tradition Today: A Synthesis*, Washington, DC: Georgetown University Press, 1999, pp.73–7.

6. George T. Montague, *Maturing in Christ: Saint Paul's Program for Christian Growth*, Milwaukee: Bruce, 1964.

7. Gustav Thils, *Christian Holiness: A Prescis of Ascetical Theology*, Tiel, Belgium: Lannoo, 1961, pp.474–7.

8. Constitution on the Church no. 39–42, in *Documents of Vatican II*, Walter M. Abbott (ed.), New York: Guild, 1966, pp.65–72.

9. Bernard Häring, 'La conversion,' in *Pastorale du péché*, Ph. Delhaye (ed.) et. al., Tournai, Belgium: Desclée, 1961, pp.65–145.

10. Synod of Bishops, 1971, *Justice in the World*, in *Catholic Social Thought: The Documentary Heritage*, expanded edn, David J. O'Brien and Thomas A. Shannon (eds), Maryknoll, NY: Orbis, 2010, p.306.

11. Poschmann, pp.178–9.

Bibliography

**A Dualistic Theophany: Nature as Source of Fear
and Love in Wordsworth—Brian Cosgrove**

Samuel Taylor Coleridge, *Collected Letters*, Earl Leslie Griggs (ed.), Oxford: Clarendon Press, vol. II, 1956.

Frederick Garber, *Wordsworth and the Poetry of Encounter*, Urbana: University of Illinois Press, 1971.

Rudolf Otto, *The Idea of the Holy*, tr. by John W. Harvey, 1923; London: Oxford University Press, 2nd edn, reprinted 1969.

Alfred Lord Tennyson (ed.), *The Poems of Tennyson*, Christopher Ricks. 1969; revd edn, 3 vols. Harlow, Essex: Longman, 1987.

Thomas Weiskel. *The Romantic Sublime: Studies in the Structure and Psychology of Transcendence*, Baltimore: Johns Hopkins University Press, 1976.

William Wordsworth. *Poetical Works*, Thomas Hutchinson (ed.); rev. edn, Ernest de Selincourt. London: Oxford University Press, 1936. Reprinted 1973. Note: the edition of The Prelude cited throughout is that of 1850.

William Wordsworth, The Prose Works, W. J. B. Owen and Jane W. Smyser (eds), 3 vols. Oxford: Clarendon Press, 1974.

Ageing Titans: Church and State in Twenty-First Century—Tony McNamara

Bobbitt, Philip, *The Shield of Achilles, War, Peace and the Course of History*, London: Penguin Books, 2002.

Evangelii gaudium, Apostolic Exhortation of The Holy Father Francis (2013). http://www.vatican.va/holy_father/francesco/apost_exhortations/documents/papa-francesco_esortazione-ap_20131124_evangelii-gaudium_en.html. Downloaded 1 April 2014.

Hardin, Russell, 'The public trust' in *Disaffected Democracies: What's Troubling the Trilateral Countries*, edited by Susan J. Pharr and Robert D. Putnam, Cambridge: Cambridge University Press, 2000, pp.31–5.

Hoban, Brendan (2013), 'Disenchanted Evenings – the mood of the Irish diocesan clergy', *The Furrow*, vol. 64, no. 11, November 2013.

Mair, Peter, *Ruling the Void: The Hollowing-Out of Western democracy*, London and New York: Verso, 2013 (References are to locations in the Kindle version).

Stout, Jeffrey (2004), *Democracy and Tradition*, New Jersey and Oxfordshire, Princeton University Press.

Taylor, Charles, *A Secular Age*, Cambridge, Massachusetts and London, England: The Belknap Press of Harvard University Press, 2007.

'What's Gone Wrong With Democracy?' (2014), *The Economist*, 8 March 2014.

Whelan, Thomas (2014), 'No Mass on Weekdays 1 – Some Reflections from Theology', *The Furrow*, vol. 64, no. 5, April 2014.

Gluais [Glossary]

Fógairt an tSoiscéil i gCultúr Briste—Breandán Ó Doibhlin

aigne	attitude
aimpléiseach	complicated
aisbheart	reaction
aisciúil	gratuitous
aisfhreagra	response
andúchasach	alien
apostátacht	apostasy
ardaigeantacht	euphoria
ardghlórach	eloquent
ardmheanma	optimism
athartha	patrimony
athchóirigh	restore
athghabh	recover
atiomnaigh	rededicate
beart a imirt	play a role
bunriachtanas	basic requirement
cádhasach	venerable
cásúlacht	contingency
céadfaíocht	sensibility
céimse	hierarchy
cinniúint	destiny
cóilíneachas	colonialism
coimhthios	alienation
coinsiasta	conscious
coinsiastacht	consciousness
coiscriú	trauma
coiscritheach	traumatic
comharthaí na linne	signs of the times
comhartha sóirt	distinguishing mark
comhluadar	community
comhroinn le (*vb.*)	communicate
cruinngh	focus
cumas téarnaimh	resilience

297

deabhóideachas	devotionalism
déchiall	ambiguity
détheangachas	bilingualism
dianchoigilt	austerity
díobháil	deprivation
diongbháilteacht	determination
díshealbhú	dispossession
dí-urchóidigh	justify
domhandúchán	globalization
éadoirmisceacht	permissiveness
eisiatach	exclusive
eispéirians	experience
faoi léas	in the light of
féinfhriotal	self-expression
féiniúlacht	identity
féinmharú	suicide
féinmheas	self-respect
féinspéis	self-absorption
follúnaigh	regulate
frithbheart	opposition
frithsheasamh	resistance
fuarchúis	indifference
giúlán	behaviour
iarmhairt	consequence
ilghnéitheach	complex
imleor	adequate
íogaireacht	sensitivity
iontamhlú	identification
léirmhíniú	interpretation
marsanta	mercenary
meanma	disposition
meanmanra	*mentalité*

meanmarc	aspiration, ideal
meathlú	recession
milleánaigh	censure
neamhchúiseach	unconcerned
neamhthuilleamaí	autonomy
nódaigh	graft
nuálach	novel (*adj.*)
oibiachtúil	objective
óraice	accepted, normal
próiséacht	project
prógras	progress
riocht	situation
róchaite	hackneyed
saeclárachas	secularism
sanas	suggestion
seachad	hand on
seadaitheoir	settler
seallach	(tv) viewer
slánchóirigh	integrate
soleontacht	vulnerability
straitéis	strategy
tátal	diagnosis
timpeallacht	environment
toilghnústa	deliberate
toise	dimension
tosca	circumstances
turgnamhaíocht	experimentation
údarásúil	authoritarian